Play School Series
Edited by Clark W. Hetherington

EDUCATING BY STORY-TELLING

SHOWING THE

VALUE OF STORY-TELLING AS AN EDUCATIONAL TOOL FOR THE USE OF ALL WORKERS WITH CHILDREN

BY

Katherine Dunlap Cather

Author of "Boyhood Stories of Famous Men," "Pan and His Pipes and Other Stories," "The Singing Clock"

Yonkers-on-Hudson, New York
WORLD BOOK COMPANY
1919

WORLD BOOK COMPANY

THE HOUSE OF APPLIED KNOWLEDGE

Established, 1905, by Caspar W. Hodgson

Yonkers-on-Hudson, New York

2126 Prairie Avenue, Chicago

The Play School Series, of which *Educating by Story-Telling* is a member, is based on the work of the Demonstration Play School of the University of California. Breaking away from the traditional idea of the subjects of study, this school has substituted a curriculum of activities — the natural activities of child life — out of which subjects of study naturally evolve. Succeeding volumes now in active preparation will relate to the other activities which form the educational basis for the work of the Play School, including Social, Linguistic, Moral, Big-Muscle, Rhythmic and Musical, Environmental and Nature, and Economic Activities. Each volume will be written by a recognized authority in the subject dealt with, as the author of *Educating by Story-Telling* is in her special field

PSS: CES-2

AUTHOR'S PREFACE

THIS book has grown out of years of experience with children of all ages and all classes, and with parents, teachers, librarians, and Sunday School, social center, and settlement workers. The material comprising it was first used in something like its present form in the University of California Summer Session, 1914, and since then has been the basis of courses given in that institution, as well as in private classes and lecture work. The author does not claim that it is the final word upon the subject of story-telling, or that it will render obsolete any one of the several excellent works already upon the market. But the response of children to the stories given and suggested, and the eagerness with which the principles herein advocated have been received by parents and teachers, have convinced her that the book contains certain features that are unique and valuable to those engaged in directing child thought.

Other works have shown in a general way how vast a field is the realm of the narrator, but they have not worked out a detailed plan that the busy mother or teacher can follow in her effort to establish standards, to lead her small charges to an appreciation of the beautiful in literature and art, and to endow them with knowledge that shall result in creating a higher code of thought and action. No claim is made that all the problems of the school and home are solved in the ensuing pages, and the title, "Educating by Story-Telling," makes no assumption that story-telling can accomplish everything. The author does assume, however, that when used with wisdom and skill, the story is a powerful tool in the hands of the educator, and she attempts to indicate how, by this means, some portion of drudgery may be eliminated from the schoolroom, and a more pleasurable element be put into it. She undertakes to demonstrate how it is possible to intensify the child's interest in most of the subjects composing the curriculum, not by advancing an untried theory, but by traveling along a path that has been found to be a certain road to attainment, not only for the gifted creative teacher, but for the average ordinary one who is often baffled by the bigness of the problem she has to solve.

Grateful acknowledgment is made for permission to use copyrighted material as follows: to the Whitaker, Ray, Wiggin Company for the story entitled "The Search for the Seven Cities" (page 149); to Dr. David Starr Jordan and A. C. McClurg & Co. for "The Story of a Salmon" (page 255) and "The Story of a Stone" (page 331); to the David C. Cook Company for "The Pigeons of Venice" (page 263), "The Duty That Wasn't Paid" (page 278), "Wilhelmina's Wooden Shoes" (page 283), "The Luck Boy of Toy Valley" (page 302), and "The Pet Raven" (page 317); and to Henry Holt & Co. for "The Emperor's Vision" (page 306).

KATHERINE DUNLAP CATHER

CONTENTS

PART ONE

Story-Telling and the Arts of Expression — Establishing Standards

PART TWO

The Use of Story-Telling to Illuminate Some Schoolroom Subjects — Stories for Telling

Stories for Telling

LIST OF STORIES BY MONTHS

EDITOR'S INTRODUCTION

THE story is a phase of communication — the instinctive tendency to signal and transmit feelings and ideas and to respond to such expressions — and communication is associated with the social complex of instincts and emotions as indicated by these responses. Through the power of social sympathy in this complex, curiosity and the imagination are brought under the sway of communication, especially in the story. Indeed, the psychology of the story reveals how deeply social sympathy influences the imagination and controls curiosity. The primitive side of this social sympathy is seen in the responses of social animals to the calls of their kind, in the rush of dogs and men to the cries of battle. Its power over the imagination is shown in the swaying of the spectator to the movements of the athlete, his ejaculations and his cries of distress or delight. Through sympathy in imagination the spectator enters the contest. Further, so socially minded are we, and so dependent upon social guidance, that curiosity is nowhere so keen, nor the imagination so active, as in the communication of a life situation. Any incident or accumulation of incidents that we call a plot in the experience of an individual or group of individuals, grips the mind. This explains the fascination of the story. Gossip and scandal are the less worthy forms. The novel is exalted gossip or scandal; the drama the same acted out. They all feed the tremendous hunger for insight into life. They unroll the curtain on the content of life, or some phase of life. Hence the story is the natural form for revealing life.

Communication, like life, may be either serious or frivolous; hence the story carries both functions. It pictures or expresses life in both phases. But the form of the story itself is pleasurable; and thus story-telling may degenerate into mere amusement. This possibly has led to both its abuse and its neglect.

The fact that the story is so enjoyable to children has led teachers and parents to use it merely as amusement, irrespective of content, or even of artistic form. This tendency has been met by publishers. As proof, note the books exhibited at Christmas time in any bookshop. They show the enormous amount of trash set up in book form for child consumption. This is a more serious danger than the trash read by adults, because they are food for hungry minds at the growing age. The importance is shown of selecting stories according to recognized criteria. While the child enjoys the story, he has no judgment of values in the story other than its pleasure-giving qualities. As judgment is a product of education, so judging values is an adult function; the adult must study all stories, but not tell all stories. The story-teller must analyze the story plot, criticize the values, select and adapt stories to age periods and to other child needs. This task Mrs. Cather has performed in her book.

The mere fact that the story amuses has caused a neglect of its larger functions in education. This is due to the traditional attitude toward the pleasurable in education. Education is life, and synonymous with the joys and griefs of life; but the traditions of the school when it was a place simply to master the three R's, and the traditions of intellectualism, monkish asceticism, and Puritanism, have conspired to perpetuate the idea of education as a "hard" process. That it is "hard" is demonstrated by the vast number of children who dislike school and drop out of it before finishing the grades, and by the small number of those who go through its process and think of education and its discipline with delight. Yet this is what all normal, vigorous children should feel. There is probably no more profound or serious issue in education or democracy — and democracy depends on education — than this conflict between the advocates of a school process that is "hard" and the advocates of a process that is "pleasurable." The arguments exhibit the two extremes in all such controversies: the advocates of "discipline," "iron," "the bitter pill" on the one hand, and the advocates of "freedom" and "enjoyment," — really soft pedagogy and license, — on the other. The truth, as is usually the case, lies between the two schools. Both are right in part, and both are wrong in part. Both see an essential, and both fail to see the reverse side of what each advocates. There is no conflict between real discipline and real pleasure; they cannot be separated in child life. This being so, the story is bound to take a large place in the teaching of the future.

The story amuses, but its function is not merely to amuse. Pleasure is not the aim of life, nor even its sole guide; it is an index of life, especially in the young.

The point needs to be emphasized that the story is the carrier, always has been the carrier, and will remain the natural carrier of racial tradition or information and ideals. The story in education has two functions: (1) it is the molder of ideals, and (2) it is the illuminator of facts.

(1) The highest and most difficult achievement in educational effort is the establishment of standards or ideals that function in judgment and behavior. The place of the story in moral education has been emphasized by many writers. Its place in developing an appreciation of artistic forms in language, in music, and in the graphic arts is splendidly illustrated in this book.

Appreciation is an emotional response, primarily instinctive, but developed through experience and according to high or low artistic standards by social approval or disapproval. In the emotional response lies interest and in the character of the emotional response lies the character of the interest. The interest may be crude, vulgar, or vicious, or it may be ideal, but in either case it is a product of developed emotional habits. In the life of the child this emotional response precedes the intellectual judgment of artistic values which comes later and only through contrast and comparison, and the former is vastly more important in social significance for the pleasure of the mass than the latter. This development of the artistic emotional response may be cleverly guided through the story, as Mrs. Cather shows, and she gives a wealth of suggestions for the use of the teacher.

But the story itself is a form of artistic expression and thus subject to the application of standardizing judgments. A good story must be judged by a double standard. It may be good in the sense that it is well told — and well told means simply that the incident or plot is related in sequence, with such emphasis and form of language that it grips the human instinctive response to the dramatic; or it may be good in the sense that it carries a good content in meaning or ideal. These two standards may not, frequently do not, coincide. A story may be so told that it is most fascinating, and yet the content be mere rubbish or even vicious; or the content may be correct and the telling so poorly done that it kills interest.

Many stories are told because of their "beauty" of form, where the content is not true. Some such stories are valuable because of the standardizing sentiments they carry, but truth is as important at least as the æsthetic. The human intellect evolved to interpret meanings and progressively perfect behavior adjustments. Each age of racial experience brings on its new interpretations, and broadly, each age makes advances upon that which preceded. Old theories fall, new truths arise; but old theories hold sway over the imagination of the masses long after the leaders have accepted higher truths because the old is well told while the new lacks the poetic expression of the artist. Literature is well-told information, yet under the guise of literature goblins and superstitions and worn-out theories parade in the imagination and thus mold ideals and behavior.

The problem of the professional story-teller of the future is to tell the best information of the age in as fascinating a form as the old myths and fables are now told after years of repetition. Only in this way can contemporary popular opinion be kept abreast of the scientific truth of the time, instead of dragging along in the superstitions of the past.

Some stories are told though untrue, because they "develop the imagination," but this by itself is a dangerous criterion. The function of the imagination is to reconstruct the world in mental terms which will guide behavior. The functioning of the imagination in any kind of images will develop "power," but the power may be detrimental individually and socially if the images cause crooked thinking. Straight thinking depends on the imagination — on the kind of emotionalized images which habitually arise in any thought situation or problem. Just so far as stories are untrue and without great moral value, yet are fascinatingly told, so far do they encourage untrue imagining and emotional attitudes, and therefore untrue thinking. And inasmuch as the emotional response to the single interpretative concept, the single vision of life, is vastly stronger through tradition than the interest in the discovery of complex relationships, — and truth comes finally only through the latter, — the emotionalized habits of imagination in interpretation are profoundly important for democracy.

Democracy cannot exist with a population of fuzzy thinkers. Story-telling, like all educational effort, must develop the imagination in mental terms that will function in life today.

(2) The story is an illuminator of facts. The child gets his information by activities in relation to the environment, by exploration, observation, experimentation, with the everlasting play of the interpretative processes, and by responding to and accepting or re-

jecting the communicated interpretations put upon phenomena by his social group. In this process of interpretation there is the immediate environment which can be sensed, but is understood only through its reconstruction in the imagination, largely in linguistic terms; and the remote environment which cannot be sensed and which can be understood only as it is built in the imagination as an extension of the reconstructed sensed environment. In these reconstructive processes the story is the most powerful correlating and illuminating educational force we have, as may be indicated by a brief analysis.

The activities of the school curriculum dealing with the environment have two natural foci of interest for the child. (*a*) The civic-geographical-historical complex (when rightly organized just one subject) and (*b*) the physical-biological complex, which is now coming to be called "general science." For the child these two groups of the environmental activities cover the whole of adult science, philosophy, and religion, and both require a tremendous reconstructive functioning of the imagination.

(*a*) The first group is a new coming correlation which naturally must carry with it organized communication or the larger share of language and literature. The investigation of the local social environment is the basis of all "civics," "geography," and "history." It expands as civics. When the child projects his interpretations of any human activity into another environment so that he is reconstructing in his imagination the life habits and customs of the people in relation to the physical and biological characteristics of the country, he is studying geography. When he goes backward in time in this process, he is studying history.

In this concentric widening of the intellectual horizon concerning human life and its relationships to the environment, the imagination must reconstruct a world which it cannot sense. The facts may be gained from pictures, maps, descriptions, but to become functional in thought in any other than in a mere commercial sense, the reconstruction must touch the emotions so that the life and conditions of living of the people will be felt. When felt the life will be dwelt upon in imagination, and when dwelt upon in imagination it will function in the life activities of the child. Giving this vivid, felt insight into the life conditions of other people is the function of the story. Through the hunger to feel life the story reveals life.

(*b*) The story also functions for children in the interpretation of the physical-biological environment or "general science."

Between six and fourteen years of age is the neglected period for science, and it is the age when the story may function in the biggest way as a natural educational tool. Yet so absorbed are school men in the problem of drilling children in the dissected elements of the written language that they do not even understand one of the two chief characteristics of child nature at this age, — the rapidly expanding curiosity concerning nature. It is the age of the first crude control of the "scientific instinct," the tendency to experiment and explore. It is the age for fixing the questioning habit and building a common-sense confidence in and familiarity with nature. These results follow from the logical processes involved in the activities, not from being presented with the formalized and logical results of adult science. The child will have none of this latter if he can help it; he wants to do his own experimenting. In this process again the story gives the larger insight. The child acquires facts by experimentation, observation, exploration, but the larger meanings and relationships require imaginative reconstruction. The child can observe the fish or the fly at different stages of their development, but the story of the life history of the fish or fly gives what observation cannot supply. It is as fascinating as any fairy tale when told with the same consideration for dramatic form, and the story is true besides. The child cannot understand evolution as presented by Darwin, or by the teacher of biology in the high schools; but the child even of eight revels in the stories that carry the facts of evolution, and thus he gains a right feeling towards the wonderful meaning of the progress of natural things, which makes later thinking true and easy. So strong is the response to the story that even the history of physical things when set in a natural story form, stimulates.

The fairy tales of the future will be well-told stories from our sciences or human life and nature, the two natural centers of interest in the environment, and we may expect as results in public opinion a broader common sense and a lessened gullibility. In this organization of science and modern thought in story form for its larger use in education the professional story-teller has still a great unfinished task to perform.

Its beginnings are in this book, and Mrs. Cather is already at work on a broader compilation of materials for a later volume. In this larger functioning of the story the old fairy tales and myths will take their place as historical data to give comparative insight into the beliefs of people in the past, a sympathetic understanding of their limitations in knowledge, and an appreciation of our privileges in civilization, due largely to the struggles of the past.

CLARK W. HETHERINGTON

PART ONE

STORY-TELLING AND THE ARTS OF EXPRESSION
ESTABLISHING STANDARDS

EDUCATING BY STORY-TELLING

CHAPTER ONE

The Purpose and Aim of Story-Telling

EVER since the beginning of things the story-teller has been a personage of power, an individual welcomed by young and old alike. Hailed as a joy bringer and heeded as an oracle, his tales have been the open sesame to admit him to any throng and his departure has always been attended with regret. During the Middle Ages he was a privileged character, free to wander at will into camp or court. The Piso manuscript in the museum at Budapest tells of the solicitous effort made by Ladislaus of Hungary to secure safe-conduct through Bohemia and Austria for a favorite narrator, and many other old chronicles attest to the fact that in France, Germany, Italy, and the British Isles passports were given to minstrels and raconteurs when no one else could obtain them. Long before this period, during the nomadic existence of the race, the mightiest men of the tribe were the chieftain and the story-teller, the one receiving homage because of his ability to vanquish his adversaries in battle, the other because of his skill in entertaining his fellows as they huddled around the fire at night. Each ability was believed to be evidence of divine gifts, and the possessor of each was revered as being a little higher than a mortal, a little lower than a god.

Primitive man, like civilized man, was fond of power, and realizing that his talents made him mighty, the narrator exercised them in such a manner as to promote their development. Every emotional response on the part of his hearers served as a key to unlock doors into the land of his desire, and as he listened to exclamations of approval, condemnation, or delight, he saw ways of arousing these emotions to even greater degrees of intensity and, possessing an elemental love of the spectacular, made the most of his opportunity. Thus he evolved from a crude declaimer into something of an artist. As the race emerged from a barbaric into a pastoral state, he grew to be more than an entertainer; he imparted knowledge to the young by keeping alive the tribal traditions.

On the Asiatic highlands, before the Aryan migration, it was the story-teller who preserved the tales of the fathers, the nature myths that were primitive man's explanation of the things he did not understand. The journey of the sun across the heavens, the shifting of clouds from one fantastic form to another, the chromatic skies of sunrise and sunset, and the starry firmament of night aroused his curiosity and awakened his awe. He wondered about them just as children today wonder about them, and just as the twentieth-century child questions his mother, so he questioned one whom he deemed wiser than himself. This consulted oracle gave as an explanation something that out of his own wondering and puzzling had grown into a vague belief, and consequently the clouds that presaged showers came to be regarded as heavenly cows from whose exuberant udders came the rains that refreshed the earth; stormy oceans and rugged mountains with ravines beset with perils held giants that avenged and destroyed; while the sun, a beneficent creature that drove away the monster of darkness, and all the saving forces of nature, were metamorphosed in the fancy of these early men into protecting heroes and divinities.

As generation succeeded generation and the young received their allotment of lore from the old, these stories became fixed so firmly in the minds of the people that they were carried with them at the scattering of the tribes, told and retold in the new-found homes, and modified to suit conditions of life in strange lands the wanderers came to inhabit; and they still survive as present-day fairy tales. There are various theories of how these old beliefs came to be disseminated, how it happened that tales supposed to be indigenous to Finland or Madagascar are found in slightly different dress among the tribes of Central Africa and in other sections of the world remote from each other; but no matter how much folklorists disagree as to the process through which the tales evolved to their present form, they do not differ as to their significance, and whether they accept the Aryan theory promulgated by Max Müller or the totemistic theory of Andrew Lang, they unite in a belief that these ancient tales represent the religion of primitive man, a religion growing out of fear of the unknown.

Always it was by the lips of the story-teller that the legends were kept alive. It was his mission to teach children the tales their fathers knew, and as the race evolved toward civilization he gave them something besides nature myths. He recounted and reiterated the achievements of the heroes of his people until youths who heard were fired with desire to emulate. Because he was deemed a man of supernal powers, his words were believed; consequently he created the ideals of the age in which he lived, and just as his own standards were fine or base, so the ideals for which he was responsible came to be high or low. Fortunately for the world, however, these old-time narrators were wiser than their fellows. They were poets and dreamers who saw life through eyes vision clear. They glorified virtue and deprecated vice, taught that right triumphs over wrong and that sinning brings inevitable punishment, and explained in a crude way the workings of the law of compensation. They fired men to achievement just as they fired boys with desire to emulate the heroes of whom they told, and as centuries passed and they grew in skill and power, their tales came to be the inspiration of some of the most thrilling chapters in the annals of man. Alexander the Great declared that the lays of a wandering bard, Homer, made him thirst for conquest. In Germany, in the twelfth century, the influence of a penniless gleeman, Walther von der Vogelweide, was greater than that of the Pope. There was no more puissant man in Ireland when Ireland was in its golden day and Tara in its glory than the low-born minstrel, Brian of Fermanagh; and the Crusades, which re-created Europe by the introduction of Eastern culture and the breaking down of old traditions, might never have been undertaken but for tales of defilement of holy places from the lips of Peter the Hermit. Story-tellers every one of them, swaying their fellows and making history, subjects of kings and nobles, yet often mightier than the masters who held their destinies in their hands.

The power of the narrator did not die with chivalry. As recently as during the middle of the last century the clergy of Scotland united in an effort to suppress story-telling in the Highlands because it kept alive beliefs of pagan origin, beliefs so deep-seated that the combined eloquence of prelates could not eradicate them, and the strength of the church was impaired because of the sheltering of these waifs of the past. To this day there are peasants in Germany who doubt not that every year at harvest time Charlemagne walks beside the Rhine under the midnight moon and blesses the vineyard region of Winkel and Ingelheim. In central Switzerland are hundreds of simple folk who believe that on the summit where they met to take the oath that fired the land against Austria, sleep the immortal "Brothers of the Grütli," and that they will slumber on until the liberty of Helvetia is imperiled; while in the southern portion of that mountain land the country folk are certain that prosperity will be the lot of every husbandman when the swan-drawn luck boat returns to Lake Geneva. Why? Because their fathers in the far-off days believed these tales; because they have come down to them by the lips of the story-teller, and wherever there is no written language, wherever the people are too unlettered to read what is written, or where they live in isolated communities and mingle little with the outside world, they still believe the legends. They love to hear them told and retold, and nothing brings so much pleasure on a winter night or in a summer gloaming as the complete family circle and the father or uncle or stranger from another community sitting in the midst repeating the old, old tales.

As it is with unlettered peasants today, as it was with tribesmen in primitive times and with the great in medieval castle halls, it still is with the child. He lives over the experience of his fathers on the Asiatic highlands and sits entranced listening to the record of it in stories. The element of suspense, the wondering what will happen next, holds him in a viselike grip, and the story hour is to him a period of joy. The here and now disappears as the narrator lifts his invisible wand, and the listener journeys by roads of never ceasing wonders into lands of enchantment. According to the skill of the raconteur, and the vividness with which he himself sees and feels the pictures he strives to portray, he makes his listeners see and feel them, rejoicing in the good fortune and sympathizing in the sorrows of the just and righteous; and they not only follow along the highroad where he leads them, but roam off into pleasant bypaths where the fancy has free play.

There is no age or racial limit to this story love. Representing, as it does, an emotional hunger that is the human heritage, it is universal. Several years ago at Five Points in New York City, a settlement worker discovered that a very effective means of gaining the confidence of immigrant women was to tell fairy tales, and recently some of the most gratifying results obtained in the Telegraph Hill district of San Francisco were made possible by a leader there gaining the good will of a group of Sicilian hoodlums because she knew the plot of *Jerusalem Delivered* and told the story magnetically and well. It was like a breeze from their native island, where they had heard it from the lips of the village story-teller and seen it pictured on the market carts, and the fact that she knew something that had fascinated them gained their sympathy and coöperation. Those who have even a limited knowledge of child life know that before the babe can read he delights in listening to a nursery tale, and that even after he journeys into bookland he is more interested in the story told him than in the one he reads for himself. Why? Because the voice and personality of the speaker make it alive and vital. Because, as Seumas MacManus says, "The spoken word is the remembered word."

The tales heard during childhood become fixed and lasting possessions. They stay with the hearer through the years, and because their ideals become his ideals, do much toward shaping his character. The child who hears many good stories and unconsciously learns to distinguish between the tawdry and the real, reads good stories when a boy and becomes a man for whom sensational best sellers have no charm.

There is much talk about the vicious tastes of the youth of this generation, and unfavorable comparisons between them and their elders at a similar age are frequently made. There is some foundation for this belief, but it is not the fault of the children that it is so. Because of the abundance and cheapness of books, many of them of questionable merit, boys and girls are left to browse unguided, and just as the range man is to blame if his hungry herd strays into a loco patch and eats of noxious weeds when he fails to drive it to the place of wholesome herbage, so it is the fault of parents and teachers if their charges acquire a taste for sensational yarns instead of for good literature. The very hunger that impels them toward that which contaminates, if satisfied in a wholesome manner would make them lovers of the best, and the reason why children become devourers of "yellow" stories is because they have failed to stumble upon a more fascinating and less dangerous highway, and no one has led them to it. There is no surer way of keeping a boy from becoming a devotee of the funny page of the Sunday supplement or a follower of "Nick Carter" than that of studying his tastes and giving him tales from good literature that will satisfy them. There is no more powerful means to use in diverting a child from the undesirable to the desirable than that of throwing a searchlight upon the attractions of the latter and presenting them to him through joyful experience. The narrator's art is in truth a magic luminary, an unfailing means of bringing hidden beauties to sight and causing them to be loved because they give pleasure.

For a number of years it has been conceded that story-telling is of value in the kindergarten and primary school, but little provision has been made for it in the educational scheme for the older child. Gradually, however, educators in America have come to realize what their European colleagues realized long ago, that the narrator's art can be a powerful element in the mental, moral, and religious development of the boy and girl and can mean as much to the adolescent child as to the tiny tot. Consequently they are now giving it an honored place. The story period has become a part of the program of every well-regulated library. Teachers of elementary and grammar grades are recognizing its value in the classroom, and in some states story-telling is included in the curriculum. Each year brings new texts and collections from the publishers, until it seems that the art so much honored in the past is coming again into its own.

Yet, with all the interest that is manifested throughout the country, story-telling is not doing its greatest, most vital work, because so little thought is given to the selection of material, so little study to the response of children who hear the tales and the effect upon them. Before even half of its possibilities can be realized, those who tell stories must know the story interests of childhood and must choose materials, not only because they are beautiful in theme and language and embody high ideals, but because they are fitted to the psychological period of the child who is to hear them. They must realize that the purpose of story-telling is not merely to entertain, although it does entertain, but that in addition to delighting young listeners there must be a higher aim, of which the narrator never loses sight. Every tale selected must contribute something definite toward the mental, moral, or spiritual growth of the child, just as each pigment chosen by an artist must blend into the picture to help make a beautiful and perfect whole. The golden age of childhood will come and fear that young people's tastes are being vitiated will die out when parents and teachers realize that much of the noblest culture of the past has been given through the medium of the story, and that it can be given through this medium now and in the future, because there is almost no type of information the child should receive that he will not receive joyously through this means, and with deep, lasting results. Story-telling planned and carried out to fit conditions will help to solve many of the problems that confront educators today. Besides developing the emotional nature and giving moral and religious instruction, it will intensify the interest in history, geography, nature study, manual training, and domestic science, awaken an appreciation of literature, art, and music, enrich the child's powers of discrimination, and teach him to distinguish between the cheap and ephemeral and the great and lasting. It will help to eliminate much of what he considers the drudgery of school life and give him information that will fit him for broad, sympathetic, useful living.

This does not mean that the teacher is to do all the work, thereby fixing children in habits of idleness, nor does it mean the addition of an extra subject to an already overcrowded curriculum. It simply means leading the child to do things for himself because of the incentive that interest gives. It means illuminating the formal subjects and sending pupils to them with greater eagerness.

In order to accomplish these ends, story-telling must be unmarred by creaking machinery, and it must be sympathetic. The narrator must rise above the level of a mere lesson giver and approach the plane of the artist, which he can do only by giving an artist's preparation to his work. The old-time raconteur swayed the destiny of nations because he was an artist, because he himself believed in the message he brought. He put heart and labor into his work, which gave his words a sincerity that never failed to convince. So too must the present-day narrator believe in the power of the story and in the dignity of his work, and he must choose material with thought and judgment instead of snatching it up indifferently, thinking that any story will do if only it holds the interest. The racial tales should be given freely in the psychological period to which they belong, but not the racial tales only. There is much modern material close to present-day life and conditions, without which the child's education is not complete, and it must be classified and graded. This entails reference work for which the non-professional has neither time nor opportunity, and to this fact is due much of the valueless story-telling of today. Experience with hundreds of parents, teachers, and workers with children has brought conviction that a belief in the value of story-telling as an educational tool is sincere and general, but that sources of classified material are not available to the average child leader. It is partly to meet this need that the present work is planned.

CHAPTER TWO

THE STORY INTERESTS OF CHILDHOOD

A. RHYTHMIC PERIOD

IF the work of the narrator is to be of real value, he must have a knowledge of the story interests of childhood, for otherwise the talent of a Scheherazade, careful preparation, and an extensive repertoire will fail to produce the desired results, because a narrative that deals with mythical heroes cannot make a lasting impression upon a child who craves animal and primitive wonder tales, even though it be written in language and style suited to his understanding. The heart or framework of the story must be made up of events that are fraught with interest in his particular period of mental development, and must introduce personages with whom he would like to companion, and whose movements he will follow with approval, pity, condemnation, or rejoicing. Under such conditions the boys or girls or dogs who contribute to the action of the tale are not strangers out of a book, but mean as much to him as the people and animals he knows, and because they do mean much he lives the tale. It becomes part of him and he of the story. His emotional nature is stirred, his power of evaluating is strengthened, and some of the foundation blocks of character are laid.

Naturally the question arises, "How is one to know which tales to choose, when there is such a wealth of stories and such a diversity of interests? Is there any rule or guide to keep the conscientious but untrained worker from the pitfalls and show him the right road from the wrong?" Such a guide there is — the psychological axiom that the child between birth and maturity passes through several periods or stages of mental growth which determines his interests.

The little child, the one from the age of about three to six, is interested in familiar things. He has not yet reached the period of fancy during which he wanders into a world of make-believe and revels with fairies and nixies, but dwells in a realm of realism. His attention is centered on the things and the personages he knows, — the mother, the father, dogs, cats, pigs, horses, cows, chickens, and children of his own age, — and consequently he enjoys stories and jingles about these creatures. He chuckles over the accounts of their merry experiences and sympathizes with them in their misfortunes, because they lie close to his interests. This is why Mother Goose has been and is beloved of little children. The rhymes do not introduce griffins and ogres and monsters that must be seen through eyes of fancy to be seen at all, but abound in accounts of creatures he has beheld from his windows and associated with in his home. Mother Hubbard and her unfortunate dog, the crooked man and his grotesque cat, the pigs that went to market, and the old woman in the shoe lie close to his world because he knows dogs and cats and pigs and kind old women, and therefore the rhymes and jingles that portray them are dear to his heart.

Especially fascinating in this period of early childhood are stories that contain much repetition. "The Old Woman and Her Pig," "Little Red Hen," "Chicken Little," "The Gingerbread Man," and "The Three

Billy Goats" delight little people, and although they have heard them again and again they always watch eagerly for the "Fire, fire, burn stick," "I saw it with my eyes, I heard it with my ears, and a piece of it fell on my tail," and are disappointed if the well-known expressions are omitted. The repetition strengthens the dramatic element and helps to make the pictures vivid, and the child loves to experience again the thrill he felt upon first listening to the tale.

Stories introducing the cries and calls of animals are much loved at this period. The squealing of the pig, the barking of the dog, the clucking of the hen, and the quacking of the duck give charm to a narrative because the child has heard those sounds in his own garden, in his own dooryard, and along the road, and knowing them, is interested in them. This is the secret of the success of many kindergarten tales that fall far below the requirements of a good story. Often almost devoid of plot and lacking in suspense element, still they hold the attention because of the animal cries and calls they contain. The little hearer chuckles as the baby pig squeals, the mother pig grunts, or the dog barks, and listens delightedly to what, without these cries and calls, would not interest him.

This too is why the racial tales fascinate today just as they fascinated five hundred years ago. They have a clearly defined plot that of itself would hold the interest, they introduce familiar characters, contain much repetition, and abound in animal cries and calls.

Broadly speaking, then, for the period of early childhood, the time of realism which extends from the age of about three to five or six, the narrator should choose stories of animal and child life, those which introduce sounds peculiar to the characters and which abound in repetition.

But he should not make the mistake of following this rule too literally or his efforts will result in failure, because children live under widely different conditions. The boy of the city slums, whose horizon extends only from his own row of tenements to the next row up the street, will not be held by tales of cows and sheep, because he does not know cows and sheep. His knowledge of four-footed creatures is confined to dogs and cats and an occasional horse that goes by hitched to the wagon of a fruit or vegetable vender, and the tales that mean something to him are those of animals of his world, and of children. Many a settlement and social worker has learned the truth of this through sad experience. A most gifted story-teller in a New York settlement house gave to her group "The Ugly Duckling," and gave it exquisitely too, but it meant nothing to the children because they never had been in the country. A barnyard was as remote from their interest as a treatise on philology is from that of a Finnish peasant. They did not know ducks and geese and chickens, and consequently punched their neighbors and grew pestiferous during the recital of a tale that would have entranced country children.

The same mistake was made by a professional story-teller who gave a coyote tale to a group of Italian children. They never had met this "outcast in gray," never had shivered as he howled in the night, and the story brought no pictures before their eyes. They were inattentive and disorderly throughout its rendition, and the narrator declared them an impossible group. Yet that same afternoon a college girl with no special training in story-telling told them of a lost nanny goat, and they sat fascinated. In the first instance the trouble was not with the children but with the narrator. She knew much of technique but little of psychology and could not hold the children's attention, while the other girl, possessed of far less native ability, entertained them because she understood the story interests of childhood. The narrator must have, not only an understanding of the psychological periods and interests of childhood, but a knowledge of the environment of the children with whom she works.

There is a wealth of sources from which to draw for this early period. Often it is necessary to adapt material, because many a tale whose framework is suited to little people is told in language beyond their understanding. "David and Jonathan," by Elizabeth Stuart Phelps, is a good example. Written for adults, yet it is so universal in its appeal that the lad of six listens to it with as much sympathy as his father or mother. The account of the affection of dog and master for each other, the pathos of the separation and the joy of the reunion, touch him as much as they touch his parents, and to receive it from the lips of one who feels and loves the tale will make him kinder to dumb animals and gentler to the aged.

This is true of many another story that is the creation of an artist. I mention particularly Ouida's "Dog of Flanders," John Muir's "Stickeen," and Ernest Thompson Seton's "Monarch, the Big Bear of Tallac," each of which I have used with children of all ages. The characters in them are living, breathing creatures, the kind that if met in real life would arouse affection and awaken both laughter and tears, and whether these stories are told in monosyllabic language or colored by fine rhetorical effects, they strike the tender places and appeal to the best. When the child meets Nello before the altar of the cathedral in Antwerp, kneeling in front of a painting by Rubens and fondling his dog, he instinctively feels that this boy is not a stranger living in a far-away land and speaking a foreign language, but that he represents all the orphaned children in the world, and that his affection for his dog is the same tie that binds every other child to the pet he loves. So too with Monarch, the majestic captive of Golden Gate Park. He is not just a bear, a creature larger and more ferocious than many other animals. He typifies wild life caged, and the boy who has pitied him in listening to the account of his tramp, tramp, tramp about the pit, never quite forgets that proud but eternal unrest, the ever present longing for the white peaks and the pines.

One need not fear that putting these stories into simple language may be deemed a sacrilegious act, or that telling the plot of a masterpiece will kill delight in that masterpiece itself. Goethe's mother, sitting in the firelight in their home, gave her boy tales from the old poets, creating in him a desire to read that helped to make him a profound student and master thinker. And the twentieth-century child will doubly enjoy reading a beautiful piece of literature at some future day, because in the magical long ago it touched his heart. Workers with little children should be ever on the alert, seeking stories that deserve the name of literature, with plot and characters that will appeal to their small charges, because such stories mold a child's taste and give a key that will unlock doors into the great treasure house of art. Whenever the mother or teacher or librarian reads a story that is a literary gem, let her analyze it and determine whether or not, if told in simple language, it would delight a child. The old-time narrators who molded national taste and ideals did this constantly, and the great story-tellers are doing it today.

Sicilian peasants, for instance, have a knowledge of the classics that amazes the average American. The stories are pictured on the market carts, those gaudy conveyances that brighten the island highways from Catania to Palermo, and the conversation of these simple folk is colored with allusions that would do credit to a professor of literature. Most of them cannot read, but they know the plots of *Jerusalem Delivered*, "Sindbad the Sailor," "The Merchant of Bagdad," and many more of the world's great stories. They heard the tales in childhood, and their fathers before them heard them from the lips of men who loved to tell them, and so they have become a national heritage. Let us do as much for the children of our land, that the men and women of the future may have a noble culture and more splendid possessions than their parents have, and let us do it in the world-old way, by story-telling.

Sources of Story Material for the Rhythmic Period

Adams, William: *Fables and Rhymes — Æsop and Mother Goose.*
Bailey, Carolyn Sherwin: *Firelight Stories.*
Bailey, Carolyn Sherwin, and Lewis, Clara: *For the Children's Hour.*
Bryce, Catherine T.: *That's Why Stories.*
Burnham, Maud: *Descriptive Stories for All the Year.*
Cooke, Flora J.: *Nature Myths and Stories for Little Children.*
Davis, Mary H., and Chow-Leung: *Chinese Fables and Folk Stories.*
Dillingham, Elizabeth, and Emerson, Adelle: *"Tell It Again" Stories.*
Harrison, Elizabeth: *In Story-land.*
Holbrook, Florence: *'Round the Year in Myth and Song.*
Hoxie, Jane: *A Kindergarten Story Book.*
Jordan, David Starr: *The Book of Knight and Barbara.*
Lindsay, Maud: *Mother Stories; More Mother Stories.*
Miller, Olive Thorne: *True Bird Stories.*
Milton Bradley Company: *Half a Hundred Stories.*
Moulton, Louise Chandler: *Bed-time Stories.*
Pierson, Clara D.: *Among the Farmyard People.*
Poulsson, Emilie: *Child Stories and Rhymes.*
Richards, Laura E.: *The Golden Windows; Five-Minute Stories; The Pig Brother.*
Skinner, Ada M.: *Stories of Wakeland and Dreamland.*
Verhoeff, Carolyn: *All about Johnnie Jones.*
Wiggin, Kate Douglas, and Smith, Nora A.: *The Children's Hour.*

CHAPTER THREE

The Story Interests of Childhood (*Continued*)

B. IMAGINATIVE PERIOD

WHEN the child leaves the rhythmic, realistic period he enters a world of make-believe and no longer desires tales and jingles that are nothing more than a recounting of facts he already knows. He delights in playing he is some one other than himself, in pretending he is doing things beyond the range of his possibilities, and because he craves a larger experience he craves also fanciful, imaginative tales in which he may have those experiences. He knows that bees sting, that the dog has a cold, wet nose, that the cat lands on its feet, and the squirrel holds its tail up. He wonders about these things, but he is still too limited in experience and in mental capacity to give them real theoretical meaning. Consequently he enjoys the wonder tale, or, as some authorities term it, the "primitive-why story." Early racial tales are those of forest and plain, varying according to the locality in which they originated, from the lion and tiger stories of India and Central Africa to the kangaroo fables of the Australian aborigine.

Primitive man through fear and fancy personified the forces of nature and gave them human attributes, and because they were less tangible than the creatures of jungle and plain that figured in his earliest fables, his mind visioned them as fantastic beings, sometimes lovely and sometimes grotesque, fairies and goblins, destructive monsters and demons, and avenging giants who preserved him from that which he feared. Thus originated the fairy story that was the expression of his religion. The child enjoys these tales.

The narrator can gather this material with comparative ease, because the science of ethnology has brought to light many of these tales from primitive literature, and not a few of them have been put into collections available to child workers.

The fairy tale that grew out of the life of the race is also rich in material for children of this period. By "fairy tale" is meant that type of story usually associated with the names of Grimm, Perrault, and Bechstein. Little people delight in it, and will listen to it again and again. Yet because of lack of understanding on the part of parents and teachers, the fairy story often proves to be the rock upon which the child craft meets disaster. Because these tales have had a mighty place in the history of the race and still have their work in the education of the child, it does not follow that they should be fed to young listeners as so much unassorted grain is fed to chickens. There are many that should not be used at all. Those that are used should be carefully graded, because a child will enjoy a narrative in which children are heroes, long before he enjoys one in which adults hold the center of the stage. The father and mother, brothers, sisters, uncles, cousins, and aunts mean much to him because they are part of his experience. But he does not know officers of the state and nation. He does not know lawmakers and magistrates and judges, and tales in which they have a part are less interesting to him than those whose characters are familiar personages. For instance, he is charmed by "Little Red Hen" or "The Three Bears" at an age when "Beauty and the Beast" or "Sleeping Beauty" mean little to him, and a good rule to guide the story-teller in the grading of fairy tales is the well-known pedagogical one, "Proceed from the known to the unknown, from the simple to the complex." Give first those stories whose heroes are familiar personages, then introduce those with characters not so well known.

The mention of fairy tales in education often raises the question, "Is there not danger of making liars of children by feeding them on these stories?" It seems to me the best answer is given by Georg Ebers, the Egyptologist and novelist, in his fascinating autobiography, *The Story of My Life.* Out of his own experience, he handles the subject of fairy tales sincerely and convincingly, and his words are worthy of consideration by every child worker.

"When the time for rising came," he says, "I climbed joyfully into my mother's warm bed, and never did I listen to more beautiful fairy tales than at those hours. They became instinct with life to me and have always remained so. How real became the distress of persecuted innocence, the terrors and charm of the forest, the joys and splendors of the fairy realm! If the flowers in the garden had raised their voices in song, if the birds on the boughs had called and spoken to me, nay, if a tree had changed into a beautiful fairy or the toad in the damp path of our shaded avenue into a witch, it would have been only natural.

"It is a singular thing that actual events which happened in those early days have largely vanished from my memory, but the fairy tales I heard and secretly experienced became firmly impressed on my mind.

Education and life provided for my familiarity with reality in all its harshness and angles, its strains and hurts, but who, in those later years, could have flung wide the gates of the kingdom where everything is beautiful and good, and where ugliness is as surely doomed to destruction as evil to punishment? Therefore I plead with voice and pen in behalf of fairy tales. Therefore I give them to my children and grandchildren and have even written a volume of them myself.

"All sensible mothers will doubtless, like ours, take care that the children do not believe the stories which they tell them to be true. I do not remember any time when, if my mind had been called upon to decide, I should have thought anything I invented myself really happened; but I know that we were often unable to distinguish whether the plausible tale invented by some one else belonged to the realm of fact or fiction. On such occasions we appealed to my mother, and her answer instantly set all doubts at rest, for we thought she could never be mistaken and knew that she always told the truth.

"As to the stories I invented myself, I fared like other imaginative children. I could imagine the most marvelous things about every member of the household, and while telling them, but only during that time, I often fancied they were true. Yet the moment I was asked whether these things had actually occurred, it seemed that I woke from a dream. I at once separated what I imagined from what I actually experienced, and it never would have occurred to me to persist against my better knowledge. So the vividly awakened power of imagination led neither me, my brothers and sisters, nor my children and grandchildren into falsehood."

Dr. Ebers' words are based on sound psychology. The child's imaginative nature should be developed, but there should never be any doubt in his mind as to what is make-believe and what is real. Let him wander at will through every realm of fancy, along its sun-kissed highways, among its shadowy glens and wild cascades, but let him realize it is a world of make-believe, not of fact, which he inhabits during that period. His imagination will be as much aroused, his emotional nature will be stirred as deeply, and there will be no discovery later that his mother or teacher deceived him, no temptation to present as fact what he knows to be purely fancy, which is a certain step toward the field of falsehood. If he questions whether a fairy story is true or not, tell him, "No, but once upon a time people thought it was true," and picture how the early tribesmen sat around the fire at night listening to tales told by some of their wise men, just as Indians and Eskimos do to this day. It will make him sympathetic toward the struggles of his remote forefathers, and he will not think the narrator tried to dupe him, nor will he regard the narrative itself as a silly yarn. It will be a dignified tale to him because it was believed in the long ago.

Since we can give only according to the measure in which we possess, whoever tells fairy stories to children ought to know something of their history and meaning. He should have some understanding of how they have come from the depths of the past to their present form, some idea of the work of notable collectors, and some insight into the fundamental principles of the science of folklore.

There are several theories about the origin of these tales, the first and oldest being that they are sun myths and can be traced back to the Vedas, and the exponents of this belief offer many arguments to prove the truth of their contention. The similarity of tales found among people of widely separated regions, they claim, is evidence that they must have come from a common source. "Little Half-Chick," a Spanish folk tale, is found in slightly different dress among the Kabyles of Africa; "Cinderella," in some form or other, is common to every country of Europe and to several oriental lands; while the Teutonic tale of "Brier Rose" and the French of "Sleeping Beauty" are modifications of the same *conte.* Therefore, the orientalists contend, they must have come from a common source and have been modified to suit conditions of life in lands to which they were carried.

Another theory is that all European fairy tales are remnants of the old mythology of the north, the nucleus of the stories having been carried abroad by the Vikings, while still another theory, the most notable advocate of which was the late Andrew Lang, traces fairy tales to the practices and customs of early man and a totemistic belief in man's descent from animals.

Then there are those also who contend that fairy tales are primitive man's philosophy of nature, his explanation of the working of forces he did not understand. The adherents of this theory admit the similarity of tales found among different tribes, but claim that the incidents, which are few, and the characters, who are types, might occur anywhere. In the French story of "Blue Beard" and the Greek tale of "Psyche" curiosity leads to destruction — in the one case of life, in the other of happiness. In the French "Diamonds and Toads," the Teutonic "Snow White and the Seven Dwarfs," and the Bohemian "The Twelve Months," selfishness brings punishment and kindness reward, while the cruel stepmother, the good prince, and the fairy godmother are common to tales of every nation.

But however authorities disagree as to the origin of these stories, they unite in declaring them to be one of the oldest forms of literature. The first collection of fairy tales of which we have any record was published in Venice in 1550 by Straparola, and was a translation of stories from oriental sources. From Italian the book was done into French and, for those early days when books were rare and costly, had a wide circulation. For almost a century this was the only collection of fairy tales in existence. Then, in 1637, a book was published in Naples, *Il Pentamerone*, which Keightley declares is the best collection of fairy tales ever written. The stories were told in the Neapolitan dialect and were drawn from Sicily, Candia, and Italy proper, where Giambattista Basile had gathered them from the people during years of wandering.

About sixty years later, in a magazine published at The Hague, appeared a story, "La Belle au Bois Dormant," by Charles Perrault, which was none other than the tale we know as "Sleeping Beauty." It did not originate with Perrault, but had been told him in childhood by his nurse, who was a peasant from Picardy. A year later seven other stories appeared, "Red Riding Hood," "Blue Beard," "Puss in Boots," "The Fairy,"

"Cinderella," "Riquet o' the Tuft," and "Hop o' My Thumb." They were published under the title, *Contes du Temps Passé avec Moralités*, and signed, "P. Darmancour." Darmancour was a stepson of Perrault, and wrote them at the older man's request from the nurse's tales; so they live in literature as Perrault's work. After this French collector came the German scholars, the Grimms, who gathered and preserved the folklore of the Thuringian peasants; Goethe, the Sage of Weimar; Madame Villeneuve; Ruskin; Andrew Lang; and several others. Each of these added to the work begun by Straparola and Basile, until now we have tales from almost every nation, tales proving that a belief in the supernatural is common to primitive people in every clime.

Another aspect wonderfully interesting in the study of fairy tales is the distinctive features of those of different regions, which are so marked that they can be classified according to the locality and topography of the region in which they originated. The largest number of these supernatural beliefs is found among nations whose scenery is wild and rugged, where there are mountains, morasses, dangerous cataracts, and tempestuous oceans, while in flat, cultivated countries away from the sea the fairy superstition is not so strong and the tales are less fantastic. This fact argues powerfully in favor of the Aryan theory that they are primitive man's philosophy of nature, the expression of his religion, and some educators claim that as they were religious stories to the race, they still are religious to the child.

Whether this theory is accepted or refuted, there can be no doubt in the mind of a thinking person that if fairy tales are given to children they should be given intelligently and with discrimination. The narrator should exercise care in their selection, and have some fixed principles to govern that selection, because of the quantity and doubtful literary and ethical quality of much juvenile material.

Many modern fairy stories are not fit to give to children. In selecting fanciful tales for this period of childhood, choose first of all the old ones, those that originated in the childhood of the race, the stories of Grimm, Perrault, and Bechstein. They have stood the test of the ages. They are expressed in beautiful language, they create ideals and arouse inspiration, they feed and satisfy.

There are some fairy tales of later origin that are the works of great writers and deserve the name of literature. First on this list come those of Hans Christian Andersen. "The Three Bears" of Robert Southey is another good example, and sometimes we find floating through magazines and in books of recent issue, fairy tales that are excellent ones to give to children, because they have all the elements of the racial tales. Notable among these is "The Wonder Box" by Will Bradley. But, if there be any doubt in the mind of the narrator about the merit of modern stories, he had better eliminate them from his list and use only those that have stood the test of the ages.

However, even among racial tales the narrator will come upon pitfalls unless judgment mark his selection. The conditions governing his struggle for existence gave primitive man a harsh standard, and consequently his literature is often tinged with a vindictive spirit wholly out of keeping with the ideals of today. Stories in which cruelty, revenge, and bloodshed have a large part should never be told to the young child, no matter what their age or origin. "Blue Beard" is a good example. Although itself a classic, and a recital of the deeds of a French ruler whose name is a synonym of infamy, this tale and all similar tales should be tabooed from the world of little people.

Charles Dickens was the first man in England whose voice carried weight to plead for fairy tales as a part of the school curriculum, and within a few years Dickens found it necessary to oppose the usage of stories that were corrupting the children of the British Isles. Because they were urged to tell fairy tales, unthinking teachers told any that they found, even those in which all the savagery of early man was portrayed. Accounts of beheadings and man-eatings became part of the daily program, and many acts of cruelty among children were traceable to these stories. Instead of teaching forbearance, courtesy, consideration of the poor and aged, and abhorrence of brute force, which the wisely chosen fairy tale will do, story-telling was turning the children into young savages. If the dominant element in a story is cruelty, strike that tale from the list; for even though the deed be punished in the end, the fact that the attention of an unkind child is focused upon cruel acts often leads him to experiment and see what will happen. And I plead also for the elimination from the story-teller's list of every tale in which an unkind or drunken parent plays a part, even though the tale itself be a literary gem. The father or mother is the child's ideal, and it is not the mission of the narrator to shatter that ideal. Even if little folk have discovered that there are delinquent parents in the world, it is a mental shock to have that fact emphasized, and the story that shocks in any way had better be left untold.

Sometimes the elimination or modification of a cruel feature of a tale makes it suitable for telling to children, as in "Hansel and Gretel." The ending Humperdinck uses in his opera, wherein the old witch turns to gingerbread instead of being baked in the oven by the orphans, is far better ethically than the original one, yet the elemental part of the story is left unspoiled. Narrators cannot be too careful in this respect; for the function of story-telling is to refine rather than to brutalize, to give pleasure and not to shock, and there is no excuse for using tales that corrupt or injure in any way when there are enough lovely ones to satisfy every normal desire of the child. Let the test of selection be the question, Does this story contain an element or picture that will shock a sensitive child or whet the cruel tendencies of a rough, revengeful one? If it does, do not use it even though the list of fairy tales may be reduced to a very limited one, but choose the other material for this period from the lore of science that will feed the fancy and not warp the soul or distort the character. (See Part II, Chapter XVI, "Story-Telling to Intensify Interest in Nature Study.")

Bibliography of Fairy Tales

Andersen, Hans Christian: *Wonder Stories Told to Children.*
Asbjørnsen, Peter Christen: *Fairy Tales from the Far North.*
Ballard, Susan: *Fairy Tales from Far Japan.*
Blumenthal, Verra X. K. de: *Folk Tales from the Russian.*
Bunce, John Thackeray: *Fairy Tales: Their Origin and Meaning.*
Chodzko, Alexander E. B.: *Fairy Tales of the Slav Peasants and Herdsmen.*
Croker, Thomas Crofton: *Legends and Fairy Tales of Ireland.*
Curtin, Jeremiah: *Myths and Folk Tales of the Russians, Western Slavs, and Magyars.*
Dumas, Alexandre: *Black Diamonds; The Golden Fairy Book.*
Edwards, Charles Lincoln: *Bahama Songs and Stories.*
Fortier, Alcée: *Louisiana Folk Tales.*
Graves, Alfred Perceval: *The Irish Fairy Book.*
Grimm, Jacob: *German Household Tales.*
Haight, Rachel Webb: *Index of Fairy Tales.*
Hartland, E. Sidney: *The Science of Fairy Tales.*
Jacobs, Joseph: *Europa's Fairy Book; English Fairy Tales; Celtic Fairy Tales.*
Keightley, Thomas: *Fairy Mythology.*
Kennedy, Howard Angus: *The New World Fairy Book.*
Laboulaye, Edouard René: *The Fairy Book; Last Fairy Tales.*
Lang, Andrew: *The Blue Fairy Book; The Orange Fairy Book; The Lilac Fairy Book; The Green Fairy Book; The Yellow Fairy Book; The Red Fairy Book.*
Macdonnell, Anne: *The Italian Fairy Book.*
MacManus, Seumas: *Donegal Fairy Stories.*
Mitford, Freeman: *Tales of Old Japan.*
Ozaki, Yei Theodora: *Japanese Fairy Tales.*
Perrault, Charles: *Tales for Children from Many Lands.*
Pyle, Howard: *The Wonder Clock.*
Ramaswami Raju: *Indian Fables.*
Scudder, Horace E.: *The Children's Book.*
Sharman, Lyon: *Bamboo: Tales of the Orient-born.*
Skeat, Walter W.: *Fables and Folk Tales from an Eastern Forest.*
Stanley, Henry M.: *My Dark Companions and Their Strange Stories.*
Steele, Flora A.: *Tales from the Punjab.*
Tappan, Eva March: *The Golden Goose.*
Williston, Teresa: *Japanese Fairy Tales.*
Wratislaw, A. H.: *Slavonian Fairy Tales.*

CHAPTER FOUR

The Story Interests of Childhood (*Continued*)

C. HEROIC PERIOD

WHEN the child leaves the imaginative period, he enters another realm of realism. The fairy world is no longer a place of enchantment to him. He is now in a condition corresponding to that of primitive man when he was not satisfied to sit by the tribal fire and listen to stories about creatures who personified the elements, but fared forth on the path of adventure, eager to know what lay beyond the lodge place of his people, feverish with desire to conquer and remove whatever obstructed his way. The barbaric, fighting instinct manifests itself, and in many children a destructive curiosity is apparent. They long to repeat the experiences of their ancestors in this same period. They want to live through nights of danger and days of daring, and since the juvenile court and probation officers hover Argus-eyed about them, ready to swoop down upon every lad who would go pirating or pathfinding, the nearest approach to the experience consists in listening to and in reading tales of adventure. This age is usually from about eight to twelve, although there are no tightly drawn lines of demarcation. Individual cases differ, and some children of ten are still delighted by fairy tales, while other lads of seven are well into the heroic period. Broadly speaking, however, this period begins about the age of eight.

There is no time in the child life during which the story-teller has a finer opportunity of sowing seeds that shall come into splendid fruition by and by than in the heroic period, and because parents and teachers do not realize this fact clearly enough, boys read stories whose tendency is to brutalize and lead them into trouble. It does not follow, because they are drawn as steel to steel to such literature, that the boys are depraved. They crave action, danger, daring. It is a cry of nature that cannot be silenced, and because the hunger is not satisfied in a wholesome way, they go where they can find the food they must have, for numerous doors are open to them.

Dozens of writers are doing pernicious work for the youth of the country by pouring forth a flood of adventure stories, perhaps not with malicious intent, but with the little knowledge that often brings dire results. Knowing the demand for the heroic, they write yarns whose only claim to recognition is a clever, spectacular plot. These books embody no ideals, and the aspirations they arouse had better be left to slumber. Sometimes, as a result of such reading, boys run away from home to fight Indians or turn pirate, and many a lad has begun a career of lawlessness ending in crime, who with a little direction might have been an individual of value to the world. Such cases are so common that they have come under the notice of almost every child worker, and the pity of it is that literature is rich in tales that satisfy the adventure craving, yet arouse high ideals and inspire to worth-while deeds. Instead of originating in the brain of some modern craftsman who is actuated by a desire for money-making, they grew out of the life of the race and perpetuate the noblest traditions of the race.

Human nature is much the same in all climes and in all ages. Until man reaches a very high state of enlightenment he is more thrilled by manifestations of physical bravery than by mental and moral courage, and he who possesses muscular strength is the hero in his eyes. A Hercules or Samson is mightier to him than a Savonarola facing persecution with sublime tenacity of purpose and dying steadfast to his ideal, because he can understand the brute strength of the one, while the spiritual fortitude of the other is beyond his comprehension. He is thrilled by action, physical action, and he craves and will have literature every page of which is colored by feats of prowess.

It is useless to try to substitute something else for children in this period. When we hunger for bread and meat, after-dinner mints will not satisfy, even though they be very delectable confections. This ravenous appetite of boys and girls must be satisfied, and if they are to grow into well-balanced men and women we must feed it with wholesome food instead of allowing them to roam unguided and eat of that which poisons.

There is no finer adventure tale in any literature than that of Robin Hood, none more satisfying to children in the early heroic period. This statement often brings a cry of remonstrance, and the objection is made that there is danger in portraying an outlaw as a hero, or in picturing the allurement of a brigandish career. But Robin Hood an outlaw? He lived in an age of injustice when might made right. The man of the people was but the chattel of a king, with no rights his lord was bound to respect. Bold Robin, in the depths of Sherwood Forest, devoted his life to redressing wrongs. He took from the oppressor and gave to the oppressed. He strove to stamp out injustice and tyranny, and his spirit is the foundation of the democracy that underlies every just government today. He was an outlaw, not because he was a criminal, but because he rebelled against the monstrous injustice of his age and strove to ameliorate the condition of the poor and downtrodden. In the time of Henry the Second he was hunted like a deer, but in the twentieth century he would be honored as a great reformer.

Robin's sense of justice appeals to boys and girls, and his fearlessness and kindliness awaken their admiration. They respond sympathetically to the story from the opening chapter, when he enters the forest and Little John joins his band, through the closing one where the hero of the greenwood goes to his final rest. If the tale is told with emphasis upon the true spirit of Robin Hood instead of with a half apology, it will prove wholesome food for the children and will help to make them juster, kinder, and more democratic men and women.

The national epics are splendid sources of story material for children in the heroic period, especially those originating in Teutonic lands and those formalized among nations not yet in a high state of civilization. Their characters are elemental, and their incidents appeal to boys and girls. Some of the stories of King Arthur and his knights, of Beowulf, of Sigurd the Volsung, of Frithjof, of Pwyll, hero of the Welsh Mabinogion, as well as many from the Nibelungenlied, the Iliad, and the Odyssey, can also be used with excellent results. Naturally the tales of an elemental type should be chosen first rather than those that are more highly refined and poetic. It has been my experience that the Mabinogion is enjoyed before the Arthuriad. Boys, especially, delight in hearing of Pwyll, lord of the Seven Countries of Dyved, and the adventures that befell him as he hunted in the forests of his dominions. These stories are of very ancient origin and are simple, strong, and dramatic. They were sung by harpers (mabinogs) in the castle halls of Wales, and finally were gathered into the Mabinogion, which was done into English by Lady Charlotte Gest. The story-teller will find *The Boy's Mabinogion*, by Sidney Lanier, an excellent handbook for this period, as it embodies the most desirable of this ancient Gaelic material, and is put into modern form by an artist.

Follow the Mabinogion with the less poetic of the King Arthur stories. The account of how Arthur won his sword and became king, of Percival and the Red Knight, and of Arthur fighting the giant mean more to the ten-year-old than does Sir Galahad and the Holy Grail. The Greek myths too should be drawn from during this period — not the highly poetic, finished tales of the Hellenes, but the elemental ones whose heroes are rugged characters that awaken child admiration. Hercules, Perseus, Achilles, and several other demigods vie for honors with King Arthur and Beowulf in the mind of the fourth-grade boy, and the story-teller should not fail to draw from the rich field of southern literature as well as from that of the north. But let her exercise care in selection and keep to the realm of heroism instead of entering that of romance.

Such stories as "Cupid and Psyche," "Pygmalion and Galatea," and "Apollo and Daphne" mean little to boys and girls of ten, yet teachers and librarians often use them and wonder why their audiences respond with so little enthusiasm. There are those who contend that all the epical stories should be given in simplified form during this period, but why spoil the romantic, poetic ones which are so much more enjoyed a little later and so much better understood, when there are hundreds that can be given without pruning them to the heart? Certain investigations and statistics show that the telling of the highly refined Greek myths to boys and girls in the early heroic period gives an erroneous idea of Greek standards, and dulls an interest in mythology later on. The story-teller should bear this fact in mind, and remember that literature rich in symbolism and formulated among people refined to a degree of æstheticism is not the literature to give to adventure-craving children, no matter to what simple language it may be reduced.

Splendidly dramatic is the tale of Roland and Oliver, which every boy loves, of Ogier the Dane, and of some of the other heroes of the time of Charlemagne. Children listen spellbound to the account of the first meeting and disagreement of the two lads whose friendship makes such a sweet and colorful story, and of Charles the Great in council with his peers and knights, and delight in the swinging lines of the old ballad:

> The emperor sits in an orchard wide,
> Roland and Oliver by his side:
> With them many a gallant lance,
> Full fifteen thousand of gentle France.

Upon a throne of beaten gold
The lord of ample France behold:
White his hair and beard were seen,
Fair of body and proud of mien.

The story of Bayard is an admirable one for this period, as well as that of the Spanish hero, the Cid; and "St. George and the Dragon" is always a favorite.

I plead, too, that more of the narrator's time be devoted to the telling of our own American epic of *Hiawatha.* The answer comes, "That is read in school." To be sure it is, and one reason why it is read so badly and appreciated so little is that it was not given in story form first. The German child uses the Nibelungenlied as a classroom text, but before he studies the epic he knows its tales. Gunther, Hagen, Siegfried, and Dankwart are familiar characters to him, and consequently he enjoys the poem.

The same principle applies to *Hiawatha.* If boys and girls are acquainted with Hiawatha himself, if they know Nokomis and Chibiabos and Kwasind and Iagoo before they are given the poem to study, it means something to them that it cannot mean otherwise. Perhaps one reason why Longfellow's masterpiece has been so little used by story-tellers is that the work of putting it into story form is a task with which the non-professional is unable to cope. Now, however, an excellent retold work is on the market — Winston's *Story of Hiawatha* — which makes it possible for every narrator to have her children know the American epic as well as German young people know the Nibelungenlied.

In considering stories for the heroic period of childhood, let us not forget the biographical and historical narratives that fulfill every requirement of hero tales. Boys and girls love the epical stories because they are true in spirit, but they love also those that are true in fact. It is a mistake to think that biography is dull and uninteresting to them, because stories of the boyhood of great men, great rulers, great discoverers and pathfinders, great lawgivers, painters, musicians, and writers, are hero tales of the highest type. Many of them have been told admirably for young people, and the narrator does no more valuable work than when he uses them freely. Sir Walter Raleigh, De Soto, Coronado, Frederick the Great, Napoleon, Garibaldi, Solyman the Magnificent, Robert the Bruce, Kosciusko, William Wallace, William Tell, and dozens of others are as fascinating as Beowulf or Hercules and have an influence even more powerful, because children know that these heroes have actually lived. Never mind what some authorities say about the man of Switzerland being a mythical personage. Let American young people know him as those of the Alpine land know him, as the defender of his ancient rights and native mountains, the embodiment of the spirit of Helvetia. They will be finer men and women because of it, and that, more than anything else, concerns the story-teller.

Then, too, there are history tales, hundreds of them, from every age and every land. There are brave deeds done by children that every child should know. The little girl on the St. Lawrence, holding the blockhouse of Vercheres against the Iroquois, the boy whose courage and presence of mind saved Lucerne, the event through which William of Orange came to be known as William the Silent, and many other similar narratives are intensely interesting to boys and girls. Some of the Old Testament tales belong in this period; for a detailed account of them see Chapter Twelve, on "Bible Stories."

At this age, when the adventure spirit runs high, when pathfinding and Indian fighting are desired above all other things, how are we to keep boys and girls from running away to lead such lives themselves? One way is by letting them live the lives of the heroes who thrill them — in other words, by dramatizing. It is the hunger for experience that causes boys to turn vagabond, and juvenile-court records show that many of the ten- and twelve-year-olds who are lured by the call of adventure come from homes that offer nothing to feed the adventure craving, whereas those who have some of the desired experiences at home are less likely to start out seeking them. It is a wise mother who encourages her boys to make pirate caves in their own back yards, to be youthful Crusoes, Kit Carsons, Daniel Boones, and Robin Hoods for a Saturday morning, and the school or public playground that provides for much out-of-door acting is doing something that will prevent many evils. In some children this desire is so strong that it is almost a fever, and if not satisfied in a wholesome manner is likely to lead to lamentable ends. I remember how much it meant to me in my own childhood, when I burned to lead the lives of some of the heroes of whom I had read or heard, to be permitted to participate in the Indian warfare of the neighborhood boys and be the maiden who was carried away into captivity. It was such a blissful experience that I joyfully contributed my small allowance to buy red ink for war paint and to help costume the braves, and when a Sioux band came to town, I ecstatically trudged after the wagon and lived for a day in a realm far removed from my accustomed one. The boys had feeling to even a greater degree, and who knows but that without this Indian play some of them might have gone forth in search of adventure and become criminals, whereas every one is now a law-abiding, useful citizen.

Sources of Story Material for the Heroic Period

Anderson, Rasmus Björn: *The Younger Edda.*
Baldwin, James: *The Story of Roland; American Book of Golden Deeds.*
Bolton, Sarah K.: *Poor Boys Who Became Famous.*
Bradish, Sarah P.: *Old Norse Stories.*
Brooks, Elbridge S.: *Historic Girls.*
Church, Alfred J.: *Stories from the Iliad; Stories from the Odyssey.*
Coe, Fannie E.: *Heroes of Everyday Life.*
Farmer, Florence V.: *Boy and Girl Heroes.*
Foa, Madame Eugénie: *Boy Life of Napoleon.*
Grierson, E. W.: *Tales from Scottish Ballads.*
Kingsley, Charles: *Greek Heroes.*
Lang, Jeanie: *The Story of Robert the Bruce; The Story of General Gordon.*
Lanier, Sidney: *The Boy's Mabinogion.*
Lansing, M. F.: *Page, Esquire, and Knight.*
Mabie, H. W.: *Norse Stories from the Eddas.*
Marshall, H. E.: *The Story of William Tell; The Story of Roland.*
Matthews, Agnes R.: *Seven Champions of Christendom* (St. George and the Dragon).
Morris, William: *Sigurd the Volsung.*
Nepos, C.: *Tales of Great Generals.*
Niebuhr, B. G.: *Greek Heroes.*
Pyle, Howard: *Some Merry Adventures of Robin Hood; Stories of King Arthur and His Knights.*
Ragozin, Z. A.: *Siegfried and Beowulf.*
Tappan, Eva M.: *In the Days of Alfred the Great; In the Days of William the Conqueror.*
Warren, Maude Radford: *Robin Hood and His Merry Men.*

CHAPTER FIVE

THE STORY INTERESTS OF CHILDHOOD (*Continued*)

D. ROMANTIC PERIOD

AT about the age of twelve or thirteen the child's rougher instincts begin to soften. Romance and sentiment develop. He becomes particular about his appearance. It is less of a task than formerly to get the boy to wash his face and hands, and he has not the antipathy toward civilized attire that he had in the days when Robinson Crusoe was the hero. Instead, he manifests a liking for being dressed according to prevailing modes, sometimes changing so suddenly from a dirty cave dweller into a dandy that it is like the metamorphosis from grub to butterfly. He craves socks and ties of bright colors and clothes that attract attention. If fashion prescribes peg-topped or straight, spare trousers, he wants them extremely wide or extremely narrow, and is willing to have his chin sawed unmercifully if high collars are the vogue, not because of a fit of hysteria, but because he has entered the period when sex awakens. He is becoming interested in the girls and wishes to be dressed in a manner that will cause them to be interested in him; and very often his taste for literature changes as completely as his personal habits. He desires stories of a higher type of heroism than those he craved in an earlier period, stories of romance and chivalry, and now is the time to give him the epic in its entirety, because of the deep racial emotions therein expressed.

He has had many of the adventure tales from the epics during the earlier period. Now he is ready for those tinged with romance, those pervaded by a spirit of fiery idealism in which knights risk limb and life in loyalty to principle, for fealty to king, or in defense of some fair lady. Percival seeking the Grail is a finer hero to him than Percival battling with the Red Knight, and the vow of the men of the Round Table means something because he can understand it. In a vague, indefinite way romance is touching his own life, and his noblest emotions are awakened by the noble words:

> To reverence the king, as if he were
> Their conscience, and their conscience as their king,
> To break the heathen and uphold the Christ,
> To ride abroad redressing human wrongs,
> To speak no slander, no, nor listen to it,
> To honor his own word as if his God's,
> To lead sweet lives in purest chastity,
> To love one maiden only, cleave to her,
> And worship her by years of noble deeds.

Boys and girls in the heroic period enjoyed only the Arthurian stories that glorify physical bravery, those of jousting and conflict into which women do not enter. But now they delight in such tales as those of Geraint and Enid, of Launcelot and Elaine, and some of the adventures of Tristram.

Here a word of caution is necessary. Like the Old Testament stories, these romantic tales will arouse the noblest emotions and highest ideals if given with wisdom, but if told thoughtlessly may create an almost morbid desire for the vulgar. Therefore the non-professional narrator should use for his work some retold version of the King Arthur tales instead of adapting from *Le Morte d'Arthur*, because there is much in the original that should be eliminated in presenting it to those in the adolescent period. The Pyle or Radford editions are excellent, likewise *The Boy's King Arthur*, by Sidney Lanier, each of which keeps the spirit of the poem, but omits everything objectionable.

The story of King Arthur, embracing as it does the Grail legend, should be followed by the German tale of "Parsifal," — not the Wagner opera version, but the original medieval legend, "The Knightly Song of Songs" of Wolfram von Eschenbach. This has been retold beautifully by Anna Alice Chapin in *The Story of Parsifal*, a book with which every child in the romantic period should be familiar. Miss Guerber, in her *Legends of the Middle Ages*, relates the tale of Titurel and the Holy Grail, which will be helpful to the narrator because of the light it throws on the origin of the legend. But for a telling version there is none equal to that of Miss Chapin, none in which the lofty chivalric spirit of the medieval poem is portrayed so faithfully.

The romantic portion of all the national epics, as well as that of *Le Morte d'Arthur*, is excellent material for the story-teller in the early adolescent period. The Nibelungenlied, the Iliad, the Odyssey, and parts of *Jerusalem Delivered* feed boys and girls in the early teens as pure adventure stories fed them a year or two before. And if the narrator would have his young listeners enjoy the epical tales to the uttermost, let him quote freely from the epic itself as he tells them. During this age, when romance and sentiment run high and life is beheld through a rainbow-hued glamour, poetry is a serious and beautiful thing. The frequent interpolation of it into a story heightens the pleasure in that story, and young people listen with the gleaming eyes of intense feeling to words like these of Siegfried:

> "Ever," said he, "your brethren I'll serve as best I may,
> Nor once while I have being, will head on pillow lay,
> Till I have done to please them whate'er they bid me do;
> And this, my Lady Kriemhild, is all for love of you."

Moreover, young people should understand that the epics were first given to the race in poetic form, and in leading them to that knowledge we can lead them also to an appreciation of the majestic, sweeping measures of the Iliad or Odyssey or Nibelungenlied, which is in itself worth thought and labor on the part of the story-teller.

The Langobardian myths, Dietrich von Bern, the story of Gudrun, of Charlemagne and Frastrada and Huon of Bordeaux, are intensely interesting in this period. Joan of Arc never fails to charm, while tales of the minnesingers, the troubadours, and the Crusaders open gates into lands of enchantment.

Oh, the romance in the lives of these medieval wanderers! Walther von der Vogelweide, too poor to buy him a coat, yet swaying the thought of the German lands; Bernard of Ventadour, among the flaming roses of Provence, making music at the court of Eleanor of Aquitaine; Richard Cœur de Lion, riding with a singing heart toward Palestine; De Coucy, Frederick Barbarossa, and scores of others who lived and achieved in that distant, colorful time! Their lives are gleaming pages in the history of their age, and their stories are glorious ones to give to boys and girls who crave the romantic.

Wonderful, too, is the account of the Children's Crusade, of Stephen, a happy shepherd on the hills of Cloyes, and that other lad of Cologne, who, fired with desire to restore to the Christian world places the Moslem had defiled, sailed away with their followers to shipwreck and slavery. In connection with this tale the children should hear, if possible, some of the music from Gabriel Pierne's great cantata, *The Children's Crusade.* It will give them a clearer, more vivid idea of the preaching of the boy apostle, of the gathering of the company, of the pilgrimage along the Rhine and Seine, of their rejoicing upon reaching the port of Marseilles, and of the light of noble purpose that glorified their eyes as they went singing to the ships. Perhaps historians have proved the account of this crusade to be just a myth. Tell it anyway, for whether it be fact or fiction the tale is too lovely for young folk to miss.

There is another type of biographical story, that of the man and woman of moral courage whose life was not so chromatically picturesque as that of him who fought the Saracens or sang in old Provence, but nevertheless thrills, fascinates, and influences. Florence Nightingale is a good example. Beautiful, the daughter of rich and distinguished parents, she might have reigned a social queen in England; yet she spent her young womanhood studying how to alleviate human suffering, toiling under the burning sun of the East, battling with disease at the risk of health and life, and well deserving the title given her by those she comforted, "The Angel of the Crimea." I have seen girls of sixteen listen with tears in their eyes to the story of this noble Englishwoman, and have watched the throats of boys throb and pulsate upon hearing the account of the British Army and Navy banquet at which the question was asked, "Who, of all the workers in the Crimea, will be remembered longest?" and every voice replied in refrain, "Florence Nightingale!" Several years ago a questionnaire, distributed at a convention of nurses, revealed the fact that ten per cent of those there had been influenced toward their life career by the story of this great English nurse. Yet there are dubious souls who wonder if story-telling pays! If the narrator can have only a few books from which to draw material for the romantic period, Laura E. Richards' *Life of Florence Nightingale* ought to be one of the number. It is sympathetically and beautifully told, an artist's tribute to an immortal woman.

Workers with youths in the adolescent period are brought face to face with one of the gravest problems educators have to solve. What is to be done about lovesick boys and girls, those in whom the elemental passions have awakened yet who have not the judgment and self-control that age and experience bring? How are we to keep them, in their first emotional upheaval, from losing all sense of proportion and from pursuing a course that may lead to disaster? The freedom given in these days of coeducation, and the unrestricted circulation of novels and stories dealing with the relations of the sexes, which may be worthy creations from the standpoint of art, but which distort the ideas of unformed youth, make possible a condition that often appalls parents and high-school teachers and sets them to wondering how to meet it.

Ellen Key suggests a remedy. In this period when the world-old emotions are first aroused, she advocates the use of love stories that are pure in tone and high in ideal. We cannot change human nature and keep the boy of sixteen from being drawn as if by a magnet to the maid who is lovely in his eyes, but we can give him an ideal that will make his feeling an elevating thing instead of a debasing one. We can put into the heart of the girl a poetry and idealism that will keep her worthy of the prince, and we can do it through literature. Instead of leaving her free to roam unguided and read whatever falls into her hand, or of sitting like a board of censors beside her and goading her toward the forbidden, which always allures, we can lead her to delightful, wholesome stories, of which there are a goodly number. This does not mean confining her to writers of several generations ago. Present-day youths know that almost every one reads current books, and they intend to have them, too. Therefore let the story-teller use the best of the new, even as he uses the best of the old. Let him refer frequently to it and tell enough of it to awaken such an interest that it will be read. A good plan is for the teacher of English to devote a few minutes each week to the discussion of some recent book or books, and to give lists of those that boys and girls will enjoy. In public libraries slips should be posted, upon which are named the most desirable of recent publications, and problem novels should be excluded from shelves to which the public has access. Thus our adolescent children may be led to glean from the best of the new. But meanwhile let us not neglect the old.

One of the lovely works with which to familiarize high-school pupils is *Ekkehard*, by Joseph Victor von Scheffel, which, aside from its value as a historical novel, is one of the noblest love stories ever written. It is a charming picture of life in the tenth century, when the Hunnic hordes swept like a devastating flame into the peaceful Bodensee region. Hadwig, proud duchess of Suabia, Ekkehard, the dreaming, handsome monk who goes from the monastery of St. Gall to become Latin instructor at Castle Hohentwiel and learns far more than he teaches, Praxedis, the winsome Greek maid, Hadumoth the goose girl, and the goat boy Audifax, all are fascinating, appealing characters. From beginning to end the book is intensely interesting, and as Nathan Haskell Dole says, "full of undying beauty."

Another charming work of a German writer is *Moni the Goat Boy*, by Johanna Spyri. The novels of Eugénie Marlitt are wholesome and well written, and give vivid pictures of life in the smaller courts of Europe. Those of Louisa Mühlbach portray in a remarkable manner the lives of some of the notable figures of history, and the intimate glimpses they give of such characters as Frederick the Great, Schiller, Goethe, Marie Antoinette, and Maria Theresa, with their reflection of the color and ceremony of a bygone day, cause them to mean in this period what adventure tales mean to boys and girls of ten.

In drawing from Germany, let us not forget Georg

Ebers, who lifts the cloud of mystery that veils old Egypt and permits us to share the romance, the loves, the joys and sorrows of men and women of the Pharaohs' time. His works are not dull inscriptions gathered from sepulchers and mummies, but moving pictures of living, breathing men and women, filmed by the genius of a master; and the triumphs of the Princess Bent-Anat, the sufferings of the captive Uarda, and the spectacular victory of the royal charioteer are so real that they seem to be in the here and now instead of in the early morning of the world.

From France we may glean without limit. Georges Ohnet, Jacques Vincent, Ludovic Halévy, and dozens of other writers have produced works that are not only a part of the education of every one who aspires to become a cultured man or woman, but are as fascinating as fairy tales to a child. Then there is the great treasure house of English and American literature, as rich in priceless things of pen and brain as the gallery of the Vâtican is rich in paintings and sculpture. Boys and girls will not draw from this wealth unguided, because they do not know where it is stored. But if we give them frequent glimpses of its brightness, if we half open the door of the repository and let them peep inside, they will follow, seeking it, as the miner follows the half-revealed ore vein, or as Ortnit of old pursued the Fata Morgana. They need not drift into pools that breed disease, when by enough story-telling to awaken their interest in the beautiful and fine they may sail into open streams where the water is clear, and where there are no submerged reefs to wreck their fragile crafts.

Sources of Story Material for the Romantic Period

Antin, Mary: *The Promised Land.*
Bolton, Sarah K.: *Famous Leaders among Men.*
Boutet de Monvel, L. M.: *The Story of Joan of Arc.*
Brooks, Elbridge Streeter: *Historic Girls.*
Buell, Augustus C.: *John Paul Jones, Founder of the American Navy.*
Buxton, Ethel M. Wilmot: *A Book of Noble Women; Stories of Persian Heroes.*
Chapin, Anna Alice: *The Story of Parsival.*
Church, Alfred James: *Stories from the Iliad; Stories from the Odyssey.*
Creighton, Louise von Glehn: *Some Famous Women.*
Gilbert, Ariadne: *More than Conquerors.*
Gilchrist, Beth Bradford: *Life of Mary Lyon.*
Guerber, Helène A.: *Legends of the Middle Ages.*
Lanier, Sidney: *The Boy's King Arthur.*
Lockhart, John Gibson: *Ancient Spanish Ballads.*
Lowell, Francis Cabot: *Joan of Arc.*
Nicholson, J. S.: *Tales from Ariosto.*
Quiller-Couch, Sir Arthur Thomas: *The Roll Call of Honor.*
Richards, Laura E.: *Florence Nightingale, the Angel of the Crimea.*
Snedeker, Caroline D.: *The Coward of Thermopylæ.*
Southey, Robert: *The Life of Nelson.*
Sterling, Mary Blackwell: *The Story of Parzival; The Story of Sir Galahad.*
Strickland, Agnes: *The Queens of England; The Queens of Scotland.*

CHAPTER SIX

Building the Story

STORY-TELLING is a creative art, and therefore a knowledge of underlying principles is as indispensable to the narrator as to the sculptor or painter. Without this knowledge he cannot hope to adapt material to his needs, but must be limited in his choice to what is already in form to give to children; with it he can avail himself of many opportunities to bring to his charges treasures of which they could know nothing but for his ability to dig them from the profound tomes in which they are hidden, polish and clarify them, and put them in a setting within the understanding of the child. For this reason a course in story-writing is a part of the training of the professional story-teller, and while the mother or teacher cannot make such extensive preparation, she may to advantage master and apply a few cardinal principles of construction.

The beginning of the oral story should never be an introduction, because from the first word the child expects something to happen, and if nothing does happen his attention scatters and interest is lost. Therefore the narrator must bring his actors on the stage and get them to work at once; he must not let them stand around waiting while he gives a detailed description of their hair and eyes and of the clothes they wear, but must have them do something. It is often necessary to make some explanatory remarks in the beginning, but it should be done in such a way that the hearer has no time to wonder when the story is going to begin. For instance, if your tale is about a boy in Holland, do not delay bringing the boy in while you tell about the country. Let him enter at the beginning, and then, by a sentence here and a clause or phrase there, give the setting with the action. The story must bristle with human interest; for while the child knows nothing about the meaning of that term, he nevertheless demands that something happen, and if nothing does happen you lose his attention. The written story may depend for its charm upon character drawing and local color, but the oral story demands *plot*, and if this plot is badly hung together the story fails in its aim, for it does not make a deep impression.

The narrative style is better adapted to beginning the oral story than dialogue, because it is more easily handled by the novice. Of course the professional story-teller is not restricted to one field, and genius is privileged to range at large and ignore rules with no dire results. But it is safe for the amateur to keep to the narrative style. In the depths of dialogue, his little craft may founder, but the much-loved words "Once upon a time" or "Long, long ago" arrest the attention immediately, even though the teller be not an artist; and having made a good beginning, he is reasonably sure of holding his hearers to the end. On the other hand, if he does not get them at the start, his story-telling time is apt to end in failure.

There are no set phrases or clauses with which one must begin a story, and it would be a mistake to say that dialogue can never be used safely in opening the oral story, for the professional often uses it with fine effect; but it is easier and safer for the amateur to use the narrative beginning, and introduce dialogue as the plot develops.

Dr. Berg Esenwein, whose excellent work, *Writing the Short Story*, will be of value to the story-teller as well as to the story-writer, lays down these rules:

"Do not strike one note in the beginning and another in the body of the story.

"Do not touch anything that is not a live wire leading direct to the heart of the story.

"Do not describe where you can suggest."

An examination of some of the perfect stories of the world shows that these rules hold good in every case. The tales of Grimm, Andersen, Perrault, and Bechstein are flawless in construction, and each plunges directly into the thread of the story. Take, for instance, "The Three Tasks" of Grimm:

> There once lived a poor maiden who was young and fair, but she had lost her own mother, and her stepmother did all she could to make her miserable.

"The Pea Blossom," of Hans Christian Andersen:

> There were once five peas in a pod. They were green and the pod was green, and they thought all the world was green.

"Red Riding Hood," as written by Perrault, begins thus:

> Once upon a time there lived in a small village in the country a little girl, the prettiest, sweetest creature that ever was seen. Her mother loved her fondly, and her grandmother doted on her still more.

"The Twin Brothers" by Grimm:

> There were once two brothers, one of whom was rich and the other poor. The rich brother was a goldsmith and had

a wicked heart. The poor brother supported himself by making brooms, and was good and honest.

It is the same in Ruskin's "King of the Golden River," in Robert Southey's "Three Bears," in all the tales of De Maupassant that are suitable for telling, and in those of Alphonse Daudet. Note the beginning of Daudet's "Last Lesson":

> Little Franz did not want to go to school that morning. He would much rather have played. The air was so warm and still. You could hear the blackbirds singing at the edge of the wood, and the sound of the Prussians drilling down by the old sawmill.

Every one of these stories begins with narrative, and every one is a perfect tale for telling.

Next in consideration comes the body of the story, which our rhetoric teachers taught us is a succession of events moving toward the climax. Until the climax is reached the oral story must be full of suspense. In other words, the hearer must be kept guessing about what is going to happen. The child does not care about a story in which he sees the end. He does enjoy hearing the same story told over and over again if it thrilled him at the first telling, because he likes to re-experience that thrill. But if a new tale holds no suspense, it falls flat. Stevenson says: "The one rule is to be infinitely various — to interest, to disappoint, to surprise, yet still to gratify. To be ever changing, as it were, the stitch, yet still to give the effect of an ingenious neatness." In other words, the succession of events must follow one another in a regular sequence, and each must contribute something to the one following it.

As a rather homely illustration of the meaning of this, we may say that plot centers around a hole, and in a well-constructed story the steps by which the hero gets into the hole are traced, and then those by which he gets out. The getting out is the climax or, as Dr. Barrett says, "the apex of interest and emotion." In other words, it is the top of a ladder, and the story must move in an unbroken line toward that topmost rung. If it does not do this, if the thread of the tale is broken to interpolate something that should have been told in the beginning, the narrator loses his audience.

The climax must be a surprise to the child. This holds good in all the great oral stories. Take as an example "The Ugly Duckling":

> And he flew toward the beautiful swans. As soon as they saw him they ran to meet him with outstretched wings.
>
> "Kill me," he said.
>
> But as he bent his head he saw reflected in the water, not a dark, gray bird ugly to see, but a beautiful swan.

In Hawthorne's "Great Stone Face" the climax lies in the discovery that Ernest is the likeness of the Great Stone Face, a delightful surprise to the child.

It is the same in "Red Riding Hood," in "Tarpeia," in "Why the Sea Is Salt." It is the same in Daudet's "Last Lesson." Note the splendid climax of that masterpiece, the surprise that comes to Franz as he sits awaiting punishment, when the teacher, in all kindness, makes this announcement:

> "My children, this is the last time I shall ever teach you. The order has come from Berlin that henceforth nothing but German shall be taught in the schools of Alsace and Lorraine. This is your last lesson in French."

With very young children the surprise element should be simple. Repetition used in a sequence, or jingle, accomplishes it well, as in the "Fee, fi, faugh, fum" in "Jack and the Beanstalk," or "Who's been sitting in my chair?" in "The Three Bears," or "The better to see you, hear you, eat you" in "Red Riding Hood." Each time the child hears the expression his interest is roused to a higher pitch, and his imagination is fired to such a point that he expects almost anything to happen.

After the climax is reached, the oral story should descend rapidly to a close. Many of the best oral stories end in the climax, and those that do not, add but a sentence or two or a paragraph at most to round out to completion. But they do not moralize and point out a lesson to the child. They leave him to see the moral for himself, and he sees it more clearly and is the more deeply impressed by it if he is allowed a few moments of silence after the completion of the story, instead of being drawn into conversation concerning it. Marie Shedlock, the English story-teller who has done so much to put the narrator's art upon the plane where it deserves to be, advocates five minutes of silence after each story period, and in my own experience I have found that it is of value to the child. Conditions under which one works will, of course, govern this; but above all, do not end a story that delights a boy or girl and then kill the whole effect by saying, "Now, Peter, what does that story teach you?" Give the child credit for being an intelligent human being, and do not spoil a tale for him by turning it into a sermon while he is still tingling with the wonder and joy of it.

CHAPTER SEVEN

Telling the Story

SINCE story-telling, like music, is an art, it is no more possible for every mother, teacher, or librarian to become a Scheherazade than it is possible for every child who takes music lessons to blossom into a Mozart or a Mendelssohn. The inspiration, the creative fire that beguiles the wrath of a sultan or gives birth to a symphony, emanates from within, from the fairy germs planted somewhere in the soul and nurtured into fruition through unceasing effort. Yet it is possible for every worker with children, provided he be willing to devote some time and labor to the study of technique, to learn to tell stories convincingly and entertainingly, although not with the artistry of the professional.

First of all, whenever possible, he should choose stories that appeal to him, those he will enjoy giving his listeners because they fit his own moods, for he cannot hope to tell every variety of tale with consummate excellence any more than an actor can be supreme in all types of rôles. The genius of Sothern displays itself to best advantage in the tragedies of Shakespeare, while that of Henry Miller, Forbes-Robertson, or David Warfield is suited to dramas of another kind. Each of these artists tried various rôles until he found his forte. Then he kept to the field in which he could excel, concentrating all his effort upon it. So it should be with the story-teller. He should experiment with every kind of narrative, then make a specialty of the one in which he can be at his best, and use it to accomplish his most far-reaching results. Of course the mother or teacher cannot confine herself to one variety of story. Her interests being varied and many, she cannot hope to reach the height of specialization attained by the artist who has but one purpose, one aim, and never swerves from it. She must endeavor to acquire a fair degree of proficiency in the rendition of every type of story, that she may not be found wanting by her youthful auditors; but she should specialize with the kind of tale that is nearest an expression of her own moods, because in this way she can obtain the most gratifying results.

Perhaps she is particularly skilled in presenting humorous material. Then let her use that ability as a magnet to draw her hearers to the story period and to hold them through it to the end. A good plan is to begin the program with a merry tale to put the group into a happy, receptive mood, follow it with a serious one containing the message or information the children should receive, and then give another humorous one. The serious narrative may be difficult for her to handle, and may not be given with the skill and charm that mark her rendition of another type of *conte*, but the children, understanding that one of her delightful "funny" stories is to follow, will listen through the less desired number and unconsciously receive its lesson, because of their eagerness to hear the succeeding one. Thus, by knowing her field of excellence and making the most of it, she can carry children into other fields because of their delight in meeting her in the one in which she is most at home.

After the story is selected, the atmosphere and setting should be studied. The teller should have a clear idea of the topography of the country in which the events occur, of the customs of the people who move through it, of their homes, their modes of life, and their manner of dress, because the more into the spirit of the tale he can put himself, the more effectively will he give it. If it be a narrative of Scotland in the days of Bruce, he should try to hear the bagpipes, see the lochs and glens of the Highlands, and walk side by side with the heroes of that time. This means gleaning many fields for materials and giving something of an artist's labor to preparation, in which, of course, he will be limited by the time at his disposal. But according to the preparation will be the result, and to believe previous thought and study unnecessary because one has natural facility for story-telling is to be gravely mistaken. Artists of the stage discovered long ago that no matter how gifted they may be, nothing can take the place of preparation. Adrienne Lecouvreur demonstrated the truth of this statement several centuries ago when she revolutionized acting, and theatrical folk are still demonstrating it, for in just this respect lies the difference between the third- and fourth-rate player and the great dramatic star. The leading man or woman who is satisfied to learn lines and do nothing more, does not get beyond stock. But one ambitious to climb to the top rung of the histrionic ladder will travel every bypath that may possibly yield him a fuller and richer comprehension of the part he has to play. Geraldine Farrar read everything obtainable about Japan and Japanese life before attempting to create the rôle of "Madame Butterfly," and Maude Adams spent months studying the life of the Maid of Orleans, following every step of her career from the hills of Domrémy to the pyre at Rouen, before being satisfied to present "Jeanne d'Arc" at the Harvard Stadium. So it must be with the story-teller. Only the professional can devote weeks, or even days, to the preparation of one program, but every one who attempts to tell stories must know more than the plot of the tale and must have felt its events in all their possibilities, if his hearers in their turn are to feel them.

The amount of preparation necessary varies with the individual. Those possessing natural facility and those who heard much story-telling in childhood need less than those whom Nature has not gifted, or who were not so fortunate in early environment. But every one needs some preparation, and there is much slovenly, valueless story-telling because this fact is not generally recognized. Many teachers do not regard story-telling seriously enough, and devote far less thought to it than to other branches of their work, because the idea is prevalent that any one can spin a yarn or two. Consequently they accomplish little through the medium of the story. But there is another group of workers who believe that story-telling means as much today as it meant centuries ago, and its members are sending children into the libraries. As nearly as time and the conditions of their work will permit them, they are following in the footsteps of the medieval narrator. Like him, they are giving an artist's labor to their work because they realize that great results come only through great effort. But the number of these story-tellers, compared with the workers with children, is very small, and consequently results are not yet gratifying. They can become gratifying only when child leaders cease to think that the story period is the one period of the day for which no preparation need be made, and realize that every minute devoted to previous thought and study will make the language come more spontaneously and fluently and will bring before the eyes of the listeners pictures that are clear because they first have been clear before the eyes of the teller.

Every scene in a story should be visualized until it is as vivid as a painting on a canvas. It must be studied and imagined until it shifts smoothly and rapidly into the succeeding one. Then there will be no danger of the teller having to pause and think what comes next, or of having to interpolate something that should have been introduced at an earlier stage of the tale. This is not equally easy for every one. Those who are imaginative by nature will find it no task, while for others it will be difficult at first. But no one need be discouraged. Each succeeding attempt will bring clearer pictures and smoother shifting of scenes, and gratifying results will follow labor and perseverance. It is a good plan for the beginner to jot down in outline form the successive events of the story and study them until he can carry the sequence in his mind.

When the pictures are clear and the order of events is fixed, the story should be practiced. This does not mean that it should be learned verbatim. Untrained narrators often make the mistake of memorizing paragraph by paragraph and sentence by sentence, and then giving the tale like a recitation, which is not story-telling at all. Story-telling is a constructive, creative art, and the tale that grips and convinces and inspires must be told in a manner that makes it seem like the teller's own. Practicing the story means facing an imaginary audience and describing so vividly and clearly what is seen that others may see the pictures that pass before the mind's eye.

Shall gesture and facial gymnastics be used? This depends entirely upon the temperament and personality of the narrator. If it is natural for him to gesticulate as he speaks, gesture will come spontaneously and will heighten the effect of the tale. But if movements of hand and head and body are not spontaneous, they will mar the rendition and scatter the interest of the listeners by dividing it between the teller and the tale. Story-telling then becomes touched with affectation and loses its artistry. It degrades the story-teller into a sort of acrobatic performer and makes him a personage upon whom the attention is centered, which is not as it should be. He is simply the medium through which the picture is made clear to the audience. He is not an actor, and should not occupy the center of the stage. As Dr. Partridge says: "The story-teller should pleasingly suggest the mood and scene of the story, then step into the background, turn down the lights on the present, and carry his hearers to a distant region, which he must make, for the time being, more real than the here and now." This is why the story-teller is at his best away from the glare of electricity, among the shadows of a summer gloaming, or by the open hearth when the firelight is dim, because then his hearers do not see him or think of him, but only of the pictures and scenes painted by his voice and words.

Therefore let the guiding rule of the narrator be, "I must describe pictures so that others will see them, and think, not of me, but of the scenes to which I lead them." And he must do it in his individual way. If gesture comes naturally, it belongs in the tale. If it is studied and artificial, it destroys the effect and value. Some of the greatest story-tellers of the past used no gesture, while others used body, head, and hands with wonderful effect. They were persons of strong individuality and did things in an individual way. Let the present-day story-teller profit by their example.

Change of voice in dialogue adds to clearness of pictures. Nothing is more colorless than a reading by one whose intonation is not in keeping with the part he interprets, and the story told in a monotone is boresome and valueless to the child. He associates tone and action and wants them to be true to each other. He is dissatisfied if the old witch speaks like a loving mother, while the heavy tones of the wicked giant, the gentle ones of the good fairy, and the mirthful, rippling notes of the joyous, beautiful maiden delight him and make him responsive to the tale. They transform the personages of the story into living, breathing creatures who walk in his presence and smile or frown in his face.

Pauses are wonderfully effective in heightening the interest in a story. Children fairly quiver with expectation if frequent pauses are used when the moments of suspense grow big. They creep nearer in their eagerness to hear about what happens next, fearing that they will miss a bit of the attractive thread. One small boy, asked why he took such delight in listening to a certain story-teller, said: "I don't know if it's the way she looks or the way she says it. She'll be going along, telling about what happens, and all at once she'll say, 'And then ——' and stop a little bit until you think all kinds of things are going to happen." This feeling is general with children, although they may not voice it, and behind the naïve words is a psychological truth. The pause heightens the dramatic effect and focuses the interest on the coming sentences.

Above all things, there should be no stopping in the midst of a tale to correct a child. If one shows evidence of lagging interest, mention his name as if the story were being told for him. "And, John, when little Red Riding Hood reached her grandmother's house she knocked on the door." This makes him feel that although many children are listening to the story, it is being given solely for his benefit. It touches his pride and grips his attention long enough to enable the narrator to muster all his forces and heighten the interest in the tale so that it will abound in suspense from that point. If it fails to do that, something is wrong, either with the selection or the presentation. Perhaps the pictures are not being made clear because they were not first clear in the mind of the teller. Perhaps the story is not an interesting one to that particular group of children. It is the narrator's business to find the reason, just as artists in Europe must learn what is at fault when their hearers hiss. Audiences on the Continent are not so polite as those in America, and there is no mistaking their feeling about a performance. When sounds of disapproval sweep over the house, the performer must rise to heights that will compel admiration or face a ruined career. Likewise, when a small boy becomes troublesome, the story-teller should not pause to correct him, but should make the tale so thrillingly fascinating that the lad forgets to be naughty. Mothers seldom meet with this problem, but settlement workers are having to solve it constantly, and they do it successfully only by knowing what lies close to the child interests and telling stories that touch those interests.

There are those who denounce story-telling in the schoolroom because they happen to have known of poor story-telling and the disorderly conduct that often ensues when the children's interest is not held. Not long ago I came across this statement in the report of a lecture delivered at a teachers' institute:

"It is to be hoped that story-telling will soon be eliminated from the primary grades, and that the spectacle of a teacher pausing in the midst of a tale to grasp a child by the arm and exclaim, 'Here, Johnny, straighten up and listen,' will become past history."

It certainly is to be hoped that such story-telling will be eliminated, but it is no more fair to condemn story-telling as an art or to deprecate its value as an educational or ethical factor because there is poor story-telling, than it is to decry painting and sculpture because there are bunglers with brushes and chisels. The remedy does not lie in abolishing it, but in elevating the standard of the workers to a higher plane and in demonstrating that story-telling syncopated by scoldings and admonitions is not story-telling at all.

When shall we tell stories? Whenever, in the opinion of the teacher, a story will do more effective work than something else. Do not depend wholly on regular periods. These have a place on every school, library, or settlement program, but the story period should not be the only time for telling stories, because often a tale told at the psychological moment will make a deeper and more lasting impression than those given during a dozen regular periods. When the children are tired, tell a story for rest and relaxation. If there has been a fight or swearing, follow up the incident as soon as possible with an apt narrative. It will do more good than moralizing. If the geography class is struggling over the map of Turkey and can see nothing but a series of dots and marks on a piece of paper, put aside the formal recitation for that day and tell them of the building of the Mosque of Ahmed the First on the Golden Horn, of the merry craftsmen who raised the dome of St. Sophia, and give them some idea of how this glorious waif of the Orient came to stand on European soil. Make story-telling fit occasions and conditions instead of trying to make conditions fit story-telling.

And above all, never moralize! As one authority says, "It is bad pedagogy and worse art." Remember what Dr. van Dyke says: "If a story is worth telling, moralizing is not necessary." It is not only unnecessary, but harmful. The child sees for himself that virtue is rewarded and evil-doing is punished. He resents not being given credit for having sufficient intelligence to understand it, and a personal application antagonizes him.

Tell the tale in a direct, unassuming manner — not as if you are talking down to a group of children, but as if you are one of the number, talking with them. Boys and girls dislike the patronizing story-teller as much as adults dislike the patronizing person, and are quick to detect affectation and insincerity. They will not receive the message a posing raconteur has to give, because his manner of delivering it irritates and estranges them. The successful story-teller must be like the poet, a joy bringer, and he can be that only when his work is marked by sincerity and genuineness as clear as brook water.

Books on Story-Telling

Allison, S. B., and Perdue, H. A.: *The Story in Primary Education.*

Bailey, Carolyn Sherwin: *For the Story-Teller.*

Bryant, Sara Cone: *How to Tell Stories to Children.*

Coe, Fanny E.: *First Book of Stories for the Story-Teller; Second Book of Stories for the Story-Teller.*

Cowles, Julia D.: *The Art of Story-Telling.*

Dye, Charity: *The Story-Teller's Art.*

Forbush, William B.: *Story-Telling in the Home.*

Keyes, Angela M.: *Stories and Story-Telling.*

Lindsay, Maud: *The Story-Teller for Little Children.*

Lyman, Edna: *Story-Telling: What to Tell and How to Tell It.*

McMurry, Charles A.: *Special Method in Primary Reading and Oral Work, with Stories.*

Partridge, Emelyn N. and George E.: *Story-Telling in the Home and School.*

St. John, Porter: *The Story in Moral and Religious Education.*

Shedlock, Marie L.: *The Art of the Story-Teller.*

Wiltse, Sara E.: *The Place of the Story in Early Education.*

Wyche, Richard Thomas: *Some Great Stories and How to Tell Them.*

CHAPTER EIGHT

Story-Telling to Lead to an Appreciation of Literature

ONE of the specific aims of education is to endow children with an appreciation of literature, and to this end much of a teacher's energy is directed. From the elementary school through the university the curriculum includes a course in English, and even in kindergarten and primary grades a point is made of introducing children to those authors whose work is conceded to have a strong appeal for them. The first, second, or third grade boy is required to read and memorize selections from Stevenson, Riley, and Eugene Field; not infrequently he is detained after school because of failure to have his lesson prepared at recitation time, and responds to the requirement in a mood that brings discouragement to his teacher.

On the other hand, there are schools in which the literature or reading hour is a period of joy, where the learning of songs of the singers of childhood is accomplished without coercion. These schools are the ones in which the teachers have learned that the acquisition of knowledge, to be of real value, must be attended with enjoyment.

It is a mistake to believe that although the function of the school is to equip the man, the aim of education is only to give enjoyment in the future. It is also the aim of education to give enjoyment now, because in this way capacity for enjoyment in the future is made possible. The boy or girl whose early association with poetry or beautiful prose is attended with displeasure and discomfort is no more likely to be drawn to the finer types of literature later than the man or woman is apt to be fond of a person, the first meeting with whom was a disagreeable experience. If we would have the man love good literature, we must first lead the child to love good literature, and we can do this only through having him enjoy good literature.

Because story-telling brings pleasure to the child, it is a most effective means of leading him to an appreciation of literature. Through the medium of the story we not only can heighten his capacity for enjoyment and elevate the standard of his taste, but we can equip him with knowledge he will never acquire if the literature period is associated with force and punishment. If a tale brings pleasing pictures before his eyes and is beautiful in theme and language, he unconsciously forms a taste for beautiful language, for he is not only getting the succession of events that make the plot, but is also absorbing words and expressions. Certain sentences stick in his memory, and teachers who have children reproduce stories know that frequently they use the exact phrases and sentences that have been used by the teller. They do not remember these for a day or an hour and then forget them; they remember them as years go by, and associate certain words with certain narratives.

William McKinley once said that the mention of willows by a river made him think of the story of Moses in the bulrushes, and brought to mind this sentence: "And she hid the basket among the rushes in a spot where willows hung over the river." The story had been told him in childhood and brought him enjoyment, and some of the narrator's expressions left a lasting imprint on his mind. "I believe that story, more than anything else," he once said, "gave me a fondness for elegant English."

James A. Garfield voiced almost the same thought, declaring that his taste for literature was shaped by stories from great authors told him by his mother during his early years, and many other men of achievement have attested to the same truth. They have proved conclusively out of their own experience that even with little children it is possible to lay a foundation upon which a noble and enduring structure can be built. We can give them an appreciation of stories and poems that are among the gems of literature.

We can also interest children in the life of an author so that they will want to know something of his work. This statement often brings the question, "How, since little children want stories that are full of action, and not biographies of men and women they never have seen?" Is it not true that the childhood of all great men contained interesting experiences, that if told as stories will lead little people to want to know about what these boys and girls did when they grew up?

Robert Louis Stevenson is a good example. Every child will listen sympathetically to the tale of the poor little rich boy who was often so ill that he could not run and play, but who made the best of things and amused himself with toys on his bed. He built cities out of blocks. He watched the lamplighter go on his evening rounds along the street, and sometimes in the summer, the dewy, Scotch summer that can be pictured so attractively to children, when he went with his nurse to the country or the shore, he put leaves and chips in the river and pretended that they were boats. He dug holes in the sand with his wooden spade and laughed to see the vagrant waves come up and fill them. The child who hears about his various experiences will become intensely interested in little Robert, and will grow to love "The Land of Counterpane," "The River," "At the Seashore," and other selections from *A Child's Garden of Verses.* Every time he reads or hears them he will see a picture of the wee Scotch lad whose story touched his heart.

This is no untried theory. Through story-telling, the author of *Treasure Island* has become a living personage and *A Child's Garden of Verses* a source of delight in more than one first grade. A teacher who had charge of forty little Italians devoted fifteen minutes each morning to stories of writers and their works, and by the end of the term the children had a knowledge of Stevenson and Field that amazed the superintendent. More valuable than the knowledge acquired was the capacity for real enjoyment of some of the works of these men, enjoyment so intense that during the half hour of song and games that was a feature of every Friday, it was not unusual for a small Tony or Gulielmo to flutter a brown hand and ask to be permitted to recite:

> Of speckled eggs the birdie sings,
> And nests among the trees.

Another teacher was rewarded for her work by hearing the mother of one of her pupils tell at a parent-teachers' meeting of how a certain little lad amused himself while recuperating from measles by entertaining the household with songs from Stevenson and stories about little Robert, who became the big Robert that wrote the book.

In doing this sort of work, however, it is necessary to keep in mind the story interests of childhood, to remember that children are interested in children, and not begin, "When Robert Louis Stevenson was a little boy," but rather, "Once there was a little boy who lived far away from here, and his name was Robert." Let the approach be from the child to the man instead of from the man to the child. Focus the interest of children upon one like themselves, then lead in a natural way to the man and his achievements.

Sometimes children can be interested in a piece of literature through a story about it or suggested by it, because often one tale helps to illuminate and clarify and add interest to another.

Suppose a primary teacher or a mother wishes to take up Tennyson's "Sweet and Low," a piece of literature that is either a succession of vivid, delightful pictures or a vague group of words, according to the manner in which it is presented. Tell of the baby who lived with the father and mother in a fishing village on the Isle of Wight. Each day the father had to go far out to sea in a boat to catch fish to sell for money with which to buy food for his dear ones, and each night the baby laughed and crowed when he came home. Once he stayed later than usual, and baby did not want to go to bed without seeing him; but the mother sang a pretty song, saying that father would soon be home, and crooned and rocked her little one until he fell asleep. It was a pleasant evening, with a big, silver moon, and a man was out walking — a rich man who lived in a house on a hill high above the fishers' huts. As he went by the cottage where the baby lived, he heard the mother singing, and the song was so sweet that he hurried home and wrote what it made him think about. Then follow with the poem, and the children will receive it gladly.

This same plan can be used with older children, but let the material be given in story form instead of as a series of disconnected incidents.

An excellent method is to give the story of a great writer's work. This is effective with children of all ages, and often leads to the reading of books that otherwise would never be opened. Sometimes the objection is made that it is wrong to substitute the story of a work for the work itself, a statement no thinking person will gainsay. But this does not mean substitution. It means whetting the appetite until the child hungers for the thing you want him to have. Instead of telling him what he should read, arouse his curiosity to the point where he wants to read it, and the desired result will follow. Fifty years ago it was safe to give a boy or a girl a beautiful piece of literature and tell him he ought to read it, but it is not safe now, not because there is anything wrong with the children of our time, but because conditions are different. Books were rare and costly then, and young people read whatever came to hand. Today books are cheap and plentiful, and present-day literature plunges directly into the complications of the story. People are in a hurry to know what it is all about, because of the spirit of the age. There is less leisure now than there was half a century ago, as there is more competition, and results must be realized more rapidly than our forefathers realized them. Consequently we travel faster, get rich faster, and move more speedily in every way. Present-day literature reflects present-day spirit, and the story must begin with the opening sentence. Boys and girls simply will not go through pages of introductions and descriptions before striking the plot of the tale, no matter how beautiful those introductions and descriptions may be. They want books that get somewhere from the beginning. So the problem confronts all who are interested in the education of children: "How can we make them as eager to read Dickens, Scott, and Thackeray as they are to read Jack London and Phillips Oppenheim? How can they be made to go as gladly to Bulwer Lytton as they go to the Henty books?" By means of story-telling. Give them an idea of the plots of the masters of literature, enough to whet the desire to know more about them.

It is not sufficient just to tell the story, because it was not the plots of these writers that made them great artists. It was their manner of handling their plots, their delineation of character, the philosophy and human wisdom they put into the mouths of their heroes, and the boy or girl who does not become acquainted with these great creators during school days is likely never to know them, because he forms a taste for reading of a more ephemeral nature, and he may go through life a devourer of books, yet be only half educated.

Why is it that so many young people never look at

the English classics after they leave high school, and would rather spend a morning at hard labor than in reading *As You Like It* or *A Midsummer Night's Dream?* Because too much attention was given to the dissecting process when they studied these plays. Instead of being taught to see the beautiful and finished creation of some master, they were made to see the skeleton and to pull it to pieces. Some teachers assign a certain number of pages or paragraphs or stanzas for a lesson, and the pupils look up the words in the dictionary, point out the figures of speech, and scan the lines. Sometimes the teacher reads the assignment when it is made. Sometimes children dramatize it after they have torn it into shreds, or write a paraphrase. But the heart and soul of the masterpiece, the sheer beauty of it, are considered least of all, and students end by heartily hating something that they might have enjoyed and loved. Yet people wonder why the average American has so little appreciation of good literature, and think something is wrong with young folk who, after a high-school course in English, will read nothing but popular novels. There is nothing whatsoever the matter with the boys and girls. They simply follow the bent of all human beings and steer from the unpleasant toward the pleasant. They go to the books of the day that they can understand, because much of our great literature, presented as it is, means nothing to them. Less fortunate than youths of fifty years ago, they are not forced to read good books if they read at all. There are verdant, if less beautiful, meadows on every side where they may browse, and into them they go.

It is infinitely better that a child's school life provide him with a capacity for the enjoyment of literature than that he have a technical knowledge of a few pieces of literature, because the latter endows him with a narrow, academic viewpoint, while the former makes possible a future growth, without a capacity for which life must be narrow and one-sided. A boy or girl may know that Shakespeare wrote *Twelfth Night* or *Macbeth,* that Milton created "The Hymn to the Nativity" or Shelley "The Skylark," be able to paraphrase each and analyze the sentences that comprise them, and not be a bit better fitted for life than he would be without that knowledge. But he is better equipped for life if he has acquired a capacity for the enjoyment of literature, so that to read a great book gives him pleasure or causes him to respond with sympathy, and the English teacher who does not develop this capacity in children has failed in his function.

The approach to the great field of literature must be through specific examples, just as the approach to an understanding of art or architecture must be through the canvases of Raphael, Cimabue, or Giotto, or the temples that were the triumphs of Egyptian, Babylonian, or Hellenic builders. But if they are to be enjoyed, acquaintance with these specific examples must be made in a pleasurable manner. They first must be beheld in a perspective that gives glimpses of them as complete and beautiful wholes, and not through the detailed workmanship of architrave or abacus or by focusing the attention on the massing of figures according to square or triangular outline. And just as the understanding and enjoyment of one great structure or painting give added interest to every other one, so, in the realm of literature, each masterpiece enjoyed gives capacity for the enjoyment of every other masterpiece met with in the future. Therefore the story, because it is a means of flashing the entire structure on the screen and making it possible for children to see the completed whole in all its beauty, is the English teacher's most valuable tool.

Take *Evangeline* as an example. Most children leave school knowing that Longfellow wrote that poem, and that Evangeline lost her lover on the wedding day and spent the remainder of her life seeking him. But you cannot coax them to read the poem again because of the memory of the time when they studied it. And the pity of it is that there is no work of American literature so appealing to boys and girls in the adolescent period as *Evangeline*, if it is presented wisely.

Before they are asked to study it, if the story of the Acadian girl is told sympathetically and feelingly they are touched by its pathos and fired by the idealism of its characters, and they feel the charm of life in the quaint old village of Grand Pré. If, before they are told to read it, they have gone with the heroine through the magic of the narrator's picturing, in her wanderings over mountain and lowland, into Indian camp and sequestered mission, living among strange peoples and sleeping by strange fires, they will read it with enthusiasm. It will become a joy instead of a burden, because they will have felt something of what was in the heart of the poet who wrote it, and not merely what appeared on the printed page.

Besides the main thread of the story, there are many

sub-stories that, if told in connection with the poem, will add to the child's enjoyment and understanding of it. Sometimes a name is rich in story material, yet often it is passed over with nothing more than a definition found in the pronouncing gazetteer, and a golden opportunity is lost.

Take, for instance, the line, "Now in the Tents of Grace of the gentle Moravian missions." There is a footnote in most editions stating, "This refers to the Moravian mission of Gnädenhütten." But what does that signify to children, since there were many missions in those early days? But if they are told of how the Moravians came from the distant German mountains to plant the tree of their faith in the Western wilds, they grow interested. They are fascinated as the tale goes on, picturing how these simple folk founded a mission in the woods of Ohio, which they named "Gnädenhütten" or "Tents of Grace," and telling how a massacre occurred there in 1790, not savages killing off whites, but a band of marauding British troops slaughtering Christianized Indians as they toiled peacefully in their cornfields. Then, as Evangeline roams over the Southwest, into the bayou country of Louisiana, if pictures of the early life there are painted vividly by the story-teller, if she gives some of the events of old Creole days, the children will look forward to the *Evangeline* period.

This same method will add enjoyment to the study of other pieces of literature. *The Courtship of Miles Standish,* aside from the main plot, is rich in stories from the Bible. The children should look up these allusions, but the teacher should put life into them by giving the story. In fact, there is no piece of literature studied below the high school, or even during the early part of the high-school course, that cannot be presented with splendid results through the story-telling method. The concrete precedes the abstract in the order in which selections are considered, those through which a story thread runs being given in advance of the essay or treatise. By making the most of this story thread, literature study will become pleasurable and bring splendid response from the children. It requires effort and preparation, but it pays. It is worth much to the teacher who loves good literature, to look back over the years and think of the children she has led to appreciate and enjoy it. It is a tremendous satisfaction to have boys come back long after leaving her schoolroom and seek her out, because through her they learned to know something of the comfort that is to be found in good old books. One teacher, speaking of her experience, said: "It made all the effort seem richly worth while, when a broad-shouldered, sun-burned man went three hundred miles out of his way to see me on a home visit to America, and thank me for having led him to enjoy poetry." As a boy he became intensely interested in *The Lady of the Lake* because his teacher gave the stories of Fitz-James and Roderick Dhu and of the clan life of the Highlands, and a pocket edition of Scott was a source of comfort to him during a surveying expedition in the wilds of West Australia, and took away the loneliness of nights spent by a camp fire with no companions save the native woodmen. He had learned to know Scott during his boyhood, and the capacity for enjoyment acquired through that association was a priceless possession to the man. If more teachers realized that story-telling is a direct road to the understanding of literature, and that it has its place in grammar and high-school grades as much as in the kindergarten, there would be less drudgery for them and more satisfying results.

Some Authors and Selections That Can Be Presented through the Story-Telling Method

Browning: Hervé Riel (Give picture of life of sailors on the Breton coast. Hervé Riel was so accustomed to taking fishing boats through the passage that the piloting of the ship did not seem any feat to him); How They Brought the Good News from Ghent to Aix; An Incident of the French Camp; The Pied Piper of Hamelin (Tell how the poet came to write this work — to entertain a child who was visiting him).

Bryant: The White-footed Deer; The Woodman and the Sandal Tree; The Donkey and the Mocking Bird, and other poems from the Spanish.

Dickens: Little Nell (*Old Curiosity Shop*); Tiny Tim (*Christmas Carol*); Nicholas Nickleby; David Copperfield, and other child characters of Dickens.

George Eliot: Maggie Tulliver Cutting her Hair, Maggie Running Away to Live with the Gypsies, Tom and the Ferrets (*The Mill on the Floss*); Silas Marner and Little Eppie (*Silas Marner*).

Irving: Legend of Sleepy Hollow (*The Sketch Book*); The Governor and the Notary (Other stories from *Tales from the Alhambra*); The Life and Voyages of Christopher Columbus (Many chapters in this contain fascinating stories, which if told to the children will lead them to read the work); Rip Van Winkle (*The Sketch Book*) (Tell also the German story of Peter Claus, from which Irving drew his inspiration to write this tale; also the Chinese story, "The Feast of Lanterns," the hero of which is an oriental Rip Van Winkle).

Kingsley: How They Took the Gold Train (*Westward Ho!*); Water Babies; Hypatia.

Longfellow: Evangeline; Courtship of Miles Standish; Hiawatha; King Robert of Sicily; St. Francis' Sermon to the Birds (Tell story of St. Francis of Assisi); Paul Revere's Ride; The Emperor's Bird's Nest; Walther von der Vogelweide (In this connection tell story of Walther and the Minnesingers. Story can be found in *Pan and His Pipes, and Other Stories,* Victor Talking Machine Company).

SOUTHEY: Inchcape Rock; Bishop Hatto and the Mouse Tower; The Well of St. Keyne.

STEVENSON: Treasure Island; Kidnapped; Island Nights' Entertainment.

TENNYSON: The Holy Grail (This poem is beyond the understanding of boys and girls of grammar grades, or even early high-school years, but they may be familiarized with portions of it, and the Grail story is a wonderful one to give them. It should include also the tale of "Parsifal" and "Lohengrin," as related by Wolfram von Eschenbach and Wagner).

This list is in no way comprehensive, but the wide-awake teacher will find it suggestive of a much longer one, which is as much as the author of a single text-book may hope for.

SOURCES OF MATERIAL TO LEAD TO AN APPRECIATION OF LITERATURE

LAMB, CHARLES and MARY: *Tales from Shakespeare.*

LANG, JEANIE: *Stories from Shakespeare Told to the Children.*

SWEETSER, KATE D.: *Boys and Girls from George Eliot; Boys and Girls from Thackeray; Ten Boys from Dickens.*

SWINTON, WILLIAM, and CATHCART, GEORGE R.: *Book of Tales from Fine Authors.*

CHAPTER NINE

STORY-TELLING TO AWAKEN AN APPRECIATION OF MUSIC

THE public school aims not only to give boys and girls a training that shall equip them with ability to gain a livelihood and provide for their material wants, but to give them resources within themselves from which to draw pleasure, broaden and deepen the emotional powers, enrich the soul by endowing it with capacity to respond to the beautiful and fine, and make them more sympathetic toward the joys and sorrows of their fellows. That is why the curriculum includes a course in music, drawing, and subjects that are branches of a great art. We do not expect to make professional musicians or painters of all the children who receive instruction, but aim to give the average child, the one who will grow to be an average, ordinary man, an appreciation of the things that give color and beauty to life and make him richer in mind and happier.

Taste is formed by what is heard in youth, and the child whose early years are associated with ragtime grows to be a devotee of ragtime, while he who hears the music of the masters becomes a man who loves great music. This is why the average European has a knowledge and love of melody that amazes Americans. He has heard good music from infancy. It is sung in the public meeting places of his town and whistled in the streets. The gamin of Naples, Rome, and Venice knows the arias from the operas as well as American children know their national anthem, and

Verdi, Donizetti, and Rossini are more than names to him. He has heard their melodies from infancy, and his father or uncle or some street story-teller has familiarized him with the plots of their librettos. He knows something of the artists who sing the rôles, also, because the tailor and the barber and the baker not infrequently go to hear them, and they are a topic of conversation in the home. Here in America we have not had such opportunities. With us the opera and the symphony orchestra are exotics which only a minority has been trained to enjoy, and consequently we cannot be regarded as a musical people.

It is natural that this should be so, because, as compared with Continental lands, we are very young, and youth cannot hope to compete with maturity. But artistic standards in the United States are being raised steadily. Most of our great cities now have symphony orchestras and a season of opera, while the municipal band concert is part of the life of comparatively small towns, and the programs are of a higher order than formerly. We are on the upward move, and meanwhile every leader of children should do his part in the great work of helping to elevate the national musical standard.

The schools are doing something, but not enough, because much of the instruction they give is of a technical nature, and although pupils can read in several keys and beat time correctly, it does not follow that they are acquiring a capacity for the enjoyment of good music. Until one has sufficient mental development to understand something of the price that must be paid for artistic success, much attention to the technical vitiates interest in music, just as the dissecting method of study kills interest in literature. Many teachers make more of an effort to have children learn to read music than they do to have them enjoy it, and this close attention to the mechanics of the art makes the music period burdensome instead of enjoyable. Before the child can see any incentive in learning do—re—mi, he must hear and enjoy music and must understand that do—re—mi is a key that will unlock gates into larger fields of enjoyment. Because the hour is replete with drudgery rather than joy, the discipline of the music class is often a good deal of a problem, and although it is not an ideal condition, it exists more frequently than most people realize. A teacher whose class distinguished itself in sight singing at an institute, was asked how she made its members so proficient.

"Simply by keeping a strap on my desk and using it about every seven minutes," she replied; "and those who did not have actual contact with it kept straight because they knew it was there."

This is perhaps an extreme case, but the schoolrooms in which the music lesson is a period of nervous strain for both teacher and pupils are numerous, and it is not strange that sometimes trustees question whether it might not be well to eliminate music from the list of public-school subjects.

An adage of the old Italian school of vocalists, whose methods have given so many glorious songsters to the world, was, "To sing, you must be happy," and one of the most celebrated prima donnas of today attributes a large measure of her success to the fact that during childhood her mother had the wisdom never to make music burdensome by forcing her to it, but played for her and sang to her without stint, giving her countless opportunities of hearing music and leading her to love it. Then when she began formal study at twelve, her teacher did not harass her with exercises, but gave simple songs that she liked to sing, songs chosen to give her voice the exercise it needed and to appeal to the natural love of melody.

We might well apply this plan to our public-school music, and arrange courses so that children will hear much good music, even if the amount of technical work has to be greatly lessened. It is here that the story may do its far-reaching work in helping to make the music period pleasurable to the children and causing them to respond with keener pleasure to a higher standard of music.

Many narrators exclaim, "It is not possible for me to lead children to appreciate the great music when I do not know the great music myself."

But it is possible. Of course it is easier for one who is familiar with the masterpieces of melody to lead children to them than for one who is not; but even though the mother or teacher was not in her own childhood familiar with Mozart or Mendelssohn, she can bring children to appreciate these artists because the talking machine has made it possible. She need not try to acquaint them with the technical terms, and mechanics of music, but she can arouse an interest that is the twin sister of inspiration, and she can do it in such a way that every minute devoted to the work is filled with delight. She can tell the life story of some great composer and familiarize the child with selections from his work that will guide him away from the cheap and tawdry. She can give him incidents connected with the composition of musical gems, and a glimpse into the great treasure house of musical literature that will cause him to want to know more of the achievements of the immortal melody makers. It is not necessary that one be a musician in order to do this. Most schools and many homes are now supplied with talking machines, and the records manufactured by the different companies bring masterpieces within the reach of all. Even the catalogs are rich in suggestion, and following the cues supplied by them, a little thought and labor will bring most gratifying results. Almost all the great composers had eventful childhoods, and the early days of Mendelssohn, Mozart, Bach, Haydn, Handel, Beethoven, Chopin, Verdi, Wagner, and many others are rich in incidents that children enjoy hearing. These biographies, sources for which are listed in the appended bibliography (page 94), if told in story form and followed by selections from the artist's works, will make an impression and arouse an interest as nothing else can do. Do not, however, make the mistake of beginning with the man and leading down to his childhood. Begin with his early years and lead up to his achievements. The child will become interested in the man only through his childhood, because children are near his own interests, while adults are not. Many inexperienced story-tellers do not understand this, and are disappointed in their failure to hold their little hearers. This was demonstrated not long ago in a university course in story-telling. An incident in the childhood of Mozart was to be given in story form to introduce some of that composer's works to a group of children. Eighty per cent of the five hundred preparing the paper began thus: "When the great Mozart was a little boy." That introduction meant nothing to the children, because they did not know "the great Mozart," and were not interested in strange men. But they were intensely interested in hearing about a child who long, long ago was sailing down the Danube with his father and sister Marianne and was very much distressed because the father would have to pay duty on the harp they carried and therefore, when they reached Vienna, Marianne could not have a new dress that she sadly needed. Little eyes sparkled and little hands clapped when the children heard how, as they reached the customhouse of the Austrian capital, young Wolfgang asked his father if he might play something on the harp, and his rendition so delighted and amazed the officials that the duty was waived and Marianne was shabbily clad no longer.

There are many musical stories besides those of lives of the composers that should be given to children: tales of the violin makers of Cremona, the minnesingers, the troubadours, the meistersingers, Pan and his pipes, Apollo and the lyre, David and the harp, King Alfred and the harp, the harp at Tara, the Crusaders bringing some stringed instruments into Europe, the development of the orchestra, the evolution of the harp from the bended bow of the early tribesmen, and the making of the piano. Stories of some of the operas, especially those based on the legends of the Grail and the Rhinegold, are delightful tales to give to children.

A good way to introduce children to a composer is by combining the story of his life with selections from his work, as in the following story about Schubert. This method may be applied to the study of any composer. Libraries are rich in materials, and the talking-machine companies bring the music within the reach of all; so there is no reason why the story-teller should not do his part in making our nation a music-loving land, as well as give pleasure to the children under his guidance.

"Whoever puts a beautiful thought or melody into the world," writes an Indian poet, "gives more than a diamond of Golconda." Whoever helps a child to understand and enjoy beautiful thoughts and melodies, gives in almost as great a measure as their creator. He too is a builder, leaving behind him something fit to stand, and labor of that kind does not go unrequited.

A BOY OF OLD VIENNA

Little Franz could hardly wait for the sun to rise. He had lain awake all night thinking of what morning would bring, and it seemed as if the long, dark hours would never end. But now it was dawn, and he knew that very soon the sun would gild the hilltops, and then the thing of which he had dreamed for days would come to pass.

"Are you up, Franz?" his mother called from below.

"Yes," he answered cheerily, "up and dressing."

The mother smiled at him as he ran down into the kitchen, for she knew how eagerly he had looked forward to this day. Josef, the kindly neighbor, had promised to take him that very morning to a warehouse where many fine pianos were kept, and he would spend hours among the beautiful instruments there. No wonder he was glad! The one his father provided for him was cheap and harsh, for Herr Schubert was just a poor schoolmaster and had few coins to spend for anything besides food and clothing. But that did not keep Franz from doing wonders with his music. He learned all he could from his brothers, and worked away at the poor piano because he could not help it. Now that he was soon to touch the keyboard of a really splendid instrument, he felt like a prince in a fairy tale.

They went out of the house and along the dingy street in which the Schuberts lived. Across the Danube they passed by the old stone bridge that led to the Ringstrasse, then northward into that part of the city where the warehouses stood. Groups of citizens in holiday attire hurried by, and now and then some great lord or lady in a fine carriage passed them on the way to worship at St. Stephen's. But Franz thought only of reaching the warehouse, and he walked so fast that Josef, who was short and fat, began to grow red in the face and pant, and he was quite as glad as the boy when they reached the building.

Franz lost no time in getting to a piano. Sunday comes just once a week, and another would not come for seven long days. He sat down at one of the lovely instruments, playing and singing as if nothing in the world mattered so much as music. He was only eleven years old, and boys of that age usually want to be out with others, engaged in the sports and games boys love. But not so with Franz Schubert. He was happiest at his music. He played and played and was so busy that he did not see a stranger come into the warehouse or hear his voice in earnest conversation with Josef.

"You say he has had no music masters?" the man asked wonderingly.

Josef shook his head. "None but his brothers, Ignace and Ferdinand, and once, for a very short time, his father sent him to a singing tutor. But he said he could teach him nothing, for when he thought to give him something new he found he had learned it already."

"Surely he is a wonder child," the stranger remarked. "Be sure to tell his father to bring him tomorrow and we will try him."

Then he passed out, but Franz did not see him. Nor did he know a word that had been spoken until on the way home, when Josef told him that the emperor's choirmaster had passed by and was so pleased with his singing and playing that he wanted him in the royal choir.

So little Franz Schubert became a choir boy, and the master wondered more and more that one so young could know so much of music.

Then he went to a boys' school. His clothes were not very fine, for he was poor. But he wore the best he had, a light gray suit that was far from handsome. Some of the richer boys thought it funny and nicknamed him "the miller." But when Franz passed the severe singing examination so well that he was given one of the gold-braided honor uniforms, they did not tease him again. No one else did as well in the orchestra as the little Schubert lad. No one else sang as understandingly as he, and his master and fellow students, like the royal choirmaster, called him a wonder child. Every boy in the school liked him, and Franz liked them all too, but especially a young man named Spaun. And Spaun's name is remembered to this day just because once upon a time he was kind to little Franz Schubert. He was almost twenty when Franz was but eleven, but they were jolly companions and the best of friends.

One day Franz said, "If I had some paper I know I could write a song."

But paper he had not, because his father could not afford to buy it. Spaun always had a little money to spend, however, so Franz got the paper and wrote the song, and after that his friend supplied him with writing material. He enjoyed doing it because he liked the lad, but he did not realize that it would mean much to the world. It did mean a great deal, however, for some of the songs Franz wrote during his school days are still sung as among the sweetest in the world, and perhaps but for Spaun's paper they might not have been written.

Well, Franz grew up just as other boys grow, and still he went on loving music and working at it, playing and writing songs. Almost everything he read or saw made him think of a melody, and every melody that formed in his brain was beautiful.

One evening he went into a restaurant in Vienna for his dinner. He had a small copy of Shakespeare in his pocket, and as he waited to be served he took it out and read. His eye fell upon the lines:

> Hark, hark! the lark at heaven's gate sings,
> And Phœbus 'gins arise,
> His steeds to water at those springs
> On chaliced flowers that lies.

They made him think of a song, and he looked about for paper upon which to write it. He asked the waiter to get him a piece, but the waiter could find nothing but a bill of fare. Schubert took that and wrote his melody, and when Shakespeare's words were sung to it, the song sounded like this:

[At this point in the story run a record of "Hark, hark the lark."]

Another time he was passing through a poor quarter of Vienna and heard a peasant serenading a girl. Schubert did not think the song a very pretty one, and he went home and wrote one that he liked better. This is how it sounds:

[Record of "The Serenade."]

When Franz Schubert was a little child, he heard his father tell an old German story. It was called "The Erl King" and was about a witchlike creature who was supposed to take children from their parents. Franz always remembered it, and after he grew to manhood and read Goethe's poem, "The Erl King," a friend told him how the master came to write it. One wild winter night the poet was visiting in the home of a physician and a man came riding through the storm, seeking help for the child he had with him. The little fellow was delirious with fever and kept clinging to his father, crying and begging him not to let the Erl King take him away. The incident affected Goethe so deeply that he wrote the poem, and Schubert, hearing the story, was so touched by it that he composed wonderful music to go with the master's words.

[Record of "The Erl King."]

Another poem of Goethe's that he read told of a wild rose growing on a heath. A boy saw the rose and said, "I will pluck you." The rose said, "No, no. If you do I will prick you." The foolish boy laughed and picked the rose, and it kept its word. This is the song Schubert made of the poem:

[Record of "Hedge Roses."]

So you see that almost everything made Franz Schubert think of music. He wrote many, many songs and much other music, and although it is almost a hundred years since he died, his name and his works will live as long as men love melody. The greatest singers in the world use his songs over and over because rich and poor alike love them, and whenever singers want to be very sure of pleasing they sing some of the songs of him who was once a boy in old Vienna, Franz Schubert.

Sources of Material to Awaken an Appreciation of Music

Barber: *Wagner Opera Stories.*
Bender: *Some Great Opera Stories* (General Operas).
Cather, Katherine Dunlap: *Pan and His Pipes and Other Stories; Boyhood Stories of Famous Men.*
Chapin, Anna Alice: *The Heart of Music; Makers of Song; Stories of the Wagner Operas; The Story of the Rhinegold.*
Crowest, Frederick James: *The Life of Verdi.*
Dole, Nathan Haskell: *A Score of Famous Composers.*
Dutton Company: *The Master Musician Series.*
Fryberger, Agnes: *Listening Lessons in Music.*
Guerber, Helène A.: *Stories of the Wagner Operas.*
Hensel, Sebastian: *The History of the Mendelssohn Family.*
Liszt, Franz: *Life of Chopin.*

Pictures to Use in Telling Musical Stories

Beyschlag: Orpheus and Eurydice.
Borckman: Mozart and His Sisters before Maria Theresa; Beethoven and the Rusmnowsky Quartette.
Carlo Dolci: St. Cecilia at the Organ.
Duncan: Story of Minstrelsy.
Giulio Romano: Apollo and the Muses.
Hamman: Mozart at Vienna; Preludes of Bach; Haydn Crossing the English Channel; Handel and George I of England.
Harpfer: Mozart at the Organ.
Leydendecker: Beethoven at Bonn.
Merle: Beethoven at the House of Mozart.
Rosenthal: Morning Prayers in the Family of Bach.
Schloesser: Beethoven in His Study.
Schneider: Mozart and His Sister.
Shields: Mozart Singing His Requiem.
Portraits of all the great musicians.[1]

[1] Brown, Perry, or Cosmos Pictures, or they may be obtained from Victor Talking Machine Company, especially the living artists.

CHAPTER TEN

Story-Telling to Awaken an Appreciation of Art

THE child who is surrounded by good pictures from his earliest years grows to love good pictures, and gaudily colored, cheap ones have no charm for him. His taste has been formed for the fine and true, and nothing else will satisfy him. To behold a beautiful painting gives him pleasure, while to see a glaring chromo produces an unpleasant sensation. This is not because he is different by nature from one to whom masterpieces have no meaning, but because he has learned to know them.

Here again we have one of the striking differences between the average American and the average European. The Italian, French, Austrian, or German laborer sees masterpieces from infancy. His earliest recollection of religious worship is associated with them. Every continental town has its art gallery or picture exhibit, and on certain days there is no admission fee. The laborer avails himself of this opportunity. On Sunday, when he is free from toil, he makes a festival of the occasion and takes his family to some park or place of amusement, and very frequently the jaunt includes a trip to the picture gallery. Consequently, even the children of those lands have a knowledge of the masterpieces of art far surpassing that of the average adult American.

In most respects the Italian street gamin does not differ from the guttersnipe of our own land, but in one he is vastly his superior. He knows the free days at the galleries as well as he knows the alleys of his native town, and is a liberal patron of such places on those occasions. I once made the acquaintance of a little chap in Rome who was an excellent guide. He piloted me among the treasures of the Vatican with the ease and security that bespeaks thorough knowledge, for he had been there so often that he knew in just which rooms or alcoves to find his favorites. He knew much of the artists, too, of their lives and times, their discouragements and successes. Yet this Roman street boy was no exception to his class. Along the Piazza di Spagna, in fact, on any of the highways, are dozens like him, rich in knowledge of the statues and fountains that glorify the streets and parks of the Holy City. The names of Brunelleschi, Michelangelo, Fra Angelico, Giotto, and those other men who built or carved or painted with marvelous power, are fraught with meaning to them, and it is not strange that it should be so. Children in Italy have grown up among beautiful things. For centuries beauty has been almost a religion to this joy-loving, sun-loving race, and the country of the Apennines, as Francis Hopkinson Smith says, is the one place in the world where a song or a sunset is worth more than a soldo. Consequently, the Italians are a nation of art lovers. Each individual regards the masterpieces as his property, and the reason the Italian people hate the memory of Napoleon is not only that he conquered parts of their land, but that he robbed Italy of some of her art treasures. These were things they and their fathers had seen and loved, and they could not forgive the vandal who carried them away, even after the wound left by the victor had ceased to rankle.

Here in America we have not had the opportunity of the average European, but already we have made a beginning, and we now possess a number of art galleries that deserve the name. At the present time these are found only in the large cities, but they are helping to form national standards. Meanwhile every worker with children ought to try to lead those intrusted to his care to a knowledge and appreciation of great pictures.

It is not enough to place reproductions of masterpieces in schools and homes and say nothing about them. If children are to have an appreciation of them, they must be led to see their beauty, to understand what they mean, to have some idea of the infinite patience and labor that made their creation possible. The child of an artistic bent will observe and study them without aid or guidance and unconsciously grow into loving them, because beauty in any form attracts him as a magnet draws a bar of steel. But teachers and parents do not work solely with budding genius, and in the great scheme of human advancement it may mean as much for many *average* children to appreciate and love art, as for one who is gifted to reach immortal heights of achievement. The average child must be led and directed. His interest must be aroused before we can hope to mold his taste as we would have it molded. He must be taught to see that a Gainsborough is more beautiful than an advertising chromo, that a face by Raphael is the expression of an inspiration that is almost divine.

Only through an association that gives pleasure will he come to see and appreciate, and here again story-telling can work wonders, because through it we can intensify a child's delight in a picture.

In the field of art the biographical tale is of immeasurable value, for the story of an artist's life, illustrated by reproductions of his works, can be made the pathway to appreciation.

In establishing standards of art appreciation, as well as those of music, we must not lose sight of the story interests of childhood, because many a picture that is a great artistic achievement is not suitable to present to little children. The "Venus and Cupid" of Velasquez is a glorious masterpiece, but we cannot expect little folk to admire it any more than we can expect those in the rhythmic period to listen to a King Arthur story and ask to hear it again. As the little child does not know Venus and Cupid, a portrayal of them means nothing to him. But he does know horses and dogs and cats. He knows other children and babies and mothers, and therefore he enjoys pictures of animal and child life and will be interested in hearing about their portrayers.

Sir Joshua Reynolds is an excellent artist to begin with, because his best work is built around themes dear to the heart of childhood. His "Age of Innocence," "Infant Samuel," "Robinetta," "Heads of Angels," "Simplicity," and "The Strawberry Girl" are ideal works to present to the small child, and this painter's early years make a charming story.

Sir Edwin Landseer is another artist with whom we can acquaint little children, through the following works: "Uncle Tom and His Wife for Sale," "Low Life and High Life," "Dignity and Impudence," "A Distinguished Member of the Humane Society," "The Sick Monkey," "King Charles Spaniels," and many other paintings, all of which will be loved by children because they love the subjects.

Rosa Bonheur and her paintings should be used in this period. Children are especially fond of "The Horse Fair," "Coming from the Fair," "Brittany Sheep," "Highland Cattle," and "A Norman Sire." In fact, everything this painter created, like all the work of Landseer, is fraught with interest to the child, because she was solely a portrayer of animal life.

An artist of whom little folk have been taught almost nothing is Gainsborough. Usually we think of him only as a portrait painter, because in America his likenesses of women are better known than his other pictures. But it is a mistake to associate him only with "the dashing, smashing hats worn by the Duchess of Devonshire." Until recently only Americans who had traveled in England had an opportunity of seeing or knowing the greater part of this artist's other work, because the British copyright law protected much of it in such a way that cheap prints could not be made. Now, however, it is possible to get good reproductions of these long-protected Gainsboroughs at a very reasonable price. Most valuable of the works of this artist to use with little children are the following: "The Market Cart," "The Watering Place," "Two Dogs," "Rustic Children," and "Study of an Old Horse."

Murillo is an ideal painter to introduce to the little child, because his childhood story is as fascinating as his creations are glorious. Children never tire of hearing about this joyous little Spanish boy, and of the time when he transformed the family picture, turning the halo of the Christ-child into a gorgeous sombrero, and making a dog of the sheep. As they laugh or sympathize with the wonder child of Seville and feel something of the charm of life in that old city, its street children, immortalized on canvas by its most illustrious son, become comrades because little Bartolome sometimes played with them and big Bartolome painted them. There is a long list of this master's works from which to choose, but the following are particularly enjoyed: "Mother and Child," "The Adoration of the Shepherds," "St. John and the Lamb," "The Melon Eaters," "The Dice Players," "Beggar Boys," "The Good Shepherd," "The Marriage of St. Catherine," and "The Immaculate Conception." No attempt should be made to interpret the two last-named pictures. Familiarize little people with them and lead them to see their beauty, but waive all idea of religious symbolism until years bring maturity of thought and the child makes his own interpretation.

All Madonna pictures are interesting to little children, so by all means acquaint them with Raphael, the king. Let them drink in the beauty of "The Sistine Madonna," "The Madonna of the Chair," "The Madonna of the Goldfinch," and as many others as can be obtained. The story of Raphael belongs more properly in the intermediate period than in the very early one, because so little is known of this painter's life before he began his career. Just tell the children of the little boy who lived in far-away Urbino long, long ago. His mother died when he was a wee little fellow, and he lived alone with his father, who was very kind to him. Instead of playing much, as the other children did, he loved to sit and listen to stories about saints and good people who lived before his time. He loved to draw pictures, too, and when he grew to be a man he became a wonderful painter.

Closely following Raphael may come Correggio, through his "Holy Night," "Repose in Egypt," and "Cherubs."

Van Dyck, too, may be made familiar to little children. From his works choose "Children of Charles I" and several details from this picture — "Baby Stuart," "Charles II," and "Henrietta." But present first the complete picture, so that when "Baby Stuart" is seen the children will know that it is only part of a painting. Many a grown person does not realize that it is a detail from another work, and this fact should be understood by every child who sees the royal baby. Other works by this artist suitable to introduce to tiny people are "The Repose in Egypt," "Madonna and Child," and "The Donators."

There are many painters whose pictures will be enjoyed by children of from five to eight, and the teacher or parent who knows art and art literature can choose for himself, keeping always in mind the story interests. To those who have little or no knowledge of art, yet who want to lead children along this path, the following list will be helpful:

Artists and Paintings That Can Be Presented to Young Children through the Story-Telling Method

Adam: Kittens; Wide Awake; The Hungry Quartette; In the Boudoir.

Botticelli: Adoration of the Magi; The Holy Family.

Bouguereau: Virgin and Angels; Virgin, Infant Jesus, and St. John; Going Home from School; The Flight into Egypt.

Delaroche: The Finding of Moses; Children of Edward IV.

Greuze: The Broken Pitcher; Innocence: Head of Girl with Apple.

Herring: Pharaoh's Horses; Three Members of the Temperance Society; The Village Blacksmith; Farmyard.

Vigée Lebrun: Marie Antoinette and Children; Girl with Muff; Mother and Daughter.

Millet: Feeding the Hens; Feeding Her Birds; The First Step; Feeding the Nestlings.

Luca della Robbia: Singing Boys; Trumpeters and Dancing Boys; Dancing Boys with Cymbals; Children Dancing to Fife and Tambor; Madonna, Child, and Saints.

Rubens: Portrait of his Wife and Children; The Holy Family; Infant Christ, St. John, and Angels; The Virgin under an Apple Tree; The Adoration of the Magi.

Children of the intermediate period enjoy the works of the great landscape painters, Claude Lorrain, Corot, Breton, and others who portrayed the woods and fields, especially when they know something of the childhood of these men. In this period, too, they should become better acquainted with some of the artists they have already met. Add to the interest previously created in Raphael by taking up such works as "Madonna of the Fish," "Madonna of the Well," and "Madonna of the Diadem." In telling the story of his life use Ouida's beautiful tale, "The Child of Urbino," which is so exquisitely told that there is nothing lovelier in literature. Show the children his portrait of himself, his "St. Catherine," "St. Cecilia,"

"St. John in the Desert," "Peter and John at the Beautiful Gate," and "The Miraculous Draught of Fishes."

Add to the interest already created in Rubens by taking up his "Portrait of Himself," "The Flight of Lot," and the paintings illustrating the life of Maria de' Medici.

Pictures representing the Crucifixion, the Descent from the Cross, and the Entombment, no matter how glorious they may be as works of art, should not be presented to children. They are too highly religious for children's understanding, and the tragedy portrayed in them should not enter into childhood. The Madonnas and Holy Families may be used freely, because they portray dear and familiar characters and are saturated with an atmosphere of happiness that gladdens the child.

The following list will aid those who are not connoisseurs:

ARTISTS AND PAINTINGS FOR CHILDREN OF THE INTERMEDIATE PERIOD

JULES BRETON: Song of the Lark; The Gleaners; The Reapers; The Weeders; The Recall of the Gleaners; Blessing the Wheat; The Vintagers; The End of Labor.

JACQUES: The Sheepfold; Pasturage in the Forest; Shepherd and Sheep.

MILLET: The Sower; The Gleaners; The Angelus; The Grafter; Sheep Shearing; Potato Planting; Bundling Wheat; Returning to the Farm; Shepherdess Knitting; Woman Churning; Labor.

There is a twofold reason for introducing children to such painters as Millet, Breton, and Jacques.

Besides giving them a knowledge of the works of the artists in question and adding to their appreciation of the beautiful, it will dignify labor in their eyes to learn that it inspired these great creators. If leaders of the "back to the land" movement would make free use of the art of the world among children, if during the years when impressions made are deep and lasting they would tell stories and show pictures that have been inspired by toilers in the fields, a sentiment would be created that would tell in results, because of boys and girls having learned to respect those who till the soil and work with their hands.

Artists and Paintings That Lead to Appreciation of the Beautiful and to Respect for Labor

Corot: Dance of the Children; Dance of Nymphs; Landscape with Willows; Paysage; Pond of Ville d'Avray; The Lake.

Rembrandt: Portrait of Himself; Portrait of His Mother; The Mill; The Burgomasters.

Troyon: Return to the Farm; Going to Work; Landscape with Sheep.

Van Dyck (Add to interest already aroused): Henrietta Maria, Wife of Charles I; William of Orange and Mary Stuart; Equestrian Portrait of Charles I; Portrait of Charles I with Groom and Horse.

Velazquez: Portrait of Himself; The Tapestry Weavers; Prince Balthazar; The Lancers; Equestrian Portrait of Philip IV; Infanta Maria Theresa.

When children reach the period during which they crave the heroic, when they are eager for the great epic stories, give them the great paintings that portray epic and mythological subjects. The following list contains names of artists and works that children in this stage will enjoy:

Artists and Paintings for the Heroic and Epic Periods

Alma-Tadema: Sappho; Reading from Homer.

Burne-Jones: The Golden Stair; The First Day of Creation; Second Day of Creation; Third Day of Creation; Fourth Day of Creation; Fifth Day of Creation; Sixth Day of Creation; Hope; Circe; Enchantment of Merlin; King Cophetua and the Beggar Maid; The Furies.

Leighton: Helen of Troy; Captive Andromache; Greek Girls Playing Ball.

Michelangelo: David; Moses; Saul; The Three Fates; Jeremiah; Ezekiel; Zachariah; Isaiah; Daniel; Jonas; The Delphic Sibyl; The Cumæan Sibyl; The Libyan Sibyl.

Raphael: St. George and the Dragon.

Guido Reni: Jesus and John; St. Michael and the Dragon; Aurora; Beatrice Cenci; St. Sebastian; The Annunciation; L'Adorata.

Rossetti: The Sea Spell; The Blessed Damozel; Ancilla Domini.

Andrea del Sarto: John the Baptist; Virgin in Glory; St. Agnes; Charity.

Tintoretto: The Forge of Vulcan; Marriage at Cana; Paradise; Paolo Veronese; Feast at House of Simon; Feast at House of Levi; Europa and Jupiter.

Titian: John the Baptist; Tribute Money; Titian's Daughter Lavinia; Flora; Head of Venus.

Turner (*Mythological*): Apollo and the Python; Jason in Search of the Golden Fleece; The Goddess of Discord; Dido Building Carthage; Ulysses Deriding Polyphemus. (*Historical*): Prince of Orange; The Death of Nelson; Boat's Crew Recovering an Anchor; Hannibal and Army Crossing the Alps; The Field of Waterloo; Agrippina Landing with the Ashes of Germanicus; The Fighting Téméraire.

Watts: Sir Galahad; Orpheus and Eurydice; Endymion.

General Bibliography of Art Story Material

Bacon, Mary S. H.: *Pictures That Every Child Should Know.*

Cather, Katherine Dunlap: *Boyhood Stories of Famous Men.*

Collmann, Sophie Marie: *Art Talks with Young Folks.*

De la Ramée, Louise: *Child of Urbino* ("*Bimbi*" *Stories*).

Ennis, Luna May: *Music in Art.*

Hartmann, Sadakichi: *Japanese Art.*

Horne, Olive B., and Scobey, Kathrine L.: *Stories of Great Artists.*
Hourticq, Louis: *Art in France.*
Hurll, Estelle M.: *The Madonna in Art.*
Menefee, Maud: *Child Stories from the Masters.*
Sweetser, M. F.: *Artist Biographies: Raphael and Leonardo, Angelo and Titian, Claude Lorrain and Reynolds, Turner and Landseer, Dürer and Rembrandt, Van Dyck and Angelico, Murillo and Allston.*
Vasari, Giorgio: *Lives of the Italian Painters, Sculptors, and Architects.*
Waters, Clara Erskine: *Saints in Art; Stories of Art and Artists.*

Sources for Moderate-Priced Reproductions of Masterpieces

The Brown Pictures, Milton Bradley Company, Springfield, Mass.; Emery School Art Company, Boston, Mass.; Maison Braun et Cie., New York, N.Y.; Frederick A. Stokes Company, New York, N.Y. (has American rights to many pictures); The Perry Pictures, Malden, Mass.; The Prang Company, New York, N.Y.; The University Prints, Boston, Mass.

CHAPTER ELEVEN

Dramatization

CONTEMPORANEOUS with what may be termed a renaissance in story-telling is a strong sentiment in favor of dramatization. Child leaders have observed that children dramatize spontaneously, and that after they have heard a tale they often play it without suggestion from an older person. They impersonate the characters, crudely perhaps, but they represent the action and portray the story as they understand it.

This they do because the dramatic instinct is a universal instinct. We are all born imitators, and we like to experience the feelings and experiences of others. That is why the little girl impersonates her mother and takes delight in dressing in grown-up attire and playing lady. It is what actuates the boy to play Indian or soldier or fireman. He wants to live through the experiences of Indians and soldiers and firemen; so he goes into the world of make-believe and acts the part. During that time he is a larger and a different personality. He is not a little boy who must go to bed before he wants to, and must stay inside the yard when he longs to be out on the highway; he is a grown man in a uniform dashing along on an engine; he is a mighty chief in feathers and war paint, leading his tribe against the enemy or speaking words of wisdom around the council fire.

There was a time when this sort of play was believed to be of no value beyond that of a romp that helped to stretch the muscles, but today there is a very different attitude toward it. Close observation of children and a more general knowledge of psychology have brought educators to realize that imitative play is a big factor in mental development. As the boy impersonates a fireman or Indian he must choose movements in keeping with the part and reject those not in keeping with it. He must select and evaluate, and in doing this he is acquiring a power of discrimination that will be of great value to him later.

The childhood of many famous men of the past was distinguished by an unusual amount of imitative play, a free expression of the dramatic instinct. Goethe, in his memories, speaks lovingly of his early years thus:

> From my father I have my stature,
> My earnest aim in living;
> From little mother, my joyous nature,
> My love of story weaving.

Continuing, he tells of the tales he heard, and what they meant to him as he played them:

> Sometimes I was a prince and sometimes a peasant. Now I was rewarded for being a bountiful and considerate king, then punished according to the deserts of a wicked and revengeful giant; and always as I played these parts I was learning the unchangeable laws of life.

What Goethe learned through acting tales his mother told him, the child of today is learning as he dramatizes stories, although not always in as great a measure as was learned by the author of *Faust* and *Werther*. But he is learning according to his ability and within his limitations. When he has played the part, the laws involved in it become fixed principles with him, and a big step is taken in the direction of his moral training. Because of a growing recognition of this truth the present strong interest in dramatization in schools is becoming general throughout the country. Teachers are beginning to realize that they can give no more eloquent sermon on truthtelling than to tell the story of "The Boy Who Cried Wolf," and then let the children dramatize it. There is no more effective means of giving a lesson in contentment than presenting the tale of the pig who thought his life hard and leading the boys and girls to play it.

Therefore it follows that dramatization should be encouraged, and to be most far-reaching in its results, it should be done by means of story-telling, because by proceeding from the story to the action the child creates the play and makes it his own.

There are many books of plays for children, carefully written and adapted to their interests in word, style, and theme. But such plays do not mean as much to the child as those he makes for himself. They are not as much his own, and consequently they contribute less toward his growth and development.

The natural way is for the child to hear the story and then act it. Therefore every story-teller should have in his possession a number of tales with dramatic possibilities. He should tell one of these vividly and dramatically, using much dialogue, and then, while it is still fresh in the minds of the children, encourage them to play it. It is well to use the published plays also, because there are many excellent ones, but the narrator should read them over, get the plot, and tell the story, before putting them into the hands of the children.

Shall dialogue be dictated by the story-teller and the children drilled in their parts? No. Conversation used in telling the tale will suggest to the children what to say, and they will make up their own parts. They must be led and directed, but help from the teacher or leader should be given in such a way that the children feel they are *making* the play themselves. Help them by questions that will lead them to think and act instead of telling them what to do and say.

Suppose "The Pied Piper of Hamelin" is to be dramatized. After the story has been told, say to the children, "Do you want to play it?" Of course they will want to. Then, by questioning, lead them to constructive effort.

How many people shall we need? Immediately the answers will come, and as the different characters are named make a list, thus getting the cast. Who can be the mayor, members of the council, the piper, rats, mothers and fathers, lame boy, etc.?

There will be two divisions, those who are forward, eager to take a prominent part, and the shy, retiring ones who will not offer. This latter group must not be ignored, and to draw its members into the work requires much tact. Sometimes when it is impossible to get a child to take a speaking part, he can be encouraged to be one of a group of "supers," as they are called on the professional stage, because although he lacks the confidence necessary to make him lift his voice, his diffidence vanishes in doing pantomime with a number of other children. He will be a rat or a citizen when he cannot be coaxed or driven into being the piper, and after many pantomime performances he gains the confidence in himself that enables him to take a speaking part.

One of the difficulties incident to dramatization in the schoolroom is that the same children always clamor to take the star parts, and sometimes sulk if not permitted to do so, or sneer at the efforts of others. This situation must be met as any other problem in discipline is met, by skill on the part of the teacher and by inculcating a sense of fairness and courtesy that holds selfishness in check. Lead the child to see that what gives him pleasure gives some one else pleasure also, and that it is the right of each member of the class to experience that pleasure. Once the boy or girl realizes that well-bred people are considerate and do not deride the efforts of others, no matter how imperfect their achievement may be, the dramatization period loses its greatest bugbear and shy children do not hesitate to take part because of fear that they will be laughed at. This result cannot be brought about instantly, but persistence and tact will finally accomplish it.

Do not be discouraged because it seems that some of the shy or less capable children will never take a speaking part. Sometimes even after they perform in pantomime they still hang back and will speak only in chorus. But this last is at least a step in the desired direction. Keep working them in groups, and gradually from group speaking they will advance to individual speaking. Sometimes this process is slow and discouraging, but the teacher should remember that mental development is never a mushroom growth, and that great achievement is not wrought in a day. The marble block yields so slowly to the shaping of the sculptor's chisel that sometimes it seems it never will take the form he visions for it, but ceaseless effort always brings results. So it is with the teacher in molding human material. Results are sure to come if persistence and patience are unflagging and faith is deep and strong. It is worth much for a shy, self-conscious child to grow to the point where he can lose himself in the rôle of a play, and no matter how crudely he does it, he should be encouraged and given frequent opportunities to express himself, because as a means of self-development his crude performance is of as much value as the artistic one of the talented child, although it may be less enjoyable to spectators.

With little children especially, it is desirable to use some play whose cast will include every member of the class. It gives the eager child a chance to be "in it," as children say, and makes it easier to draw the diffident child to participate, because he wants to do what all the others are doing. "The Pied Piper" is ideal for this, because of the flexibility of groups. There can be enough rats, parents, children, or council members to include twenty or forty children, and the larger the groups the more intense the interest.

After the cast is decided upon, plan the scenes, again by questioning the children. What is the first thing to be done and where is it done? Thus, by question and suggestion, work up the lines. In other words, have the children create the parts themselves and they will play them spontaneously. The production may not be highly artistic, but it will have greater educational value than one worked out by an adult and merely acted by the children. After it has been created in this way it may be put into finished permanent form. Little children may practice it until they memorize the lines, while those in the grammar grades may write parts, thus making a play that can be used many times. This sort of work is very valuable, and may form a composition or language exercise that will be enjoyed by the class.

Another method is to have the various members suggest lines to be spoken by the different characters and choose the best for the play. Sometimes a child who does little in the usual composition work and never gets a high mark, will suggest an excellent line or sentence, and to have it go into the play is a tremendous joy to him, especially if he doubts his own ability. Another plan that makes the class interest keen, is for each member to plan or write a scene, and without the members knowing the authorship of the various papers, have them read, and select the best by vote, whereupon the name of the writer is revealed. This method can be used in writing parts for one character or for all the characters, and in several other ways that will be of much value to the children.

Of course the teacher or leader must be the guiding spirit, because a well-built, correctly proportioned plot is necessary. But her suggestion should be chiefly by way of question, leaving the children to feel that they, and not the instructor, are doing the work, although in reality the teacher's judgment is the foundation upon which the structure stands, and she must use it in building the play just as she uses it in telling the story.

For little people there are many stories with dramatic possibilities, some of which may be acted wholly in pantomime, some with combined pantomime and spoken parts, and others entirely of spoken parts. In working with foreign children it is well to begin with pantomime plays, as the child who knows he cannot express himself easily in English will always balk at taking a speaking part. Some of Æsop's fables lend themselves particularly well to pantomime, especially "The Lion and the Mouse," "The Fox and the Grapes," "The Dog and His Shadow," and "The Hare and the Tortoise." *The Dramatic Festival*, by Craig, and *Festivals and Plays*, by Chubb, give valuable suggestions for pantomime work, as well as a list of plays adapted to it, and the worker with older children will also find these books to be excellent guides.

There is an equally large amount of material for dramatic work with older children. *Hiawatha* never fails to delight fourth and fifth grade boys and girls. *Robin Hood* in dramatic form is loved even more than in story, as are some of the exploits of King Arthur and his knights and of Pwyll, the hero of the Mabinogion. Any of these tales may be carried out simply or may be worked into elaborate performances with costumes and stage settings. If the latter be the choice, much pleasure and useful experience will come to the children through making the properties. Any boy who can whittle can fashion spears and swords, and gold and silver paper is wonderfully effective in supplying glitter. Does a knight need colored hose to be in keeping with his doublet? Let him borrow a pair of his mother's or sister's white ones and coat them with blackboard crayon of the desired hue. One laundering will make them spotless again, and there is no outlay of money for something that must be discarded at the end of the performance. Helmets, shields, and pilgrim hats can be made by the manual-training boys, and girls in the domestic-science class will enjoy sewing the costumes.

The teacher in the ungraded school is particularly fortunate in opportunities for this kind of work, because she can correlate it with other subjects in ways that workers in schools using the departmental system cannot do. One country teacher had her eighth-grade history class give a pageant portraying the French exploration in the Mississippi Valley. The class devoted a term to the preparation; the subject was made the nucleus of their reading, language, history, and manual work, and the results were most gratifying. Boys who never had written a readable paper did some astonishingly good work in composition because of their interest in the play and their desire to contribute to it, and the standard of class scholarship was raised, to say nothing of the joy the children derived from it.

Many other historical subjects are equally rich in possibilities. The Spanish exploration in Florida, the Dutch in New York, the Spanish settlement of California, the framing and adoption of the Declaration of Independence, John Smith and Pocahontas, Ponce de Leon seeking the fountain of youth, the story of Columbus, and many similar themes afford good opportunities for class play-making and correlation of school subjects.

Sometimes a picture will suggest an entire scene in a dramatization, or even an entire play; the following are especially good for this purpose:

BACON: The Burial of Miles Standish.
BALACA: Departure of Columbus from Palos.
BOUGHTON: Pilgrims Going to Church; Pilgrim Exiles; The Return of the Mayflower; Priscilla.
KAULBACH: The Pied Piper of Hamelin.
PILOTY: Columbus on the Deck of the Santa Maria.
VAN DER LYN: The Landing of Columbus.

Those wishing to make a specialty of dramatization will find the following books helpful:

CHUBB: *Festivals and Plays.*
CRAIG: *The Dramatic Festival.*
CURTIS: *The Dramatic Instinct in Education.*

The following are excellent stories for dramatic work with little children, and are included in so many books that they are available to every teacher:

Three Billy Goats Gruff; The Wolf and the Seven Little Kids; Chicken Little; The Old Woman and Her Pig; The Pig Brother; The Gingerbread Boy; The Boy Who Cried Wolf; The Town Musicians; Mother Goose Rhymes; The Three Bears; The Pancake; The Discontented Pig.

Many others will be found in the list of story collections for children in the rhythmic period, and in the bibliography on the following page.

Bibliography of Material for Dramatization

For Primary Grade Children

Bell, Florence E.: *Fairy Tale Plays and How to Act Them.*
Chadwick, M. L. Pratt-, and Freeman, E. Gray: *Chain Stories and Playlets.*
Nixon-Roulet, M. F.: *Fairy Tales a Child Can Read and Act.*
Noyes, M. I., and Ray, B. H.: *Little Plays for Little People.*
Perry, S. G. S.: *When Mother Lets Us Act.*
Stevenson, Augusta: *Children's Classics in Dramatic Form, Books 1–3.*
Wells, Carolyn: *Jolly Plays for Holidays.*

For Intermediate Grade Children

Harris, F. J.: *Plays for Young People.*
Sidgwick, Ethel: *Four Plays for Children.*
Spofford, Harriet Prescott: *The Fairy Changeling.*
Stevenson, Augusta: *Children's Classics in Dramatic Form, Books 4–6.*
St. Nicholas Book of Operettas and Plays.

For Grammar Grade Children

Frank: *Short Plays about Famous Authors.*
Lansing, M. F.: *Quaint Old Stories to Read and Act.*
Lütkenhaus, A. M., and Knox, Margaret: *Plays for School Children.*
Rucker and Ryan: *Historical Plays of Colonial Days.*

CHAPTER TWELVE

Bible Stories

ONE of the glaring defects of our modern educational system is that almost no provision is made for the study of the Bible as a great classic, and as a result boys and girls complete grammar and high-school courses without sufficient knowledge of the epic of the Hebrews to enable them to understand the world's best literature. The myths of Greece and Rome are studied because of their cultural value, yet from universities throughout the country comes the complaint that many of the works of famous authors are beyond the enjoyment of students because the Biblical allusions have no meaning for them. What should be as familiar as "Red Riding Hood" and "Cinderella" is known in name only, and the immortal book is regarded as a repository of golden texts and maxims instead of as a glorious artistic creation.

The masses of children know almost nothing of the story of Israel, because outside of the Sunday school and the exceptional home, it is rarely told. Yet educators emphasize its need in the intellectual as well as in the spiritual development of the child, and declare that the Old Testament tales should be as much a part of the school curriculum as are the myths of Greece and Rome and the northland. Rein, the great German educator, advocates using them in the third and fourth grades to the exclusion of all others, which is done in the state schools of Baden, while in America Dr. G. Stanley Hall pleads eloquently in behalf of Bible stories.

"To eliminate the Bible from education," says this famous psychologist, "is as preposterous pedagogically as it would have been in the days of Plato to taboo Homer from the education of Greek youth. It is not only a model of English, but it is impossible to understand the culture history of Europe without it, as it has influenced the literature, history, and life of Western nations as no other book has begun to do."

The secular narrator, as well as the teacher of religion, should use the Bible tales freely, that men and women of the future may have a broader knowledge of literature, history, and life than they can have without them. This is no impossible task, even for the amateur, because the Biblical narratives are perfect ones for telling. Nowhere else in literature do we find such thrilling tales of adventure, such exquisite idylls, such sublime ballads, such annals of high purpose and noble achievement, as in the epic of Israel. Nowhere else are there more spectacular, perfectly constructed plots. Ruskin said, "It would be pre-eminently the child's book even though it had no religious value above other books"; and Dr. Fuchs of Vienna declares that we might, if we lacked material, give children nothing but Bible stories and yet satisfy every craving of their natures, because the Bible contains every type of tale that appeals to the child. From Genesis to Revelation it is an incomparable record of human desire, human endeavor, human failure, and human success. In the Old Testament we find myth, fairy tale, fable, romance, legend, and history, told in simple, elemental beauty by the Hebrew story-tellers, tinged with that varied color and imagery so characteristic of oriental literature and so fascinating to children, — stories that, as Mrs. Houghton says, "are the product of a child nation, and therefore very close to the heart of the child."

The Old Testament, rather than the New, is the child's storybook, because it is the expression of a primitive people, and its tales picture primitive, rugged heroes that boys and girls can understand, whereas the second division of the Bible, except that portion centering around the childhood and boyhood of Christ, is adult in character. But it is a mistake to think that all Old Testament tales can be presented with gratifying results. To tell the story of Ruth and Boaz to tiny tots would be as absurd as to give them the *Decameron* of Boccaccio or Goethe's *Faust*, because the characters and incidents are remote from their interest. In using material from the Bible, as from any other source, it is necessary to keep in mind the story interests of childhood, and to remember that the skeletons of tales, not the style and vocabulary in which they are written, must be the test for selection. If the framework is suited to the period of mental development, the language can be adapted, while otherwise no amount of simplifying can bring it within the understanding and powers of enjoyment.

The Old Testament is particularly rich in stories for children, because it was formulated in a period when the Hebrew nation was a child nation. The men and women of Israel were grown to adult stature, but they had the hearts of children. They thought concretely, as the child thinks, and consequently their literary expression is concrete and illustrative. This, added to the facts that they, like all other orientals, loved the story and brought it to a high artistic point, and that the Old Testament heroes are not refined to the point of æstheticism, but are strong, rugged, elemental men, thoroughly human and far removed from goody-goodies, makes it an ideal book for the child. Gideon and Joshua possess virtues, but they possess faults also. They are punished and they are rewarded, and because they have much in common with children, the lessons learned through their victories and defeats are more valuable than a thousand admonitions.

In advocating the use of Bible stories a word of caution seems necessary, lest the narrator, actuated by the laudable desire to enrich the intellectual and spiritual life of the child, may harm instead of benefit. The Hebrew people were in a state of advanced barbarism when their tribal achievements grew into an epic, and the deeds of their heroes are often so bloodthirsty and revengeful that they cannot be reconciled with modern views. Boys and girls are quick to realize this, and consequently many of the Old Testament tales must be softened by the elimination of objectionable features, just as many fairy and epical tales must be softened.

Nor are gore and revenge the only elements we must cut away from these old tales. Those who give the narrative of Israel to boys and girls of twelve and fourteen should be careful to eliminate from it everything that may be suggestive of the vulgar, for which, at this age, many children are on the lookout. It is better to omit than to veil and modify questionable portions of a tale, because young people are very discerning, and to see through gossamer is to arouse curiosity. Dr. Bodley cites instances of youths in the romantic period reading the Bible because of lewd thoughts. This danger leads some persons to decry the use of Bible stories by the average narrator, in whose hands they believe them to be dangerous. However, if he uses judgment, if he makes it a rule to omit whatever awakens a doubt in his mind, even the amateur may tell Bible stories with beneficial results. It is possible to eliminate from many an Old Testament narrative without breaking the thread of the story, just as it is possible to give boys and girls a clear idea of the man Chopin without introducing the George Sand episode. So much of the Old Testament is pure adventure tale that the story-teller may use the portion that feeds the elemental hero love without touching upon what might arouse morbid curiosity or desire, or that which sanctions gore and revenge.

Those who have not had training in gathering and adapting story material from the Bible will be aided greatly in their work by Frances Jenkins Olcott's book, *Bible Stories to Read and Tell.* Miss Olcott gives the stories as they are given in the King James Version, preserving all the beauty of language of the Hebrew story-tellers, but she has excluded everything that might prove objectionable; and with this book as a guide there is little danger of making a mistake in telling the Hebrew hero tales to children.

Bible stories should be graded as carefully as fairy stories are graded. In choosing for little children, select those whose heroes are children, and give to the boy who craves the heroic the incomparable tales of the Hebrew wanderers, those men whose lives were a varied succession of adventures. For the child of each period there is a wealth of material. The stories of the baby Moses, little Samuel, the boy Joseph, the boy Timothy, the boy David, and the baby Isaac are very appealing to six- and seven-year-olds. They love also to hear of the mother and the baby Samson, of Ishmael and Hagar, and those other mothers and babies of long ago, and especially dear to them is the story of the Babe of Bethlehem. This lovely narrative is a part of the birthright of every child, and is exquisite enough to merit careful preparation on the part of the story-teller. The Bible itself should be the storehouse to which the narrator goes for material, but those not especially gifted in visualizing and imagination will derive much help from the work of modern literary artists who have told again the story of the Christ Child. The eleventh and twelfth chapters of the first book of *Ben Hur*, the creation of a man whose reverence was as great as his talent, should be re-read by every one who attempts to tell of the song and the star in Judea, and the works of Henry van Dyke, Selma Lagerlöf, and John of Hildesheim will aid greatly in giving color and atmosphere. This means time and labor, but no amount of preparation is too great to put upon the world's noblest stories. The narrator should approach them, not arrogantly, and satisfied of his ability to tell them because he has known them from childhood, but as the artist approaches the masterpiece he aspires to copy, willing to labor that he may be worthy of the task, willing to read them over and over again and count each reading a return to the fount of inspiration. This should be the attitude toward all great stories, but especially toward the immortal ones of the Bible.

For the child in the heroic period the Old Testament is a gold mine, and it is a pity that its superb adventure tales are so little used by story-tellers, since they are so fascinating to boys and girls. Even when told as separate stories they arouse interest and hold the attention, but they are most valuable when given in a sequence, because then the child regards the Old Testament as a great human drama, the epic of a people.

A good plan is to begin with the call of Abraham, as related in the twelfth chapter of Genesis. Picture the patriarch, with Lot and Sarah, going into exile out of the land of Haran, through Canaan to the plain of Moreh, building there the altar under the soothsayer's oak, and journeying southward over the desert to Egypt. Tell of the banishment by Pharaoh and the return to Bethel, of the strife between the herdsmen and the survey of the land, of the captivity and rescue of Lot. Paint vividly the highway along which they traveled, now over the desert, now across the fertile plain skirting the sea, often footsore and weary, often suffering from heat and thirst as wanderers in the East suffered, and the story will cause children to turn from the cheap adventure tale of today as music lovers turn from ragtime to a Chopin prelude.

Then there are tales of those other Old Testament wanderers, Isaac, "the Ulysses of the Hebrews," and Jacob, whose life was so eventful. Take the boys over the routes these men traveled. Let them share their exploits and adventures, resting in fertile places where the wanderers rested, now by the well outside Nahor, the servants praying beside the kneeling camels as Bethuel's lovely daughter came down the hillside with the pitcher on her shoulder, now moving as the caravan moved, over roads the Hebrew armies traveled on their way to war, along which tradesfolk journeyed in times of peace. There is marvelous color and romance in these Old Testament thoroughfares, and they are highways of fascination even today. Still across their yellow sands turbaned Arabs go up and down, singing praise to Allah just as men sang to God in the remote time of Israel. They bear with them skin bags filled with water from the pools and streams, dates, figs, and dried goat's flesh, such as formed the noontide repast of Isaac and his men, for in the changeless East life is today as it was in the beginning of things. When the caravans rest, they sit under the palm trees in some oasis, telling stories their fathers told, and using the Old Testament forms of speech. Still in that land of nomads to see is to "lift up the eyes," and maidens go to draw water when the day's heat is over just as Rebecca went to the well of Nahor.

The book of Joshua is a glorious adventure story. The siege and destruction of Jericho, the victories of Joshua, the slave boy from Egypt who became the first soldier of the Hebrews, the distribution of Canaan among the tribes of Israel, and Othniel's valor and reward satisfy every desire of the child who craves hero stories. They satisfy now as they satisfied two thousand years ago, because they grew out of the life of a people and run the entire gamut of human emotion as only racial tales can do.

The book of Judges is a collection of incomparable narratives. The enslavement of Israel by Jabin, the defeat and death of Sisera, and Gideon's deliverance and victory never fail to hold boys and girls who crave the heroic. Moreover, these stories will arouse interest in perhaps the finest ode known to any literature, the song of Deborah in the fifth chapter of Judges. Give the children some idea of what it has meant to the world. Ruskin said the memorizing of it in his boyhood shaped his taste for literature, and Macaulay declared it inspired him to write "Horatius at the Bridge." Read the work of the English poet, and bring out the lovely pictures in the great Hebrew ode, for it is not fair to our young people that we allow them to go through life without knowing this gem, without leading them to see the beauty of these exquisite words:

> Speak, ye that ride on white asses, ye that sit in judgment and walk by the way.
>
> They that are delivered from the noise of archers in the places of drawing water, there shall they rehearse the righteous acts of the Lord.

Visualize the scenes in those lines: sumptuous, haughty Hebrews, traveling as only the prosperous traveled; men in the fine linen of lawgivers, holding places of power in the land; vagabonds lounging along the highways, begging alms of passers-by; husbandmen tilling fields far from the sound of conflict; men in every walk of life, widely separated by material conditions, yet brothers in a common weal, rejoicing in a common blessing, the victory of Barak over the foe of Israel. It is as rich in color as a canvas by Titian, and pupils in the upper grammar grades will grow to love it if it is presented as it should be, through the medium of the story.

The books of Samuel, with their tales of Saul and of David, of the shepherd boy from the Hebron hills making music for Israel's king, his meeting and slaying Goliath, Saul and the Witch of Endor, and all the eventful life of David are glorious materials for the story-teller. Here again inspiration may be obtained from the work of a modern writer. Browning's "Saul" will greatly aid the narrator in telling the story of the boy David, for the picture the poet gives of the afflicted monarch in his tent, the son of Jesse standing beside him singing the Hebrew gleaning songs, is as vivid as it is exquisite.

Where can we find a more splendid narrative than that of Solomon, in the second book of Kings? Where is the boy or girl who does not delight in listening to the account of the visit of Hiram, king of Tyre, when two sumptuous monarchs met; of the collection of materials and the building of the temple; of the visit of the Queen of Sheba, the adversity and death of Solomon, and that succession of events that led to the captivity of Israel? Here, too, we find the great story of the invasion of Judah and the destruction of Sennacherib; and Byron's poem will vivify this tale just as Browning's "Saul" vivifies that of the boy David.

The only reason why children look upon the Bible as a dull, ponderous book is that they are not familiar with the Old Testament adventure tales, and it is a mistake to think that present-day boys and girls will turn away from them. If playground and settlement workers would give more time and attention to the stories of the Hebrews, they would have less difficulty in reaching hoodlumish boys. It is necessary to use tact in presentation, — "sense," as Lilian Bell says, "of the brand commonly known as horse," — for to preface a narrative with, "Now I shall tell you a Bible story," might mean an insurrection. The only way is to bring the hero on the stage and tell his tale so vividly that the listeners are held by it to the end. After they come to know such men as Gideon and Joshua, they will regard the Bible as a great storybook.

A settlement worker had this experience not long ago. She told the tale of Joshua to a group of young ruffians, who sat through it as if held by a spell, and at its conclusion the leader of the band remarked, "That was some story!" Other Old Testament heroes were then introduced with excellent effect, and the lads were amazed to learn that the Bible contained such stories. But results of this kind cannot be obtained without effort and preparation on the part of the raconteur.

Bible stories, being the perfect tales of the world, should be told as nearly as possible in the language and style in which they were written. Some modification is necessary for the purpose of clarifying, but the Biblical expressions should be used frequently. Quote freely from the original or follow the story with a Bible reading, that the child who hears the tales may catch something of the majestic beauty of expression of the Hebrew story-tellers. There can be no more pitiful mistake than to tell these matchless narratives in the vernacular of the street. To use modern slang in recounting the wanderings of Isaac or the passing of the Children of

Israel through the Red Sea is to profane a marvelous artistic creation, even though it had no religious significance, and unfortunately story-tellers sometimes do this, thinking they will make the tales more interesting to children. That sort of narration will amuse and hold young folk only as long as it lasts, and leaders of children are not working merely for the here and now. Their effort is for time and eternity, and they should have sufficient vision to see beyond the present, sufficient sense of proportion to estimate values. The Old Testament tales need no modern strokes to make them attractive, because they abound in color and incidents that lead to superb climaxes, and never fail to fascinate when given with sincerity. Therefore they should be told in simple, dignified language, as the men of Israel told them when the world was young, and while they fire the imagination, they will lead children unconsciously to an appreciation of beautiful English, which is one of the cardinal aims of every story-teller who is worthy of the name.

The teller of Bible stories should draw from music and art, as well as from literature, because to follow a tale with a picture or musical number inspired by it is to heighten enjoyment and strengthen the impression already made. If children see Bendemann's masterpiece, "By the Waters of Babylon," after they have heard the story of the captivity of Israel, they will have a sympathy for the exiled Hebrews that they cannot have otherwise. Saul, David, and many other Old Testament heroes will seem more than ever like living, breathing men when viewed as Michelangelo portrayed them, while Giulio Romano's frescoes, "The Story of

Joseph," or Pellafrino da Modena's "Story of Solomon," will intensify their color and romance and help to lead to an appreciation of art. Cheap reproductions bring these and other masterpieces within the reach of the narrator, and he should travel every bypath in which he may glean materials that will help children to love these old tales. He should keep ever before him the thought of how they have enriched the world, and how powerfully lives are influenced by stories heard in childhood. When Bertel Thorwaldsen was a blue-eyed boy in Copenhagen, he heard a tale that long afterward became the inspiration of "The Lion of Lucerne," and young Richard Wagner, playing in a Dresden street one day, crept into a group to which a strolling bard was telling the medieval legend of "Parsifal." It was a seed planted in a creative mind, and years afterward it flowered in two noble operas of the Holy Grail. So it was with Goethe, with Browning, with Byron, and many other great men. Perhaps in your group of youthful hearers there may be a boy or a girl who will listen as gifted children of the past have listened to an old, old story, and perhaps your telling it may result, long after your work is ended, in his giving to some branch of art a creation that will enrich the world through generations yet to come. But even though there be no budding genius among your auditors, sincere, artistic telling of the Bible stories cannot fail to produce great results. It will develop the emotional nature of the average child; it will broaden his sympathy and increase his capacity for feeling, make him more sympathetic, more responsive to the joys and sorrows of his fellow men, and better fitted to become a useful citizen.

Sources of Material for Bible Stories

Abbott, Lyman: *Life and Literature of the Ancient Hebrews.*
Aguilar, Grace: *The Women of Israel.*
Baring-Gould, S.: *Lives of the Saints.*
Canton, William: *A Child's Book of Saints.*
Dearmer, Mabel: *A Child's Life of Christ.*
Doane, T. W.: *Bible Myths.*
Fiske, John: *The Myths of Israel; The Great Epic of Israel.*
Hodges, George: *A Child's Guide to the Bible.*
Houghton, Louise S.: *Telling Bible Stories; Hebrew Life and Thought.*
Kent, Charles Foster: *Heroes and Crises of Early Hebrew History.*
Lagerlöf, Selma: *Christ Legends.*
Olcott, Frances Jenkins: *Bible Stories to Read and Tell.*
Sangster, Margaret E., and Yonge, Charlotte M.: *Stories from the Best of Books.*
Smith, George A.: *A Historical Geography of the Holy Land.*
Smith, Nora A.: *Old, Old Tales from the Old, Old Book.*
Van Dyke, Henry, Abbott, Lyman, and Others: *Women of the Bible.*

CHAPTER THIRTEEN

Story-Telling and the Teaching of Ethics

THE function of education is not only to give the child knowledge and a capacity for acquiring further knowledge that shall equip him for the life struggle and make success a possible attainment, but also to give him an ethical standard that shall make him fit to live among his fellows and a respect for the rights and feelings of others, or, as Goethe says in *Wilhelm Meister*, "Reverence for what is above, reverence for what is beneath, reverence for what is equal." He must be taught to realize that he is part of a great unit and that individual desires must often give way to the welfare of the many. He must be taught that as an individual he owes to society obedience to the laws that govern society and allegiance to the principles that make possible a harmonious family, civic, and national life. Consequently it is required of every teacher that she give ethical instruction, that she endeavor to bring children to an understanding of what is generally accepted as right and wrong, and implant in them convictions strong enough to cause them to adhere to those standards.

In establishing ethical standards, as in establishing standards in art, literature, or music, we must appeal to the emotional side of the child as well as to the intellectual side. We must lead him to feel that the right act is the one that he wants to do, and this cannot be accomplished by a presentation of dry facts and precepts. Every teacher knows that the time spent in admonishing a child what he *ought* to do brings no gratifying results. He is not swayed to repugnance for one act or to admiration for another by being told "Thou shalt," or "Thou shalt not." At the time the command is given, fear may cause him to obey it; but conduct that is the result of force does not strengthen the character or teach high standards of action. It tends instead to harden the child and make him determined to act differently at the first opportunity. Ethical training does not mean to attempt to control the child, but to enlighten him and direct his volition to the point where he will attempt to control himself. As Ella Lyman Cabot says, "Its aim is to make the best there is so inviting to the child that he will work eagerly and persistently to win it." The ideal that is held up to him must be so beautiful that he will be willing to sacrifice and endure hardship in order to attain to it, and through story-telling he may be led to see this ideal more vividly than in any other way, because the story makes right acts appealing and wrong acts repugnant. Moreover, through the narrator's art the child lives the experiences of the tales he hears. He suffers with the evildoer and is rewarded with the virtuous, and because he is powerfully moved by a narrative, his character is lastingly affected by it.

In giving ethical instruction, it is necessary to use the right material. Tales selected for this purpose should be suited to the child's particular period of mental development, they should contain a lesson the boy or the girl ought to learn, and they should be strong and virile and true to life. Much harm is done by telling stories of unusually good children. Such young folk are unpopular with boys and girls, and the story about them is as distasteful as is the "goody-goody" that is met with in real life. Instead of being an influence toward commendable action and the acceptance of a higher standard of right and wrong, the over-idealistic tale antagonizes the child and goads him toward that from which we would have him veer aside. Perhaps this accounts for the fact that girls often enjoy boys' stories more than those written especially for girls. The normal girl wants to read and hear about live, natural young folk, and the heroine who has drawing-room manners and nothing else is very far from her ideal. Story characters that influence children must be human, full of human faults and virtues. From their failures and successes young people will learn many valuable lessons, but they will learn no lesson from one who poses as an unnatural young saint.

Moral training should begin with the babe, and therefore the mother and primary teacher need stories that have ethical values as early as they need Mother Goose tales and jingles. Very early in life the child must be brought to realize that there is a higher law than that of its own will or desire. It must be taught obedience, cleanliness, kindness to animals, consideration for the rights of others, truthfulness, industry, honesty, and courtesy, and these lessons can be inculcated more effectively by means of story-telling than in any other way. The tale of "The Little Red Hen" doing the work and reaping the reward of her labor is a sermon on industry that little people do not forget. The story of the farmer boy who rolled the stone out of the highway because he feared it might cause injury to some one, and then of the compensation that came to him at the hands of the lord of the village who placed it there, will help to make children thoughtful and kindly.

In telling stories of this type, the narrator should emphasize the fact that the greatest reward is the mental satisfaction that follows a good action, because the child who hears much of material reward sometimes thinks chiefly of the money or picnic or good time commendable conduct may bring, and if it happens that he does not receive remuneration, decides it is useless to perform good deeds. A case of this kind that came under my observation was that of a boy in a country school, a lazy, thoughtless little fellow. One day when a man drove through the school yard, his brother, who was very considerate, ran to open the gate. The stranger tossed a penny to the child, and the teacher, thinking to give a lasting lesson in consideration to the thoughtless boy, dwelt at length upon the stick of candy the money would buy. Several days later another man drove through the school yard and the thoughtless boy ran to open the gate. He received a smile and a "Thank you" but no money, and he could not be persuaded to open the gate again.

It is well to give stories in which children are materially rewarded, but they should be taught to see that material reward is not the only reward, and that desire for it should not be the motive that prompts a good action. The fireman who risks his life in saving the property or life of another is not bountifully paid, and seldom does he receive a purse for bravery. But he is true to his duty. He is giving to society the thing that he owes it, service, and his greatest guerdon is the satisfaction that comes from being steadfast to a trust. Examples of this kind are of great value to the child who is inclined to be selfish, and they are very effective in bringing all children to realize the truth of Alice Cary's words:

There are no fairy folk who ride about the world at night,
To give you rings and other things to pay for doing right,
But if you'll do to others what you'd have them do to you,
You'll be as blest as if the best of fairy tales were true.

Very young children can be taught to realize that the true reward of right conduct comes from added self-respect and from winning the esteem of others, and whenever a child is given a tale in which a boy or a girl receives some wonderful treasure for kindness or courtesy or truthfulness, the narrator will do well to interpolate a sentence like this: "And the best part of it was that Albert was happy because he had done what was right. That thought gave him a glad feeling even more than the big, shiny dollar."

Many fairy tales and fables are of particular ethical value for little children, and the narrator can draw much from the field of general literature; biography and history hold many good examples, while the Bible is a rich storehouse of material. Ella Lyman Cabot's excellent work, *Ethics for Children,* discusses the ethical side of story-telling in such a detailed and complete way that it should be in the hands of every mother and teacher. The book gives valuable suggestions, not only to workers with little folk, but to those who have the training of grammar grade and high-school pupils also. Carolyn Sherwin Bailey's *Stories for Sunday Telling* contains some good material for the mother and the primary teacher, while the several books by Sara Cone Bryant (listed in Chapter Seven, "Telling the Story") will be helpful.

The following list is one that has been used with good results:

Stories to Develop or Stamp out Certain Traits and Instincts

Deceit

Æsop: The Fox that Lost Its Tail (Adams, William: *Fables and Rhymes — Æsop and Mother Goose*).

Malice

Æsop: The Dog in the Manger (Adams, William: *Fables and Rhymes — Æsop*).

Sympathy and Compassion

Cabot, Ella Lyman: A Lesson for Kings (*Ethics for Children*).
Sawyer, Ruth: The Gipsy Mother's Story of Joseph and Mary (*This Way to Christmas*).

Honesty

Cabot, Ella Lyman: The Little Loaf (*Ethics for Children*).

Faithfulness to Duty

Bryant, Sara Cone: The Little Hero of Haarlem (*How to Tell Stories*).
Cary, Phœbe: The Leak in the Dike (*Poems*).

Inattention

Bryant, Sara Cone: Epaminondas and His Auntie (*How to Tell Stories*).
Grimm, Jacob: Stupid Hans (*German Household Tales*).

Obedience

Partridge, E. N. and G. E.: The Little Cowherd Brother (*Story-Telling in the Home and School*).

Generosity

BAILEY, CAROLYN SHERWIN: The Boy Who Had a Picnic (*Stories and Rhymes for the Child*).

BAILEY, C. S., and LEWIS, CLARA M.: The Woodpecker Who Was Selfish (*For the Children's Hour*).

BRYANT, SARA CONE: The Cloud (*How to Tell Stories*).

BULFINCH, THOMAS: Baucis and Philemon (*The Age of Fable*).

CABOT, ELLA LYMAN: Margaret of New Orleans (*Ethics for Children*).

CARY, ALICE: The Pig and the Hen (*Poems*).

GRIMM, JACOB: The Star Dollars (*German Household Tales*).

GRIMM, JOSEPH: The Elves and the Shoemaker (*German Household Tales*).

WILDE, OSCAR: The Happy Prince.

Love and Sweetness

BRYANT, SARA CONE: The Mirror of Matsuyama (*How to Tell Stories*).

TOLSTOÏ, LEO: Where Love Is, There God Is Also (See BRYANT: *How to Tell Stories*).

Forgiveness

BIBLE: The Prodigal Son.

CABOT, ELLA LYMAN: Lincoln and William Scott (*Ethics for Children*).

HUGO, VICTOR: The Bishop and Jean Valjean (*Les Misérables*).

MOULTON, LOUISE CHANDLER: Coals of Fire (In CABOT: *Ethics for Children*).

TOLSTOÏ, LEO: A Spark Neglected Burns the Whole House (In CABOT: *Ethics for Children*).

Cleanliness

BAILEY, CAROLYN S.: The Child Who Forgot to Wash (*Story-Telling Time*).

KINGSLEY, CHARLES: Tom, the Chimney Sweep (*Water Babies*).

LINDSAY, MAUD: Dust under the Rug (*Mother Stories*).

RICHARDS, LAURA E.: The Pig Brother (*The Pig Brother and Other Stories*).

Perseverance

CABOT, ELLA LYMAN: The Story of Helen Keller (*Ethics for Children*).

CATHER, KATHERINE DUNLAP: Old Jan's Twilight Tale; The Joyous Vagabond; The Whittler of Cremona; The Border Wonderful; Jacopo, the Little Dyer (*Boyhood Stories of Famous Men*).

HOLLAND, RUPERT S.: The Boy of the Medici Gardens (*Historic Boyhoods*).

Industry

BRYANT, SARA CONE: The Gold in the Orchard; The Castle of Fortune; The Sailor Man (*How to Tell Stories*).

Contentment

BROWNING, ROBERT: Pippa Passes (*Poems*).
BRYANT, SARA CONE: The Rat Princess (*How to Tell Stories*).
CABOT, ELLA LYMAN: The Discontented Pendulum (*Ethics for Children*).
CATHER, KATHERINE DUNLAP: The Discontented Pig.
MENEFEE, MAUD: Pippa Passes (*Child Stories from the Masters*).

Kindness

ÆSOP: The Lion and the Mouse (ADAMS: *Fables and Rhymes—Æsop and Mother Goose*).
ANDERSEN, H. C.: Five Peas in a Pod (*Wonder Stories Told to Children*).
BAILEY, C. S.: The Little Brown Lady (*Story-telling Time*).
BROWN, ABBIE FARWELL: St. Francis of Assisi and the Wolf (*Book of Saints and Friendly Beasts*).
BRYANT, SARA CONE: Prince Cherry (*Stories to Tell to Children*); Why Evergreen Trees Keep Their Leaves (*How to Tell Stories*).
CABOT, ELLA LYMAN: Dama's Jewels (*Ethics for Children*).
GRIMM, JACOB: Snow White and Rose Red; Snow White and the Seven Dwarfs; Queen Bee (*German Household Tales*).
LONGFELLOW, HENRY: The Bell of Atri (*Poems*); (see also WIGGIN and SMITH: *The Children's Hour*).
PARTRIDGE, E. N. and G. E.: The Stone Lion; Little Paulina's Christmas (*Story-Telling in the Home and School*).
RICHARDS, LAURA E.: Florence Nightingale and the Shepherd Dog (*Florence Nightingale, the Angel of the Crimea*).
STOCKTON, FRANK R.: Old Pipes and the Dryad (LYMAN: *Story-Telling: What to Tell and How to Tell It*).

Greed

ÆSOP: The Dog and His Shadow (In ADAMS: *Fables and Rhymes — Æsop and Mother Goose*).
HAWTHORNE, NATHANIEL: The Golden Touch (*Wonder-Book*).

Courtesy

CABOT, ELLA LYMAN: A Four-Footed Gentleman (*Ethics for Children*).

History and biography offer a particularly rich field from which to draw material for older children, for nothing drives home with more force a lesson in patriotism, loyalty, faithfulness, heroism, or obedience than to read of some one who has been put to the test and has triumphed. Dozens of characters worth emulating will occur to any teacher, and the following books will be found of particular value:

Sources of Material to Use in the Teaching of Ethics

Baldwin, James: *American Book of Golden Deeds.*
Bolton, Sarah K.: *Famous Leaders among Men; Lives of Poor Boys Who Became Famous; Lives of Girls Who Became Famous.*
Lang, Andrew: *The True Story Book.*
Lang, Jeanie: *The Story of Robert the Bruce.*
Richards, Laura E.: *Florence Nightingale, the Angel of the Crimea.*

PART TWO

THE USE OF STORY-TELLING TO ILLUMINATE SOME SCHOOLROOM SUBJECTS — STORIES FOR TELLING

CHAPTER FOURTEEN

Story-Telling to Intensify Interest in History

IT has been said by Walter Prichard Eaton, "The pupil who gets a mark of one hundred and thereafter hates Shakespeare, has failed — rather, his teacher has," — and it is equally true that the instructor also has failed whose classes look upon history as a series of dates and dull facts instead of a colorful story.

To teach history successfully means to give the child vivid pictures of the past, to enable him to see as a whole the march of a race or of a nation across the canvas of time, to watch the legions of warriors go to victory or defeat, to hear the voices of statesmen whose wisdom has builded empires, to walk side by side with the men and women whose lives make up the annals of the world. To be of value to the child, history must be felt, just as a work of literature must be felt. He must live it, must approve the worthy and disapprove the unworthy, must rejoice in and sympathize with the fortunes and misfortunes of its characters, else it cannot be anything more to him than the chronology in the almanac, disliked during his school days and forgotten as soon as they are over.

Story-telling can make history alive and vital because of its power to convey the child to distant scenes and ages, and through it he may become, not only a spectator, but a participant in every human activity. If our libraries were to be swept away and publishing houses should shut their doors, we could still teach history to children, and teach it successfully, through the art of the narrator. By the medium of the story we can make the child see what has been done by his ancestors and other people in the past; by it we can interpret to him how his forefathers lived and acted, how other people have attempted to do what he is trying to do or sees done, and give him a vivid idea of human ways of living and conduct. This is history in the larger sense, and it was taught successfully by the story-teller in the past.

Before the days of printing, when books were manuscripts that no one but monks could read and kings could afford to own, story-telling was the only way in which this subject was taught. Tales of bygone days were told in castle halls and to groups of eager listeners on the village green, and boys and girls of King Alfred's time knew as much of their country's story from the lips of wandering bards as those of our generation know from cramming the contents of textbooks. They knew it because through the tales they heard they were able to relive it, and what has been done before can be done again. Because of the story's power to vivify, modern children can relive the world's story just as those in medieval times relived it, and history can be made a subject fraught with delight to the child.

Child attention centers first upon familiar things, and radiates from them to the unknown. Through his interest in creatures that are a part of his environment, the kindergarten tot becomes interested in those of other regions, in the men, women, children, and animals that are part of the life of some other child. Through knowledge of his immediate surroundings he comes to acquire knowledge of life in other surroundings, and according to the appeal it makes to his imagination, he understands and sympathizes with it, and his social sense is broadened. Therefore, in the study of history, the attention should be focused upon local environment, and from it should radiate to other sections of the world. In other words, by what the child sees happening around him, he must be led to see what has happened in the past and what is happening now in distant regions. This requires imagination, and a boy or a girl cannot see or feel these events if they are presented as a dry chronology, because under those conditions they do not arouse the imagination. He must behold them flashed on a canvas like a colorful picture, and because the story can do this, because it can make real to the imagination situations that cannot be experienced, through it he can be led to see and feel all that we desire him to see and feel.

The biographical story, the tale of the leader who towers above his fellows like the Matterhorn above the Valais foothills, is a boon to every teacher of history. Because it is unified in plot and dramatic in appeal to the imagination, it is the most easily handled of all the history material, and should be used freely. But if children are not to have a distorted idea of the story of the human race, we must not stop with the biographical tale. We must give them also a conception of the part the masses have had in the making of the great human story, of the yeomen of England, upon whose sturdy shoulders the foundation of British liberty stands, of the vassals of Italy, France, and Germany, of the army of unknown toilers who built the Pyramids and the Chinese Wall. Sometimes, in satisfying the child's hero-love, we make him one-sided by laying too much stress upon individual achievement and not enough upon the work of the multitude. We do not lead him to value the importance of the humble who toil in the rank and file. This is not as it should be. We should make it clear to him that the stokers who feed the furnace of the man-of-war are as splendidly patriotic as the admiral who commands the fleet, and are as necessary to their land, because, were there no coal heavers, there could be no navy.

Sometimes, too, because martial events are more spectacular than those of peace, we give the impression that they are the only important and heroic ones, and fail to convince the children of the fact that the peasants of Lorraine, who tilled their fields until they blossomed like gardens, served their land as loyally as the soldiers who marched to victory under the oriflamme of Henry of Navarre. We are too prone to center the child interest around military affairs, and neglect to emphasize the importance of conflicts of another kind. The history of every modern industry, of every achievement that has meant anything to the world, is a story of struggle, of victory over opposing forces. It has its succession of events, its periods of triumph and defeat, its moments of suspense, and its thrilling climax, and if presented in all its possibilities, is as fascinating to childhood as Napoleon's Russian campaign. Let us not fail to give these narratives of struggle that are unstained by human blood, and in doing it lead children to understand that there are other ways of serving one's land besides riding a war horse or carrying a musket.

We teach that Robert Fulton invented the first steamboat, but it is only the exceptional child-leader who makes the most of that event, who throws upon the canvas, for youth to behold, the story of the struggle and disappointment, the triumph and despair, of the young American engineer. To give them the fact that the *Clermont* made a successful trip from New York to Albany in 1807, is like telling the end of a story without the beginning or intervening chapters, and a snatch of a tale never has the effect of the whole. But if the children have all the light and shade of that splendid narrative of invention, of the labor beside the Seine, of the hope and discouragement there, it becomes a fascinating, unforgotten tale. They remember the *Clermont* episode because they have enjoyed a story, and years afterward, when they see a ferryboat or an ocean greyhound, they will think of the New Englander through whose dreams and labor it came to be.

To the teacher who looks upon history as a great, fascinating tale, who regards it as a narrative instead of a mere bunch of dates and periods, who knows the story of man's inner development as well as that of his outer, and who uses the myths, legends, and epics of a land as side lights to illuminate its true story, great results are possible. There is no phase or period of history that he cannot make intensely interesting to the child, no page of the world's story that will not teem with life and color to the boy or girl who receives it from such an instructor. It may be an account of events in his own land, of happenings in the stern, white north country or in the opalescent south, it may be of knights in glittering armor or of serene-faced, brown-cowled friars, of men from the masses or from the ranks of the exalted, but it will breathe and pulsate for him, it will give him the information that he should receive, and it will give him an understanding that no memorizing of dates and outlines can give, because he has lived with those who made history, because he has suffered, rejoiced, and achieved with them.

Every great historian is more than a recounter of events of the past. He is an artist who fits himself into the moods of men and women who lived and accomplished before his time, puts them into his pages as creatures of flesh and blood, and gives to their activities as much freshness and interest as have the events that happen before our eyes. Motley, Guizot, Hume, Hallam, Froissart, and our own Parkman, Lodge, Prescott, and Bancroft created as splendidly as ever Hugo, Corneille, or Balzac created, because they endowed characters of fact with as much life as these other men gave to characters of fiction; and consequently, with sources rich in inspiration from which to draw, the teacher who aspires to vivify history by story-telling is confronted by no hopeless task. He need only go to the works of the standard historians for his background, and then, by giving the imagination sufficient play to supply setting and detail of situation, he can carry a joyful lesson to the children. This is well illustrated in the following story of Western discovery. Children love it and ask to have it told again and again, while if the bare facts are given them in outline form, it means little to them. Not every teacher is gifted to the degree of Miss Hood and can hope to weave a fact of history into a tale that deserves to rank as a children's classic; but every teacher can put history into story form with enough skill to make it hold delight for his pupils and cause them to go from his instruction with a fondness for history, an understanding of what history really means, which is worth infinitely more than a thousand dates or outlines crammed into the mind for an examination or recitation, or stored there permanently to rust and grow useless, because they have no meaning, and therefore no broadening or illuminating effect upon his life.

THE SEARCH FOR THE SEVEN CITIES

By Margaret Graham Hood

The Story of Tejos

In the year 1530, when Nuño de Guzmán was governor of New Spain, he had an Indian slave of whom he was very fond and who was likewise fond of his master. He was a good servant and different in many ways from all the other slaves in the palace, and it often pleased Nuño de Guzmán to talk with him.

"Tejos," said De Guzmán to him one day, "tell me of your home when you were a boy, and tell me of your father and mother."

Then Tejos turned away from his master and stood for a long time silent.

"Master," he said at last, "when Tejos was a boy he lived not in this land, nor was he a slave. His home was in a land far, far to the northward. My lord, it was a great land. Beyond the home of my father there was yet another country greater still. In that farther land were seven great cities, and even the smallest of them was as great as this city of Mexico. So rich were the people of those cities that they made arrowheads of emeralds, and scraped the sweat from their bodies with scrapers made of gold, and put precious stones over their doors. Their houses were wide and high. My father carried to these people the feathers that they wore upon their heads, and in return they gave him gold and turquoises and emeralds. My father took Tejos with him twice, my lord, when he journeyed with feathers to those cities, and though Tejos was then but a small boy, he still remembers the long streets where were only the stores of jewelers who sold the precious stones and made them into ornaments for the people."

"And where," asked Nuño de Guzmán breathlessly, "where is this land?"

"It is far away from here, my lord," answered Tejos, sadly. "Forty days you must journey to reach it, and the land through which you must travel is a desert lying between two seas, and there is neither water nor food to be had."

Scarcely waiting to sleep, De Guzmán began to gather a force to march in search of this wonderful land. Far and wide the story spread and on all sides the talk was of

The Land of the Seven Cities

With four hundred Spaniards and twenty thousand Indians, De Guzmán marched from Mexico, and the people waited each day to hear that he had conquered a great empire in the north.

As he went, rumors of the Seven Cities kept coming to him, and his men were often so excited he could hardly get them to sleep enough. For days they pressed eagerly forward, hoping each day to find the Seven Cities at hand; but instead of this, the country each day grew more desolate, the mountains grew steeper and the roads harder to find, while the Seven Cities, instead of coming nearer, were always farther and farther to the north.

Then the Indians began to desert and the Spaniards to complain. "We have been deceived," they said, "and we shall all die in this bleak land. Let us return to Mexico."

For a while Nuño de Guzmán cheered them by holding ever before them the reward that awaited them, but at last he too grew discouraged and afraid; they all turned about and marched sadly back to Mexico.

"We will go back now," said Nuño de Guzmán, "but some day I will have the right sort of an army and I will come again. Tejos himself shall lead me, and I will yet find and conquer those Seven Cities."

But when he returned to Mexico, Tejos was dead, and the story of Nuño de Guzmán's misfortunes discouraged others; so for six years no one went to seek the Seven Cities. Then a strange thing happened.

The Wanderings of Cabeza de Vaca

Into the town of Culiacan there one day came wandering four strange men. They were barefooted and almost naked. The little clothing they wore was made of skins and hung in rags about them. Their hair lay in a tangled mass upon their shoulders, and their beards reached almost to their knees.

They fell at the feet of the first Spaniard they met, crying, "Thank God! Thank God! At last! At last!" Then they seized his hands and kissed them, kissed each other, and danced about, clapping their hands and shouting for joy.

"They are madmen," said the people who gathered around to look at them. "What shall we do with them?"

"No, no," cried the oldest of the strangers. "No, no! You do not understand. We are poor wanderers who have been lost for years among the Indians. We have been slaves; our companions have died, but at last we have escaped and now, for the first time in years, we see Christians and Spaniards and our joy overcomes us. Can you wonder at it, dear friends?"

"Lost among the Indians!" murmured the people in astonishment. "Made slaves by the Indians! Terrible! What can it mean?"

"There is something very strange about it," said one.

"Let us take them before our Capitán," said another, and they took them at once to the Capitán.

"Who are you?" he asked rudely, looking with disgust at their dirt and rags.

"I am Cabeza de Vaca," said the oldest man. "I am a noble of Castile who came with Narvaez to conquer Florida. The fleet was wrecked and all were lost save these three companions and me. We have been all these years since among the Indians."

"I do not believe a word of it," said the Capitán. "There is something strange about it. These men may be criminals. Put them into prison until we find out."

For three months they lay in the prison. Then they were sent for by the Alcalde Melchior Diaz. He received them with all kindness, and to him they were allowed to tell their story.

"Is it true," he said to the oldest man, "that you are Cabeza de Vaca of Castile?"

"It is true," answered Cabeza de Vaca. "Ten years ago I sailed with Narvaez to the Florida coast to take part in his great expedition, but, alas! all our ships were wrecked and only a few of us escaped to the mainland. There most of those who did escape died, and we four, three of us Spaniards and one a negro, have wandered ever since among the

Indians. We wept for joy at sight of our own people when we reached your town, but they have treated us worse than did the Indians."

"Do not think of that now," said kind Melchior Diaz. "It was a mistake; you shall now be treated with all the kindness that is your due. Tell me your story."

Then Cabeza de Vaca began the story of his wanderings:

"After Narvaez and the ships were lost," said he, "we escaped to the mainland and were taken captive by the Indians. They were a poor, starved people who lived on roots and berries and whatever they could get, and who often went for days without a mouthful. I do not know how many years they held us as slaves, but it was for many years and our sufferings were great.

"We tried always to get to the north, and little by little we got further westward and northward.

"At last we escaped from those Indians who held us as slaves and fell in with others farther west who had never seen a white man. We had with us a rattle such as is used by their medicine men, and this, with our beards, made them think we were from heaven. They fell on their faces before us and gave us all that they had.

"We told these people we wished to go to where the sun sets, and they said, 'No, you cannot go there. The people are too far away.'

"'It makes no difference,' I said, 'you must still lead us there.'

"We saw they were in great fear, but at last they sent off two of their women to see if they could find the other people and tell them of our coming. In five days they came back. 'They have found no people,' said the Indians to us. 'Then,' said I, 'lead us to the northward,' and again they said: 'There are no people there. Neither is there food or water.'

"At this I became offended and went apart from them,

and at night went away by myself to sleep. But they came at once where I was and remained all night without sleep. They talked to me in great fear, telling me how great was their fright, begging us to be no longer angry; and they said they would lead us whatsoever way we wished to go, though they knew they should die on the way.

"We still pretended to be angry, lest their fright should leave them, and while we were thus pretending a remarkable thing happened: the very next day many of them became ill, and eight men died. They believed we had caused their death by willing it, and it seemed as if they must all die of fear.

"In truth, it caused us so much pain to see them suffer that it could not be greater, and we prayed to God, our Lord, to relieve them, and they soon got better.

"News of our strange power spread through the land, and the people trembled at our coming. Sometimes they would come to meet us, and bring all they owned and offer it to us. Or, again, when they heard we were coming, they would go into their houses and pile all their goods in a heap in the middle of the floor for us, and then sit down, with their faces to the wall, their heads bowed, and their hair drawn over their eyes. Thus they waited until we came and spoke to them. Then they gave us whatever we would take from them.

"Wherever we went, they brought their sick to us and begged us to cure them. We always examined them carefully, and treated them as best we knew how, and prayed earnestly to God to help us, and they nearly always got well. Whenever a sick man got well, he not only gave us all that he had, but all his friends did likewise.

"As we pressed westward and northward we came all the time to finer Indians who had more wealth and better homes than those farther east.

"At last we came to a land of plenty. The people lived in houses and had beans, pumpkins, and calabashes for food and covered themselves with blankets made of hides. They were the finest-looking and strongest people we had seen and intelligent beyond any of the others. They had nothing they did not give to us. They begged us to pray for rain and told us that for two years not a drop had fallen. When we asked where they had got their food, they told us from the land of the maize. Then I bade them tell me of this land of the maize, and they told that beyond them was a land of many people and large houses, where maize grew all over the land; that the people of that land were wealthy and wore beautiful plumes and feathers of parrots, and used precious stones for arrowheads and to decorate their houses. And they brought to me five beautiful emeralds cut into arrowheads, and many fine turquoises and beads made of coral such as come from the South Seas. When I asked whence they got these stones, they pointed to some lofty mountains that stand toward the north and told us that from there came the precious stones, and that near those mountains were large cities. They said that in those cities the houses were so large that there were sometimes three or four lofts one above the other."

"And did you not go to those cities?" asked Melchior Diaz, eagerly.

"No," answered Cabeza de Vaca. "I did not go because I heard that toward the sunset were other men of my kind, and I hurried westward, hoping to meet them. Therefore I did not go to the land of the cities. I longed once more to look upon the face of a Spaniard."

"You have suffered much," said Melchior Diaz, "but do not think of it, and now rest."

Then Melchior Diaz sent off a messenger to Mexico to carry a letter to the Viceroy de Mendoza, telling him of Cabeza de Vaca and his strange tale.

Forthwith the messenger returned with a letter commanding Cabeza de Vaca and his companions to come at once to Mexico and appear before the viceroy.

To Mexico they went, and again Cabeza told the strange story of their wanderings.

"It is a wonderful story," said the viceroy, when he had finished, "and you certainly deserve to spend the rest of your life in ease. Say the word, and I myself will send you home to Spain."

Cabeza de Vaca almost wept for joy at these words. "Gladly will I go, dear friend. Gladly will I go, for I am weary of wandering and would once more see my own country."

So Cabeza de Vaca and two of his companions sailed off to Spain, and the Viceroy de Mendoza thought much of the wonderful cities far to the northward.

The Journey of Fray Marcos

The story of Cabeza de Vaca set all New Spain talking once more of the Seven Cities.

"Of course," said the people, as they talked, "of course they are the same seven cities Nuño de Guzmán learned of from Tejos, the Indian. He did not get the right directions, and so he failed to reach them. But now we know they are there," and many were eager to set out at once.

But the Viceroy de Mendoza was a quiet and careful statesman.

"There have been many lives lost already," he said, "and it will be better not to be in too great a hurry. I believe these are the seven cities sought for by Nuño de Guzmán, but I shall not send an army until I am sure."

Then he thought of a monk called Fray Marcos of Niza, who had been much among the Indians of the north, and he sent for him to come at once to Mexico.

Fray Marcos came, and the Viceroy de Mendoza told him the story of Cabeza de Vaca.

"Now, Fray Marcos," said the viceroy, after finishing the story, "if we should send an army, these Indians would surely make war upon us and both for them and for us there would be many lives lost. You understand them, and it might be that they would let you come among them and learn what we desire. Perhaps there lies to the northward as great a nation as Peru or Mexico. It must be taken for the church and the crown. Will you not be the one to carry the message of the cross and to take possession of the country for the king of Spain?"

"I will," said Fray Marcos, eagerly.

"Very well," said Mendoza, smiling. "The negro Stephen who was with Cabeza de Vaca is here, and he shall be your guide. Remember that this expedition is to be undertaken more to spread our knowledge of God than for great wealth. Therefore, bear in mind that the natives are to be treated with the utmost kindness, and my displeasure will fall heavy upon whosoever shall offend them. Say to them that the Emperor is very angry at those Christians who have been unkind to them, and that never again shall they be enslaved or taken from their homes.

"Take special note of their number, and of their manner of life, and whether they are at peace or at war among themselves. Notice the nature of the country, the fertility of the soil, and the character of its products. Learn what wild animals there are there, and find out if there are any rivers great or small. Search for precious stones and metals and, if possible, bring back specimens of them. Also make careful inquiry if the natives have any knowledge of a neighboring sea.

"If you shall succeed in reaching the Southern Sea, write out an account of all your discoveries and bury it at the foot of the tallest tree and then mark the tree with a cross.

Do the same at the mouth of all rivers, and those who are sent after you will be on the lookout for such a sign. Take enough Indians with you so that you can send them back from time to time to bring to us reports of the route you have taken and how you are treated by the Indians you meet. If you shall come to any great city, do not send back word but come yourself and tell me about it. And lastly, although all the world belongs to the Emperor, be sure and plant the cross in those new lands and take possession of them in the name of the Spanish crown, and never forget that your life is of great value to your church and your country, and do not risk it needlessly. Now, go. Make all your plans and set out as soon as may be."

Fray Marcos hastened to make his plans, and on the seventh of March, 1539, he set out from Culiacan with the negro Stephen and a few faithful Indians.

Several months went by; then, at the end of September, 1539, a traveler in a monk's gown came walking alone into Culiacan.

"It is Fray Marcos!" cried the people. "It is Fray Marcos, who went to search for the Seven Cities!" "Did you find them, Fray Marcos?" "Where is Stephen, the negro?" "Are the Seven Cities full of wealth?"

But Fray Marcos would not answer. "I have much to tell," he said to them, "but I will tell it only to the Lord de Mendoza himself."

To the Lord de Mendoza he told a story even more wonderful than the story of Tejos, the Indian, or that of Cabeza de Vaca.

"All the way," he said, "I found great entertainment, for after I told the Indians they were not to be enslaved, they could not do enough to show their love for me. I went where the Holy Ghost did lead me. The Indians guided me from place to place, and some went ahead to tell others that I was coming. Everywhere they came to meet me and gave me welcome. They had food ready for me; and where there were no houses, they built bowers of trees and flowers that I might rest safe from the sun.

"I saw naught that was worthy of notice until there came to me some Indians from an island off the coast, and these wore about their necks great shells that were of mother-of-pearl. To these I showed the pearls which I carried with me for show, and they told me that in their islands there were great stores of such, and that there were thirty islands.

"And then I passed through a desert of four days' journey, and there went with me the Indians from the island and from the mountains I had passed. At the end of this desert I found other Indians, who marveled much to see me, because they had not before seen a white man. They gave me great stores of food and sought to touch my garments, and called me Hayota, which in their language means 'A man come from Heaven.'

"As best I could, I told to all these Indians of our Lord God in Heaven, and of our great Emperor over the sea. Then I asked them if they knew of any great kingdom thereabout or of any great cities.

"And they told me that farther on were high mountains, and at the foot of those mountains was a large and mighty plain on which were many great towns and people clad in cotton. Then I showed them metals that I carried with me and said to them, 'Have the people of those cities any of these?' And they took the gold metal from my hand and said: 'Of this do the people of those cities make the vessels from which they eat, and also do they make of it thin plates to scrape the sweat from their bodies, and the walls of their temples are covered therewith.'

"Then I asked concerning the precious stones known to the people of the cities, and the Indians answered that they had round, green stones that they prized much and wore hanging from their noses and ears.

"The Indians offered to take me to the cities, but because it was a long journey from the sea, and your lordship had commanded me to keep close to the coast, I did not go.

"It was now Passion Sunday, and I felt inclined to tarry among the people I was with. I did so, but I sent on ahead of me the negro Stephen.

"I told him to go to the northward fifty or threescore leagues, and to take with him Indians, of whom he should send back from time to time messengers bearing me news of all that he learned.

"We agreed that if it were the mean country of which he learned, he should send me a cross no longer than my hand; but if it were a great country, he should send me a cross the length of two hands; and if it were a country greater and richer than New Spain, he should send a great cross.

"Stephen went from me on Passion Sunday, after dinner, and within four days there came to me messengers bearing a cross as high as a man. He sent me also word that I should at once come after him, for he had news of a mighty province; that he had with him certain Indians who had been to that province, and one of them he sent to me.

"The Indian whom Stephen had sent told me it was thirty days' journey beyond the town where Stephen was, to the first city of the province, which was called Cibola. He said there were seven great cities in this province all under one lord. The houses, he said, were made of stone and the smallest of them were of two lofts, one above the other; and the house of the lord of the province had four lofts and was wide and long. He said, too, that the gates of the finest houses were cunningly wrought with turquoises, whereof they had plenty.

"The same day that Stephen's messenger came to me there came also another Indian from the seacoast, and he told again of the many islands in the sea and of people who have many pearls and much gold.

"And that same day there came to me three Indians with their faces and breasts and arms painted.

"They came, they said, from a province toward the east that bordered upon that of the Seven Cities. They had heard of me and wished to see me. They told me of the Seven Cities of Cibola, the people, and the houses, in the same manner that Stephen had sent me word. I sent back the Indians who had come from the islands on the seacoast, and hurried on after Stephen.

"Each day messengers came to me from Stephen, all carrying large crosses and all telling of Cibola.

"At last came Indian messengers who told me of three other kingdoms called Marata, Acus, and Tonteac. They said that the people of those provinces dressed even as the people of Cibola, with gowns of cotton that hang to their feet, and they bound them with girdles of turquoises. And they told me much more, to make me know that these provinces were in all ways as great as Cibola.

"I traveled on for days, stopping to know the people among whom I passed and always being received by them with all tenderness.

"They brought me their sick that I might heal them and sought always to touch my garments. They gave to me cowhides so well tanned that I could not well believe them to have been dressed by savage people.

"As I went on, I came to great crosses set up in the ground by Stephen to let me know that the good news of the country increased. I came to a pleasant town at last where indeed were people clad in cotton, both men and women, and they wore turquoises in their noses and ears. The lord of the village came with his brethren to greet me, and they were well dressed in robes of cotton and hides and wore collars of turquoises about their necks.

"It was a fair country, better than any I had yet seen; so I set up two great crosses and took possession of it for

His Majesty, the Emperor. They offered me gifts of all they had, but I took not one thing save food.

"I came now to a desert and went into it, and I found that the Indians had gone on ahead of me and built bowers beneath which I ate and slept, and in this manner I traveled for four days.

"Then I entered a valley where were many people; men and women came to meet me with food. All of them had turquoises hanging from their noses and ears and collars of turquoises three or four times double about their necks.

"Here they knew of Cibola as much as we in New Spain know of Mexico and could answer all I wished to ask about the people.

"As I went on I met more and more people, and passed through a fine country where is much grass and water. The people were in all ways civil and kind and told me about Cibola and Acus, and Tonteac and Marata and Quivira. Here I saw a thousand oxhides all nicely dressed and chains of turquoise, and they told me they all came from Cibola.

"And now I had two deserts to cross and was fifteen days' journey from Cibola.

"I entered the desert, and many Indians went with me, and others went on ahead to make ready for me; and each day there came word from Stephen, telling me all was true and to hurry after him.

"For twelve days I journeyed thus, and then there came running to meet us an Indian in great fright — his body covered with sweat and dust and his face showing the greatest sadness.

"He told us that the day before, Stephen had reached Cibola, and had sent messengers into the city with presents for its lord, and to let him know they came in peace.

"But the lord of the city fell into a great rage, and dashed the presents of Stephen to the ground. In his fury he drove the messengers out of the city, and told them that if they again appeared they would surely be killed, as would also Stephen, if he dared to come near.

"The messengers hurried to Stephen and told him what had happened, but he was in no wise afraid; he answered he should go, nevertheless, and bade the Indians fear not, but to come with him.

"They went on, but as they were about to enter the city, many of its people met them and seized them and cast them into a great house that stood just outside. They took from them all that they had, and left them all night without food or drink. The next morning Stephen and his Indians tried to escape, but they were scarce outside their prison when the people of the city set upon them, and Stephen and all the Indians, except the messenger and one other, were killed. These two had been struck down and left for dead, but were only stunned. They had lain under the dead bodies of the others until the angry people had gone back into the city. Then they had crept away.

"My Lord de Mendoza, so great was my grief at this terrible news that it seemed for a moment I must indeed die, but when I saw all my Indians begin to weep and lament, I knew I must not give way.

"I straightway gave to them many of the presents I had intended for the people of Cibola, and then I resolved that though I might not enter the city I would still look upon it, and I told them I would nevertheless go on. They begged me not to go, but when they saw I was firm two of them agreed to go with me. Se we left the others to await our return and journeyed forwards. We traveled one day, and then we came to a round hill. This I climbed, and on looking down saw at its foot the city of Cibola. It was a fair city, my lord. The houses were as the Indians told me, of two and three and four stories and built of stone. The people were somewhat white and dressed in white garments. Greatly was I tempted to risk my life and go thither, but knowing that if I were killed all knowledge of the country would be lost, I gave it up and contented myself with planting a cross upon the hilltop in token that I took possession for the crown of Spain."

"You have done well, Fray Marcos," cried Mendoza, "and now it is time to send an army."

The Disappointment of Coronado

When Mendoza wanted to send an army, the first person he thought of was a brave soldier and fine nobleman named Francisco de Coronado, who sat by his side, listening eagerly.

Coronado knew all about the expedition of Nuño de Guzmân, and had heard the story of Cabeza de Vaca. Also, he had talked with Mendoza before the viceroy had sent Fray Marcos on his journey, and had said he would be willing to spend a fortune in fitting out an army to take the Seven Cities.

So Mendoza turned to Coronado and said: "Is it still your wish, my noble friend, to lead an army against this kingdom of Cibola?"

"It is," said Coronado.

"Well, then, make ready at once, and I will help you in every way that I can," said the viceroy.

The news spread rapidly, and again all New Spain was talking of the Seven Cities. In a short time three hundred Spaniards and eight hundred Indians had enlisted, and so many gentlemen of noble birth had offered to go that the viceroy was much embarrassed in choosing officers, for of course he must take the noblest gentlemen, and there were too many!

A fine sight they were — those cavaliers of Spain — in their glittering armor, mounted on prancing horses, their lances gleaming in the sunlight and their banners flying. Out of Compostela they marched in the gayest spirits, thinking of the loads of gold and jewels they would bring back with them.

But it was very different when they reached the desert and the mountains. They did not know how to bear the fatigue of such a journey, nor how to care for their horses and cattle and sheep. The animals died in large numbers, and the courage of the soldiers weakened rapidly as they grew weary.

The soldiers had come with the thought of conquest, so they did not treat the Indians they met so kindly as Fray Marcos had done, and of course the Indians did not like them very well, and in a little while there began to be trouble.

At last they came to a narrow pass in the mountains.

"I am afraid the Indians will try to keep us from passing," said Coronado to the Master of the Field. "Go you with a company of soldiers and guard that pass until all the army come up. Then we will go through."

The Master of the Field took his company and stood guard at the pass. But that night, while all but the sentries were asleep, the Indians crept down upon them and the sleeping camp was roused by a shower of stones and arrows and the wild yells of the Indians.

Now the men had lain down with their guns beside them; so they were ready, and they sprang up and began fighting bravely. For a while the battle raged hotly, the Spaniards firing their guns and the Indians replying with stones and arrows. But when the Indians saw some of their number falling dead, they were frightened and fled away in the darkness, and the Spaniards held the pass.

After that the Spaniards had little peace, but nevertheless Coronado managed to keep up their courage. On they went, up through that country we now call Arizona, over almost the same road that Fray Marcos had traveled. They paused where is now the city of Tucson, and then marching northeastward, crossed the Gila River and moved on toward

Cibola. At last, where today stands the town of Zuñi, they reached the first city of the kingdom whose fame had so long filled with golden dreams the minds of the Spaniards. But instead of the great, fine, glittering city they had expected they saw only a village of a few hundred houses.

The hearts of the Spaniards sank as they gazed upon it. Coronado called three of his men and said to them, "Go into the city and say to the people that we are not enemies, but have come in the name of the Emperor, our lord, to defend them and to join with them in friendship."

The messengers went into the city and delivered Coronado's message, but the people of Cibola received it with scorn.

"We did not ask you to come," they replied, "and your lord had no right to send you. This is our land and we can defend it. Go back to your lord and to your own land, for if you stay here you shall not one of you live."

The messengers turned to go back to Coronado, and even as they went the people of Cibola began firing arrows at them.

Coronado got his men quickly together and gave the command to attack. The people of Cibola were gathered upon the walls of their city and rained down arrows and stones upon the Spaniards as they came. The Spaniards were many of them so weary from their long journey that they had not strength enough left to pull a crossbow. Indeed, for a time it seemed they must be beaten, so fiercely did the Indians battle against them. The glittering armor of Coronado and the earnestness with which he cheered on his men, told the Indians that he was the leader of the Spaniards, and they tried particularly to kill him. Twice they felled him to the ground, and once he must surely have been killed had not a brave knight stood across his body and guarded him from the rain of stones until he recovered. He would not give up. Weak from the blows he had received, aching in every part, and with an arrow sticking in his foot, he led the last charge, shouting "Santiago!" as he rode.

"Santiago!" echoed his soldiers as they followed him straight into the town. The Indians fled as the Spaniards entered, and the battle was over.

The Spaniards almost wept with rage and despair as they looked about them. The houses, it is true, were made of stone and were large, as had been said, but there were no jeweled gates, no vessels of gold and silver, no fine city, no stores of wealth to carry back to Spain.

So great was Coronado's despair that he fell ill almost unto death. He could not bear to give up. It seemed he must find those seven wonderful cities. As soon as he was able he sent out parties in all directions to see what could be found.

For almost two years they searched. Whenever an Indian told them a new tale, they started off at once to see if it were true. They heard of a great river to the westward, and Arellano, one of the brave officers, led a party at once in search of it. Across the dry, hot desert of Arizona they went, and never stopped until they came to the Grand Cañon of the Colorado. Below them flowed the mighty river between walls hundreds of feet deep and so steep they could not descend to the water, though they were almost dying of thirst as they stood over it.

Scarcely had they got back before the army was again all excitement because an Indian had told a tale of a great city to the northeastward. Coronado himself led them in search of it. Up they went through New Mexico, traveling for days among herds of buffaloes that reached farther than they could see.

They went so far north as to enter that part of our country now called Kansas. They found in reward for their long journey only a few Indian villages.

At last, when more than two thirds of his men were dead, Coronado gave up and marched back to Mexico. And this was the last search for the Seven Cities that were not.

CHAPTER FIFTEEN

Story-Telling to Intensify Interest in Geography

IN the study of geography the story means as much as in history. The child is keenly interested in what he is doing and in what those around him are doing, and when he discovers that people in China, in South America, in Australia, or in Russia are doing the very things he is attempting to do or sees done, that they are engaged in industrial occupation very much as his father or uncle or neighbor is engaged in it, that distant occupation loses its remote quality, and the country with which it is associated becomes real and near to him. In the larger sense geography is something that must be felt and imagined. It is an interpretation of foreign activities and the regions in which they take place, and because the story can interpret these activities, because it can make situations real and familiar instead of aloof, it is of inestimable value in teaching the subject. Here the myth and fairy tale can be used with excellent results, because through them the child sees something of the struggle of man in his effort to interpret the world and comes to have a broader sympathy for the ideals of people of other regions. Moreover, in many instances it tends to fix definite information concerning a certain locality and to invest distant regions with vivid interest, for to the boy who associates the Rhine or Danube or Himalayas with the tale of a hero or people who once lived and did brave deeds there, those rivers and mountains will be more than black specks on a map.

If he hears of the two frogs in Japan who started out to see the world, he will not say that Kioto is somewhere in South America, because the spot has been fixed in his mind by a story. Because it is associated with something he has enjoyed, it stays there, and while the highest aim of the study of geography is not merely to stuff the mind with facts, but to broaden the horizon and bring the world within the child's own dooryard, the acquisition of certain information tends to give him that broad outlook which makes all people seem creatures of his world and all activities a part of his own experience. Unfortunately, however, teachers sometimes lose sight of this fact, and the larger aim is made subservient to a memorizing of data.

Geography and history are so closely related that it is difficult to separate them, and in making one vivid we must draw constantly from the other. The field is limitless. In fact, there are so many stories to give the geography class that teachers sometimes say, "When are we to have time for formal recitations?"

Too much recitation and not enough story is responsible for the fact that boys and girls sometimes give startling information about the location of places. Shorten the recitation period, if necessary, but do not fail to give the stories that bring far-away places as near as one's own dooryard, and let tests and examinations prove which method is better. We must possess before we can give, and the pupil who is assigned a number of pages and expected to recite about them often fails miserably, because interest, which must underlie the acquisition of knowledge, has not been aroused. We may tell him to study the course of the

Rhine and locate the cities that dot its banks, and one will mean no more to him than the other. But if he hears the tale of the building of the king of German cathedrals and the legend of the architect's compact with the Evil One, Cologne will have an individuality very different from that of Coblenz with its bridge of boats. If he listens to the tale of Maui fishing up New Zealand from the bottom of the ocean, of the demigod chieftain who was the discoverer of Hawaii and the patriarch of his people, there will pass before his eyes at the mention of places among the Pacific Islands pictures of a dark-skinned, sea-loving race with a history fully as fascinating as that of his own people.

If there is not time for him to recite it all, let him write about it. This will help to solve the composition problem, because the reason for much of the miserable written English work is due to the fact that the child has nothing to give. He is told to elaborate upon a subject that lies far from his interest, one of which he has little knowledge, with results that every English teacher knows. But if he has been interested in it by a story, he can give that story back in oral or written form, even though the construction be far from perfect.

Another value of using stories with a geographical or historical background is that they develop the child's social instinct and give him something of a realization of the brotherhood of man. Through hearing and reading them he becomes broader and more tolerant. He sees that in every part of the world men have their standards and ideals, which, although they may be greatly at variance with his own, are entitled to respect because they represent deep convictions and desires. Instead of viewing the world through a keyhole, he sees it across unobstructed fields and comes to have a bigger human understanding. In the study of geography there is a finer opportunity than anywhere else in elementary education to divert the child's feet from a narrow, provincial trail into the broad highway of cosmopolitanism.

As in the study of history, so in geography the story should radiate from local environment to other sections of the world, and every worker with girls and boys, whether mother, teacher, or librarian, should endeavor to give them some idea of the story of their own locality. The child should know something of the legends of the people who built their camp fires on the spots that are his public parks and gardens, and teachers especially should aid the earnest group of men and women that is patiently collecting and preserving our American folklore, by giving some of it to the children. It will not only heighten pride in their own locality, but it will broaden their understanding of other lands and races and their sympathy with the struggles of different peoples. This kind of work belongs to the field of history, but it so greatly increases interest in geography that the teacher should not miss the opportunity of using this material.

There are legends clustering about every section of our country that the people of that locality should know, and it is a matter of regret that the average man or woman has seldom heard of them. Europeans are inclined to say we are a people of no traditions.

While the charge is untrue, and our land is rich in legendary lore, it is true that only a small percentage of Americans are familiar with it. One reason for this general ignorance is that much of it has been buried in scientific treatises, which are unavailable to the layman. But within the last few years a large amount has been put within reach of the story-teller. The unceasing work of the American Folklore Society has resulted in unearthing and preserving much that would otherwise have been lost and that is important enough to have a place in our schools. Nothing is more fascinating to the child than stories of his own region, and our young people ought to be privileged to share in that joy with boys and girls of the Old World.

There are peasant lads in France, Italy, and other European countries who can entertain by the hour with tales of their rivers and mountains — not those of some distant province, but the peaks that tower above their native village, the streams along which they trudge on their way to school. California, Washington, and Oregon children should be given legends of the Yosemite, of Lake Tahoe, of Mount Shasta, of the Columbia River, and of Mount Rainier. Boys and girls among Southern bayous should be taught the traditions of their region, of the Indians and Creoles who made history there when that section was a province of France; while along Northern lake and inland river are tales of forest folk, of pathfinder and black-robed message bringer, of knights of the Old World come to seek fortune in the New, that are a part of the heritage of every youth living there. Let us give them to our young people, that they may love their home spots, not just because they are beautiful and are theirs, but as the French child loves the Rhone or the Austrian the Danube, because of the stories that tend to make them enchanted ground.

In using the story in geography the teacher's work does not end with telling the story. The places mentioned in it should be located on the map, that their exact position may be fixed in the mind of the child. Interest in the story will make this a pleasure rather than a task for the boy, just as it becomes a delight rather than a hardship for him to follow the route taken by his father or uncle when he goes on a journey, or to work out the itinerary of a trip he hopes to take himself. One small boy studied the geography of Virginia with keen interest after reading *Lord Cornwallis' Silver Buckles*, and more than one man and woman attest to the fact that some book read and loved during their school days did more to fix the location of river, city, and mountain in their minds than hours of classroom recitation spent in bounding states and countries and tracing the courses of rivers.

The following legend of Niagara Falls is illustrative of one type of tale that will greatly add to the child's interest in geography by investing certain localities with story associations. Much other material is given in the appended bibliography, and the wide-awake teacher will be able to glean much more from libraries and adapt it to her work.

THE GOD OF THE THUNDERING WATER

Retold from an Iroquois Legend

Before the white man sailed westward across the Atlantic, in fact, before Columbus was born or anybody even dreamed about a short route to the Indies, a little Indian girl lived on the shore of Niagara not so very far above the cataract. She was a happy little thing, and as she grew to maidenhood she became the fairest girl of her tribe, and her father, who was a mighty chieftain, promised her in marriage to the most powerful of his braves. This Indian was a swift runner, and around the council fire not another tongue was so nimble or eloquent as his, and never did his arrows fail to pierce the heart of the deer at which he aimed them. But that mattered little to the girl. He was not her ideal of a husband, and she could think of nothing more dreadful than becoming the mistress of his wigwam. Yet her father had spoken and she must obey, and with a sad heart she made ready for the wedding, weaving the handsomest of wampum belts and ornamenting her moccasins with gay beads and bits of woodpecker feather.

The wedding morning dawned, and the Indians began the games and merrymaking that always marked a marriage. The bridegroom and the young braves vied in races and wrestling matches, and the women too had a part in the festivities, singing and chanting weird songs as they tended the fire and roasted venison for the feast. Everybody was happy, — every one but the bride, who did not want to marry, and who sat in her wigwam looking sadly out upon the sport. Suddenly came the decision that she would not be the squaw of the man she detested.

Quickly, softly, she crept from the wigwam and hurried to the river bank. The others were so busy with their merrymaking that they did not see her go, and soon she came to where her canoe was moored to some bushes. She stepped into it, pushed it from shore, and began drifting down the stream. It was good to be there on the water, for, like all Indian girls, she loved to paddle, and in her joy of skimming along with the current she began to sing.

Suddenly a whoop went up from the village of her people. It was not the cry of those victorious in a game, it was a shout of anger, a cry of alarm, for they had seen her and believed she was trying to escape from the marriage every one knew was distasteful to her. The bridegroom started in pursuit, then another Indian and another, until every man in the village was rushing to the river and some had already begun the chase in canoes.

"They shall not take me back," the girl murmured. "I will not go back to the village and become Kunawa's squaw."

With swift, powerful strokes she paddled down the stream. She forgot that the cataract was roaring below her, forgot that her canoe was going rapidly and surely toward the bright foam from which no boat could come back. She thought only that she was fleeing from a wedding, and not until she saw the rapids beneath her did she realize her fate. Then she began her death song, and those in pursuit heard it for a moment, loud, clear, and plaintive as the canoe cut into the cataract, then suddenly silenced as it shot down to the rapids. Some of the women wailed and joined in the funeral dirge, and some of the others cried out in fear to the Great Spirit.

"It is the last of Kunawa's bride!" they exclaimed. "She is now on her way to the Spirit Land."

But it was not the last of the girl. Far down in the mist of the cataract, Heno, the Thunder God, had seen her. He held forth his arms, and as the canoe dropped to the rapids, she went into them, and bearing her through the watery depths, he placed her in a cavern behind the fall where he had lived since the beginning of things, and where the girl would live with him henceforth.

Many years passed. She was no longer a young maiden, but a tall, sturdy woman, and Heno gave her to one of his sons to be his squaw. She lived there in happiness with him in the cavern under Niagara, and often she thought of her people and her native village above beside the river. Because she remembered and loved them, Heno was kind to them, and when pestilence came to the region he lifted her to the shore that she might tell them where to go to escape the disease.

Once a great monster, a snake all green and white, came trailing his body through the forest like a river between hills, and made straight for the village by Niagara to feed upon the people there. But through the Indian girl Heno had told them of the coming danger, and they fled before the monster so fast that when it reached the village it found only a place of deserted camps. The great creature hissed with wrath, but Heno saw it from the mists and struck it dead with a thunderbolt. The great mass rolled to the river, floated down the stream, and lodged so tight above the cataract that a fold in its body sent a great volume of water out of its course, forming the Horseshoe Fall. The flood centered there destroyed the home of Heno too, but the Thunder God arose with his children and the Indian girl, and ascending to the heavens, has lived there ever since, where he thunders in the cloud mists as he once did in those of the fall. His voice is so mighty that the echo of it is always sounding above Niagara, and although white men say it is nothing but the noise of falling water, the Indians know better. They know it is the song of the god of the Thundering Water.

Sources of Material to Use in History and Geography

The history and geography references have been combined because each of the books listed here is valuable in both lines of work. This plan also carries out the Play School idea, which is that there is no line of demarcation between the two subjects.

Baldwin, James: *The Discovery of the Old Northwest.*

Becquer, Gustavo Adolfo: *Romantic Legends of Spain.*

Brabourne, Lord (Edward Knatchbull-Hugessen): *River Legends* (London and England).

Converse, Harriet Clarke: *Myths and Legends of New York State Iroquois.*

Griffis, William Elliot: *The Unmannerly Tiger and Other Tales* (Korean).

Guerber, Helène A.: *The Story of the English; Legends of the Rhine; Legends of Switzerland.*

Hardy, Mary E.: *Indian Legends from Geyser-land* (Yellowstone).

Hearn, Lafcadio: *Kwaidan* (Japan).

Janvier, Thomas A.: *Legends of the City of Mexico.*

Johonnot, James: *Ten Great Events in History.*

Judson, Katharine B.: *Myths of California and the Old Southwest; Myths and Legends of the Great Plains; Myths and Legends of Alaska; Myths and Legends of the Pacific Northwest.*

Lang, Andrew: *True Story Book.*

McMurry, Charles A.: *Pioneers of the Mississippi Valley.*

Perry, F. M., and Beebe, Katherine: *Four American Pioneers.*

Pitman, Leila Webster: *Stories of Old France.*

Skinner, Charles M.: *American Myths and Legends; Myths and Legends beyond Our Borders* (Mexico and Peru).

Smith, Bertha H.: *Yosemite Legends.*

Warren, Henry Pitt (Ed.): *Stories from English History.*

Westervelt, H. D.: *Legends of Old Honolulu.*

CHAPTER SIXTEEN

Story-Telling to Intensify Interest in Nature Study

NATURE study, as a formal subject in the elementary schools, is often uninteresting to the child, because many teachers think that there the bare truth should prevail, and present information concerning the sciences as a series of dry, emasculated facts. The result is indifference toward what might be a keen pleasure, and sometimes even distaste for it. But if the nature lesson is presented in a manner that brings vivid pictures to the mind of the child, if he is given some vision of what cannot be understood by mere description, it becomes a living reality, and not only fixes information that is the foundation for scientific study later, but enlarges the emotional life and quickens the imagination. It gives him a feeling of close contact with nature and makes him so responsive to its varied life, moods, and aspects, that he comes to love it.

Those who understand nature love it more than those who do not. The man who knows the elm, the beech, the hemlock, and various other forest brethren, finds a pleasure in the woods that is impossible to him to whom a tree is just a tree. The latter is like Peter Bell, of whom Wordsworth wrote:

A primrose by a river's brim
A yellow primrose was to him,
And it was nothing more.

He goes on his way thinking that trees are good for lumber, to produce shade and break the force of winds that might otherwise blight his crops, but he has little conception of how they affect human happiness and human life. When tired and nerve worn, he does not yearn for the peace of the redwoods, but for some artificial stimulus in a city distant from the one in which he has his cares. Why? Because he was not born with a love of nature that is as rare as genius, and was not fortunate enough to be led along the path on which it is acquired. That there are many men and women of this type is proved by the ruthless way in which our forests have been destroyed, by the abuse of privileges in public parks and gardens, by the way in which trees are slaughtered in city streets. It is certain that love of nature is not born with every one, and that what is the fortunate heritage of the few must be instilled into the many. This can be done, and it can be done through story-telling. The careless child, the unobservant child, to whom a flower is just a flower or a bird a bunch of feathers, can be led to open his eyes and see what he did not see before, while the one who has already found joy in the life of field and stream will respond with intense pleasure because a new and roseate light is flashed upon what is already familiar.

Children learn to love nature just as they learn to love a picture, a dog, or a swimming hole, through experience with it that gives joyous results. The country lad, whose Saturdays and vacation days are associated with cowslips, dragon flies, and quiet hours beside a trout stream casting a line for the elusive catch, is not likely to find schoolroom nature study a dull subject, because, through hours of enjoyment, he is equipped with an emotional and imaginative background that gives color to every fact presented. But he who has not had this opportunity, who knows as little of wild life as a cormorant knows of the Colorado crags, will not respond eagerly to a series of facts, because experience has not previously aroused his imagination concerning them, and he cannot comprehend their mystery and wonder. If these facts are presented through the medium of the story, if they depict the life of the open as vividly as some painting that meets the eye, they will give pleasure and furnish incentive for further investigation. They will not only awaken the uninformed child to a realization of the wonders and delights nature holds for him, but they will give the other, more fortunate child additional pleasure, just as a favorite fairy tale does when told again and again by one who loves it and can make its moods his own.

This does not mean that all information should be presented through the medium of the story. The story should be used only to give such information as is natural to the story form. But nature study can be wonderfully illuminated by the story, because many of the truths of science do lend themselves to plot, and where they have been put in parallel literary form, they are as replete with beauty and imagery as the fairy tale, and afford the fancy as free play as do the adventures of sprites and goblins. The marvel of the brown bulb or seed metamorphosing into the brilliant-hued blossom, of the homely caterpillar evolving into a bit of flying color, of the majestic movements of stars and planets through worlds remote but as exquisitely constructed as our own, fascinates the child and furnishes wide, untrammeled avenues along which his imagination may roam. There is almost no branch of science that is not rich in material for the story-teller. Dr. Carrel, the great French specialist, once said that some day an artist will arise who will weave the facts concerning the circulation of the blood into a tale as fascinating as any *conte* from the *Arabian Nights*.

It is not likely that physiology will ever be the nucleus of stories to give to children in the early years of school life, but Dr. Carrel's words hold a valuable hint for the narrator, who should not fail to draw from truth as freely as he draws from myth and fable. An overdose of one kind of food, no matter how wholesome, disarranges the digestive apparatus, and an overdose of one kind of literature makes a one-sided man. There are some facts to show that a too free feeding on fairy tales has led to crooked thinking and susceptibility to superstition, and the story-teller should balance his work in improbable tales with those of fact that fire the imagination because of the marvels related in them.

This is not so difficult as it may seem, for many of the truths of science have been put into simple language by men who were poet enough to bring to children something of their mystery and beauty, and there is no dearth of books that can be used with gratifying results by workers among children as young as those of six to nine years. Part of the story of evolution is enjoyed in this period. The boy in the age of fancy is fascinated by listening to an account of early man's struggle with nature, and tales of the tree dwellers, of cave and cliff dwellers, of the discovery of fire and the adventures of the first wanderers, mean as much to him as any fairy tale, because they have the very characteristic that makes the fairy tale delightful — an element of mystery that permits the fancy to roam unchecked.

Older children revel in the truths of science, if they are presented in story form. Take, for instance, David Starr Jordan's "Story of a Stone." Where is there a fairy tale more fascinating than this narrative of "a bit of petrified honeycomb," plowed up by a Wisconsin husbandman as he made ready to sow his winter wheat? The style and language have the charm of Andersen, the plot is as well sustained as that of any Thuringian folk tale collected by Grimm, and it begins as fairy tales have begun since the beginning of time:

Once upon a time, a great many years ago, so many, many years that one grows very tired in trying to think how long ago it was; in those old days when the great Northwest consisted of a few ragged and treeless hills, full of copper and quartz and bordered by a dreary waste of sand flats, over which the Gulf of Mexico rolled its warm and turbid waters as far north as Escanaba and Eau Claire; in the days when Marquette harbor opened out toward Baffin's Bay, and the northern ocean washed the crest of Mount Washington and wrote its name on the pictured rocks; when the tide of the Pacific, hemmed in by no snow-capped Sierras, came rushing through the Golden Gate between the Ozarks and the northern peninsula of Michigan, swept over Plymouth Rock, and surged up against Bunker Hill; in the days when it would have been fun to study geography, because there were no capitals, nor any products, and all the towns were seaports, — in fact, an immensely long time ago, there lived somewhere in the northeastern part of Wisconsin a little jellyfish.

Dr. Jordan has also woven into story form information concerning the animal life of sea and stream, of a mother and baby seal, in the delightful tale of "Matka and Kotik," and there is not a boy or a girl in the heroic period who does not listen eagerly to the adventures of a salmon, "a curious little fellow, not half an inch long, with great, staring eyes which made almost half his length, and with a body so transparent that he could not cast a shadow." The account of the battle of the fish there under the ripples of the Cowlitz, the beginning of the eventful journey down the river, the merry conflict with the herring and the terrible one with the sea lions, swimming always and always, growing larger and more daring, and having in his watery realm as many adventures as bold Robin had in his greenwood, hold the children from the beginning to the end of the story. They sympathize as he struggles up the stream again, "growing poor and ragged and tired," and through his life and adventures they come to have an interest in the world of fishes that they will not have without the tale. Such stories demonstrate the fact that information concerning the sciences can be put into fascinating story form, and every worker with young folk should endeavor to present some of it through this delightful medium.

The child will find such tales far more appealing than the so-called nature stories in which animals are over-personified and in which they meet man in situations that every intelligent boy or girl knows are impossible. A lad is not brought into harmony with nature by being given yarns that caricature nature, and many of the modern nature stories do this very thing. Children know that a wild bear does not walk into a little girl's flower garden, and then politely say "I am sorry" and back out because the small mistress of the garden is kind and instead of throwing stones at him explains in elegant English that it is rude to go into another's property unbidden. They know that animals and children do not converse together in the same language, and that bears do not have courses in ethics. The nature story that fascinates the child must be true to nature's laws. He may listen to some of the sugary, impossible yarns written to point a moral, but they do not give him keen pleasure, and because they are ridiculous in his eyes, he draws no lesson from them. One of the aims of story-telling is to give ethical instruction, but there is a wealth of tales that reflect nature and life correctly that should be used for this purpose, and the facts of science should not be distorted in an attempt to emphasize a lesson.

Tales pervaded by over-sentimentalism will not stir deep response in children. This is why the nature story that is true to the facts of science is the one that interests the boy or girl. It is like the racial tale, full of conflict, of temporary defeat and final triumph. The young salmon grown old, struggling up Snake River to the foot of the Bitter Root Mountains, was sore of muscle and unsightly of skin, and his tail was frayed and torn, but the desire of his nature was fulfilled at last. He scooped out a nest and covered the eggs of his companion, and then, because the work of his life was done, was free to drift downstream.

Such stories give insight into nature and engender a love of nature; and besides quickening the imagination and enriching the emotional life, they help to give stability to the child character, because through them he learns the workings of certain inexorable laws.

There is such a vast amount of material to use in teaching nature study, that the suggestions and bibliography given in this chapter can by no means be comprehensive. In the realm of geology there is the story of limestone, of slate, of quartz and granite, of rock salt and sandstone, and particularly interesting to the child is the story of coal. For him it abounds in color, and beautiful indeed are the pictures that he sees as he listens to this narrative of the carboniferous forests that grew in the beginning of time, of the lush, dank swamps of the Permian or Triassic or Miocene Period, and the strange animal life that peopled them. From astronomy and botany one may glean as much as from geology, while entomology, zoölogy, and ichthyology hold untold delights for the child.

A wonderful science story is that of the coral polyp, building from some submerged cliff or crag until a little island rises above the blue water. In my own childhood it meant as much as ever a fairy tale meant, and I can still feel the pleasure I experienced the first time I heard it. It is full of mystery and wonder, and a story of rare beauty for the child. I have used it often in story-telling, and it never fails to bring enthusiastic response; and very popular with the children is this song of the insect builders, of which I do not know the authorship, but which is one of the fragrant memories of my childhood:

Far down in the depths of the deep blue sea,
An insect train works ceaselessly;
Moment by moment and day by day,
Never stopping to rest or play,
Rock upon rock they are rearing high,
Till the top looks out on the sunny sky:
The gentle winds and the balmy air
Little by little bring verdure there,
Till the summer sunbeams gayly smile
On the birds and flowers of the little isle.

Older children enjoy hearing about the different forms of coral, of the characteristics of that of the Mediterranean Sea and the Indian Ocean, and of the Caribbean Sea and the Atlantic. They enjoy, too, hearing about the coral industry, of the fishing for it along the shores of Africa, of the departure of the seekers from Sicily, of the Feast of the Coral Fishers that is such a picturesque feature of the island life, of the polishing and carving and preparing the product for trade; they like the legend the southern Italians tell of how the first medallion in Sicily was made as an offering of gratitude by a fisher lad to the young Princess of Naples. From beginning to end the coral story is a narrative that charms the child, and it is but one of the forms of sea life, which holds rich opportunities for the narrator, while sea life is but one of the fields of science from which he can glean with splendid results. In fact, the possibilities for story work in the teaching of science are almost beyond imagining until one begins to survey the field and enumerate sources of material, and the story-teller will be restricted in it only by her ability to organize material and present it to the children in story form.

Sometimes writers, thinking they will make nature stories more enjoyable to boys and girls, people them with supernatural folk who are supposed to be responsible for the marvels that occur in them. It is a practice that scientists decry, and it is condemned by all who believe that a story fit to give to children must be worthy of the name of literature, and consequently, whether fact or fiction, must be true in spirit. The tale that portrays a fairy up in the sky keeping the planets in motion like so many checkers on a board, or one in which enchanted creatures bury their beads in the ground, causing them to send up roses and lilies and other beautiful blossoms, is not a nature story. It may be a charming fanciful tale, but it should not be given to teach the truths of science. Science stories, like Bible stories, need no sugar coating to make them attractive. When given as stories, and not as a string of facts, they are full of suspense, and accounts of actual happenings in star land, under the waves, or deep in the earth are as fascinating to the child as the fancied ones of nature's forces were to primitive man in the forest, when he crept close to the tribal story-teller and in big-eyed, wondering awe sought to know the meaning of the great globule that gleamed in the sky by day and the numberless tiny ones that gleamed there by night. The primitive animal tale, which gives early man's belief as to how certain creatures came by their characteristics, is very interesting to the child, and while in a broader sense it belongs to the field of geography, my own experience has been that if told in connection with animals or flowers studied, it is received with enthusiasm by boys and girls. But the child should understand that these narratives are primitive man's conception, and that the science stories are the real "why" and "how" stories.

THE WONDERFUL BUILDERS

Out in the heart of the Pacific, far out where the blue waves roll their shining masses between Samoa and the Australian mainland, where the brown-skinned islanders and the white-winged sea birds seem always happy, a little animal floated around one day, floated from among the shoals of Tutuila toward the open sea. It was a tiny creature, and as curious as it was tiny, for it looked more like a spot of clear jelly than anything else, and its name was Polyp.

Quite lazily it floated about in the water, now under a stretch of seaweed, all purple and opalescent like ropes of wonderful colors, now through the clear, bright current past the gaping mouth of a shark. But the shark, although always on the watch for something to devour, did not get the little polyp, and soon it came to a submerged rock deep under the waves. This seemed a very good resting place, and there the polyp stayed.

Days passed, weeks lengthened into months, and still the polyp kept to its place on the under-sea rock. But it was not drowsing and sleeping like a lazy creature. It was busily at work, for the very minute it landed on the rock it decided to make a house.

Now you must not think that it could not work, because, although it did look like a drop of jelly and was small and curious, it was alive. It had arms, very, very tiny arms, finer than the finest silk thread in your mother's workbasket, and so thin and delicate looking that nobody could see them. But those arms were stronger than they looked, and with them it held on to the rock tight and fast.

Then, what a queer house-making! The little, jellylike body began to swell. It raised itself up in the shape of a tube, and around the edge of the tube came a little rim. This rim was the beginning of the house of the polyp.

The waves rolled on. The sun beat down brightly and hotly as it always beats down in the South Sea country, and then came another change. A knot rose in the middle of the jelly, and out of that knot reached a mouth and feelers.

Now the work began in earnest. The polyp began to eat, to eat as greedily as a boy who has had not a bit for a whole day. It took in chalk and phosphorus from the sea food that came its way, yet it seemed never to get enough, and all the while the little feelers kept reaching out for more food and pouring it into the open mouth. As it ate, the chalk it took in piled around the little rim, which I told you was the beginning of the house, and although the polyp wanted much to hold some of that nice chalk food in its mouth long enough to get the full taste, it could not. The white substance went right down and piled up on the rim; so it is no wonder that the little creature was always hungry.

Well, it ate and it ate. The rim kept growing and growing, as of course it must with so much chalk piling up on it, and as the house grew higher and higher the polyp kept moving to the top. The part below was hard and white like stone, and still the polyp kept eating, eating, and building, building.

For a long time it kept on, until finally it died. Then one day another drop of living jelly floated that way, and finding the chalk house of the other polyp, stopped there and began building on top of it. The waves rolled on. The sun shone, and all the while the house went steadily higher. Other polyps too came and began building beside and above it, and as they died they left their hard, white homes behind them as the first polyp had done. Others and still others came, until, as many, many years passed, the chalk houses reached the top of the water and men called them an island.

The waves rolled by. Seaweed drifted that way and lodged itself on the chalk reefs. It decayed and turned to soil. Sometimes the water and sometimes the wind brought bits of plant and seed from some other older islands, until at last there were flowers and trees and birds singing in the branches.

Now the ships of the world sail by, going toward China or Australia or to the American shores far, far away, and sometimes they stop at the little island, and sometimes those on board rest there among the palms and think it so delightful a land that they wish they never had to go away, but might stay there always and always. Yet but for a wee, curious sea creature that island would not be, for it had its beginning in a tiny animal, more like a drop of jelly than anything else, that floated one day between Samoa and the Australian mainland, and made its house upon a bit of submerged rock.

Sources of Material for Science Stories

Beard, James Carter: *Humor in Animals.*
Bergen, Fanny Dickerson: *Plant Work.*
Burroughs, John: *Squirrels and Other Fur-bearers.*
Collins, Archie Frederick: *The Book of Stars.*
Comstock, John Henry: *Insect Life.*
Du Chaillu, Paul B.: *The World of the Great Forest.*
Fabre, Henri: *Insect Adventures; The Life of a Fly; The Hunting Wasps; The Mason Bees; The Life of a Caterpillar.*
Frye, Alexis Everett: *Brooks and Brook Basins.*
Grinnell, Joseph and Elizabeth: *Birds of Song and Story.*
Grinnell, Morton: *Neighbors of Field, Wood, and Stream.*
Groos, Karl: *The Play of Animals.*
Hawkes, Clarence: *Shovelhorns: The Biography of a Moose.*
Holder, Charles F.: *Stories of Animal Life.*
Ingersoll, Ernest: *Wild Life of Orchard and Field.*
Jordan, David Starr: *Science Sketches.*
Lea, John: *The Romance of Bird Life.*
Miles, Alfred H.: *Animal Anecdotes.*
Miller, Ellen R.: *Butterfly and Moth Book.*
Morley, Margaret W.: *Butterflies and Bees.*
Porter, Gene Stratton: *Moths of the Limberlost.*
Porter, Jermain G.: *Stars in Song and Legend.*
Roberts, Charles G. D.: *Earth's Enigmas; Haunters of the Silences; Kindred of the Wild; Kings in Exile.*
Thompson, Jeanette May: *Water Wonders Every Child Should Know.*

CHAPTER SEVENTEEN

Story-Telling in Domestic Science and Manual Training

PEOPLE are likely to smile when a story-telling enthusiast suggests that his art will intensify the interest in manual training and domestic science, but a little investigation usually convinces them that this contention is not merely a wild theory. Cooking and sewing and wood, metal, and leather working each has an interesting story, and through understanding how these crafts originated and how they have developed with the progress of the race, he comes to have an appreciation of their true dignity and value. In a broad sense these tales belong to the field of history and geography, for domestic science and manual training have a background in history and present-day geography. But since the school gives them as separate subjects, a consideration of story materials touching them will be valuable to teachers of these subjects.

It is a far cry from the first roast meat of primitive man, discovered by accident to be more delectable than that untouched by heat, to the banquet of the twentieth-century gourmet, but they are chapters of the same tale, each intervening portion of which is interesting. There seems to be no relation between the grass skirt of the prehistoric belle and the creations of Worth or Paquin, but they are links in the same chain, beads strung upon the same thread, as are the rush mats of the cave woman and the rugs of Teheran. There are dozens of stories to give to girls that will increase their interest and delight in household crafts.

Tales of the lace makers of Italy and Spain, of medieval tapestry weavers, of dower chests of European peasant maids, the contents of which pass from generation to generation, of royal costumers and court tailors, their problems, patience, and artistry, all tend to give a touch of romance to something many girls are inclined to hold in contempt. They enjoy hearing about cookery in foreign lands, of ways of serving meals that are very different from our own, and no one is more amused by Lamb's "Dissertation on Roast Pig" than she who deals with problems of roasting and baking.

Domestic-science girls who are told something of the legends clustering around various foodstuffs enjoy the cooking class more than those who hear nothing but lectures on chemistry, dietetics, and comparative nutritive values, and they take more pleasure in preparing a meal because they know stories about the various dishes that comprise that meal.

This is no unproved theory, but one that has been tried successfully with a group of fourteen-year-old girls, who took keener delight in bread making after being told of the bakers of Nuremberg and who brewed coffee with more interest when they knew the tale of how Arabians discovered the use of coffee.

There are stories of wood, metal, and leather workers that should be given to every boy, not only because they throw new light upon what he is doing and add interest to it, but because they lead him to respect those who toil with their hands. Stories of medieval carving, of house building in different lands and ages, now of the brush hut of the Australian aborigine, now of the workmanship in the palace of a sultan or czar;

of the poet craftsmen of Nuremberg, of the pottery making of the Aztecs, of the building of Venice upon piles hewn from Tyrolean forests, these and dozens of kindred subjects are rich in materials that will give children pleasure and knowledge. To the boy or girl who loves the work in manual training and domestic science they bring additional pleasure, while in the indifferent they awaken interest; and, moreover, the snobbish child who is inclined to think handcraft beneath his respect, will be led to see that the carpenter who strives to make each effort more worthy than the preceding one, or the housewife who puts the best of herself into the preparation of a meal, is in the same class with Phidias or Shakespeare in earnestness of purpose, even though not in results, and is as deserving of honor. The first step toward success with these branches is to dignify them in the eyes of children, and nothing accomplishes this as effectually and rapidly as the story. To know that the crafts were worthy of the best efforts of those of other times and lands is to make them feel they are worthy also of their best effort.

There is another reason why these stories should be told. In the midst of the agitation in favor of vocational training, the force of which is sweeping away and modifying some of the old educational standards, there is danger that in catering to the demand for the practical in schools we neglect that which conduces to dreams and ideals.

A man may advance beyond the ranks of a journeyman joiner and make a good living if he has no thought beyond the work of each day as it dawns, but without vision he cannot become the master builder, and romance is the corner stone upon which the temple of vision stands. The palaces of old Hellas were built to strains of music, for the beauty-loving Greeks knew that melody gave men lofty thoughts, and believed work performed to its accompaniment would be of higher order than that performed without it. Bands were hired to play as the toilers worked, and boys who were to become builders were inspired to emulate the efforts of great craftsmen by being told stories of their achievement. In our day we cannot expect the state to provide bands and symphony orchestras to inspire toilers, but during the days of their apprenticeship we can give them tales that will have a tendency to glorify their chosen craft. We can cause them to feel that only the best efforts of hand and brain are fit to go into this craft, because it is a monument to the memory of those who lived and died in its ranks, and that every worthy effort of each succeeding toiler helps to make that monument nobler and more enduring.

THE DERVISH OF MOCHA

Retold from an Arabian Folk Tale

The dervish Hadji Omar was a fortunate man. No one of his day was so well versed in lore of the ancients and in the knowledge of his own time, no one was so highly esteemed by his people or so loved and trusted by the caliph. At every royal banquet he sat in a seat of honor, and whenever he went through the streets of Mocha the populace shouted, "Hail, Omar!"

But there came a time when the fortunes of the dervish

changed. One afternoon as he sat in the court garden he heard a conversation that dismayed him. Beyond the palm trees that screened him from their sight, the caliph and his council were planning how to defraud the common people and enrich themselves. Hadji Omar listened, grieved, and that night went to his friend, told what he had heard, and tried to dissuade him from a course of dishonor.

Then the caliph forgot all the happy hours he had spent with the dervish, forgot that he had loved him even as a brother, and remembered only that the dervish was trying to interfere in his plan. He flew into a rage and declared that Omar should be exiled from Mocha, and that a price would be upon his head should he ever return. Never again should he sit at the royal banquet table. Never again should he pass through the streets amid cries and calls of endearment. He should live in the wilds like a hunted creature and get his food as the birds of the field get theirs.

So out from the city that he loved went the wise and righteous dervish. He took the camel trail into the desert, and after a time came to an oasis where he stayed. A miserable existence he had there, because few food plants grew in the spot. Sometimes a caravan came by, and a merchant or camel driver pitied him and gave him dates or milk. But sometimes he had nothing to eat, and always his meals were so scanty that he grew thin and weak and haggard.

One day — he had been a long time without food and was faint from hunger — he found some berries growing on a tree beside a spring. They were so bitter that he could not eat them; so he tried the experiment of roasting them over the coals. This made them more palatable, but still they were viciously hard. Hadji Omar was so hungry that he was willing to do any amount of work to get food; so he boiled the berries, hoping they would soften. Still they were hard, but he managed to eat a few of them and drank of the water. His hunger and fatigue seemed gone, and he realized he had made a great discovery.

Hastening back to the city, he told the guard his story and was allowed to go into the presence of the caliph. There he produced some of the roasted berries, which were boiled according to his direction, and the governor and council drank of the water. They pronounced it a kingly beverage, and the decree went forth that Hadji Omar was to go free.

Thereafter he lived with the caliph, who loved and trusted him as before and led a more exemplary life because of the influence of the goodly dervish.

Hadji Omar was honored during his remaining years, and after his death was revered as a saint, not only because he was wise and righteous, but because he discovered to Arabia the beverage of the coffee berry.

Sources of Material to Use in Domestic Science and Manual Training

Clinch, George: *English Costume from Prehistoric Times to the End of the Eighteenth Century.*

Goldenberg, Samuel L.: *Lace, Its Origin and History.*

Knight, James: *Food and Its Functions.*

Lowes, Emily Leigh: *Chats on Old Lace and Needlework.*

Morse, Frances Clary: *Furniture of the Olden Time.*

Norton, Edith Eliza: *Rugs in their Native Land.*

Planché, James Robinson: *History of British Costume.*

Ransom, Caroline Louise: *Studies in Ancient Furniture.*

Singleton, Esther: *Furniture of Our Forefathers.*

Stories of the Ancient World Retold from St. Nicholas (Clothing).

CHAPTER EIGHTEEN

Does the Work of the Story-Teller Pay?

AND now arises the question, Does all this effort on the part of the story-teller pay? Is it worth the labor required for the domestic-science supervisor, the manual-arts director, the music, literature, geography, or history teacher, to prepare stories that touch upon his work? That question can best be answered by estimating results.

As stated in the opening chapter of Part One, story-telling can simplify the entire education problem. It will create noble ideas in boys and girls of today just as it created ideals and established standards in those of the past. It will arouse an ambition to live and to achieve so that they may be worthy of the emulation of children of the future even as they emulate the heroes of days gone by. In no other way can such deep desire be awakened as through story hearing and reading. In no other way do children realize so completely the truth of Longfellow's words:

> Lives of great men all remind us
>   We can make our lives sublime,
> And, departing, leave behind us
>   Footprints on the sands of time.

Yet in many homes story-telling is almost unknown because the mother does not deem it of sufficient value to make some sacrifice of her time and provide for it. She does not know that the story-telling mothers of the past have been those whose children have risen up and called them blessed; that the confidence of their boys and girls, won around the fireside as old-time tales were told, has been held unshaken to the end.

The force that in the long ago moved men to great achievement has lost none of its power. Twentieth-century children respond to stories as eagerly as did boys and girls by the sea of Hellas when Greece was young, as they did in medieval castle hall to the strains of minnesinger and harper, because child nature does not change. The story hour in the home is a formidable rival of the street and the nickelodeon, and the teacher whose fund of tales is large and who tells them joyously has little trouble with discipline. Her charges know that she holds the key to Magic Land, and that if they are good she will open the gate. They remember her with affection, and best of all remember the dreams that came into being under her spell. She is queen of her little realm through the royal right of the minstrel, and no pretender can dislodge her from her throne in the hearts that she has won.

Yet some school officials, men of education and refinement, regard story-telling as a very good means of entertainment, but unworthy of a place in the curriculum, and when urged to include it ask, "Does it pay?"

If it is worth anything to make formal schoolroom subjects joyous instead of boresome, then story-telling pays; if it is necessary to give the child something that will be a perennial rainbow in his soul, something that will keep him sweet and full of faith and hope when disappointments come and illusions go, that will cause him to laugh at age even in the time of white hairs and wrinkles, then story-telling is vitally necessary. He cannot grow bitter who possesses Aladdin's lamp. Dark skies may lower over his head and the thunder crash ominously about him, but if the seeds of romance have been planted in his soul, if poesy has been nurtured into flower there by the world's best stories heard in his youth, he will retain, even in the midst of blackness and tempest, a vision of turquoise skies behind the clouds, a dream of sun-kissed fields where grow everlasting flowers of fragrance and beauty.

Is the reward to the worker not worth the price? One guerdon lies in the thought that he who joins the ranks of story-tellers becomes a member of a glorious company, one with which the greatest souls of the world were not unwilling to be identified. Goethe never felt it beneath his dignity to gather a group of children about him and delight them with a tale, and nothing speaks more eloquently of the sweetness of Verdi's nature than one of his letters to his librettist that relates how, in his visits back to the hill town where he was born, it gladdened him to see gamins swarm from every quarter, exclaiming, "Una favola, signor, una favola!"

"He is a happy man," says Châteaubriand, "who keeps through a turbulent lifetime the heart of a child, who carries with him to the end of his journey some of the illusions stored up in his youth, for contact with envy and calumny and deception are apt to cause them to take flight." The author of *Faust* and the creator of *Otello* each had his share of brushing against the things that make men bitter. They had sounded the depths of discouragement and disappointment, yet they had the hearts of children, and who knows but that telling stories to children had something to do with keeping them young? During Verdi's period of struggle and heartbreak, when Milan jeered at his compositions and critics declared him a man of no talent, when obstacles piled so high it seemed beyond mortal power to remove them, when no one in the city but himself and his wife believed in him, instead of becoming sour and worthless, as any but a granitic nature like his would have done, he returned to his native highlands and told stories to children who thought him more wonderful than a king; then he went back to his labor strong and fit. Forgetting himself in delighting the village *bambinos* bolstered up his courage and his faith and helped to make him an exuberant giver. Perhaps the present-day story-teller, like that master at Roncone, if he approach his work reverently and keep in mind a thought of what it has meant to the world, may receive as much as he gives.

STORIES FOR TELLING

THE STORY OF THE MAN IN THE MOON

(Alsatian Folk Tale — Christmas Story — Ethics, teaching honesty)

The man in the moon was once a merry peasant, who ever so long ago lived quite amicably with his good wife and children, and had a hut with a wooden floor and a roof whose thatch was as thick as any in the village. Always there was plenty of black bread and goat's milk, and sometimes on Sundays or holidays the family felt rich enough to afford a bit of pork. But one Holy Night that peasant turned dishonest, and then something happened.

"What shall we have for the Christmas feast?" asked his wife, who was fat and jolly. "Shall it be our good rye bread and a fine joint of meat?"

"To be sure," the merry husband answered, "but that is not enough. There shall be cabbage too."

At his words the wife opened her mouth so wide that it looked like a big round window in her face.

"Cabbage!" she gasped. "Pray, how can that be, since we have not a leaf in the hut?"

The peasant nodded in a knowing way and answered, "To be sure, there is none there now, but there will be by and by."

Then he held his tongue as if he thought it unwise to talk too freely to a woman, took a basket, and went out of the door. His wife was much excited. She was sure he had some secret message from the fairies, for it was in that far-away time when strange and marvelous things happened.

Down along the road the peasant hurried, smiling like a village maiden on the way to meet her sweetheart at the fair. Everywhere lights gleamed from the windows, and he laughed at the sight of them, for he knew people were inside, thinking of the feast and the Holy Night.

"Which makes it safe for me," he murmured. On and on he went, never stopping until he came to a cabbage patch, the largest and finest in the village. They were bigger than his head, those cabbages, and every one of them belonged to the mayor.

"But some shall go into my good wife's pot," he laughed as he saw them, and climbing the fence he went into the patch and began to help himself.

Then suddenly along the road came a child on a snow-white horse. He rode as if nothing could halt him, but seeing the man in the patch, he stopped and shouted, "What are you doing?" The peasant looked to right and left and began to stammer, "Just b-b-b-borrowing some of the m-m-m-mayor's cabbages," he replied, as he threw a plump one into his basket.

The clear, strong tones rang out again, "You steal, and on the Holy Night too! So you and your basket shall go to the moon."

Then, whisk! Up the peasant started and never stopped until he came to the middle of the moon, and there he has stayed ever since. Whether or not he ate the cabbages, no one knows, but he and his basket are there to this day, and every night when the moon is full you may see them.

THE DISCONTENTED PIG

(*Thuringian Folk Tale — Ethics, teaching contentment*)

Ever so long ago, in the time when there were fairies, and men and animals talked together, there was a curly-tailed pig. He lived by himself in a house at the edge of the village, and every day he worked in his garden. Whether the sun shone or the rain fell he hoed and dug and weeded, turning the earth around his tomato vines and loosening the soil of the carrot plot, until word of his fine vegetables traveled through seven counties, and each year he won the royal prize at the fair.

But after a time that little pig grew tired of the endless toil.

"What matters it if I do have the finest vegetables in the kingdom," he thought, "since I must work myself to death getting them to grow? I mean to go out and see the world and find an easier way of making a living."

So he locked the door of his house and shut the gate of his garden and started down the road.

A good three miles he traveled, till he came to a cottage almost hidden in a grove of trees. Lovely music sounded around him and Little Pig smiled, for he had an ear for sweet sounds.

"I will go look for it," he said, following in the direction from which it seemed to come.

Now it happened that in that house dwelt Thomas, a cat, who made his living playing on the violin. Little Pig saw him standing in the door pushing the bow up and down across the strings. It put a thought into his head. Surely this must be easier and far more pleasant than digging in a garden!

"Will you teach me to play the violin, friend cat?" he asked.

Thomas looked up from his bow and nodded his head.

"To be sure," he answered; "just do as I am doing."

And he gave him the bow and fiddle.

Little Pig took them and began to saw, but squeak! quang! No sweet music fell upon his ear. The sounds he heard were like the squealing of his baby brother pigs when a wolf came near them.

"Oh!" he cried; "this isn't music!"

Thomas, the cat, nodded his head.

"Of course not," he said. "You haven't tried long enough. He who would play the violin must work."

"Then I think I'll look for something else," Piggywig answered, "because this is quite as hard as weeding my garden."

And he gave back the bow and fiddle and started down the road.

He walked on and on, until he came to a hut where lived a dog who made cheese. He was kneading and molding the curd into cakes, and Little Pig thought it looked quite easy.

"I think I'd like to go into the cheese business myself," he said to himself. So he asked the dog if he would teach him.

This the dog was quite willing to do, and a moment later Little Pig was working beside him.

Soon he grew hot and tired and stopped to rest and fan himself.

"No, no!" exclaimed the dog, "you will spoil the cheese. There can be no rest time until the work is done."

Little Pig opened his eyes in amazement.

"Indeed!" he replied. "Then this is just as hard as growing vegetables or learning to play a violin. I mean to look for something easier."

And he started down the road.

On the other side of the river, in a sweet green field, a man was taking honey out of beehives. Little Pig saw him as he crossed the bridge and thought that of all the trades he had seen, this suited him best. It must be lovely there in the meadow among the flowers. Honey was not heavy to lift, and once in a while he could have a mouthful of it. He ran as fast as he could go to ask the man if he would take him into his employ.

This plan pleased the bee man as much as it pleased the pig.

"I've been looking for a helper for a year and a day," he said. "Begin work at once."

He gave Little Pig a veil and a pair of gloves, telling him to fasten them on well. Then he told him to lift a honeycomb out of a hive.

Little Pig ran to do it, twisting his curly tail in the joy of having at last found a business that suited him. But buzz, buzz! The bees crept under his veil and inside his gloves. They stung him on his fingers, his mouth, his ears, and the end of his nose, and he squealed and dropped the honey and ran.

"Come back, come back!" the man called.

"No, no!" Little Pig answered with a big squeal. "No, no, the bees hurt me!"

The man nodded his head.

"Of course they do," he said. "They hurt me too! That is part of the work. You cannot be a beekeeper without getting stung."

Little Pig blinked his beady eyes and began to think hard.

"It seems that every kind of work has something unpleasant about it. To play the violin you must practice until your arm aches. When you make cheese you dare not stop a minute until the work is done, and in taking honey from a hive the bees sting you until your head is on fire. Work in my garden is not so bad after all, and I am going back to it."

So he said good-by to the bee man and was soon back in his carrot patch. He hoed and raked and weeded, singing as he worked, and there was no more contented pig in all that kingdom. Every autumn he took his vegetables to the fair and brought home the royal prize, and sometimes, on holidays, the cat and the dog and the bee man came to call.

THE BAT AND HIS PARTNERS

(*Old Bavarian Folk Tale—Helpful in Nature Study*)

Once upon a time a strange thing happened. A cormorant, a bat, and a bramble met at the mouth of the river Elbe one day and told a sorrowful story. Each was almost bankrupt; so they decided to postpone paying their debts, put their remaining possessions together, and share in the consequent weal or woe.

They bought a merchant vessel, a ship large and strong, and so seaworthy it seemed it could sail to the nethermost parts of the Spanish Main. Wool was precious then as now, and in a country far away a hundredweight of sheep's fleece brought many a gold doubloon. So they freighted the vessel with the best wool that was to be had and joyfully watched the white sails disappear in the pearl-gray mist. But a storm arose and angry winds dashed their galleon against demon-like rocks. Instead of reaching a distant land of gold doubloons the ship went to Davy Jones's locker, and her precious cargo made couches for the mermaids.

Then sad indeed was the plight of these partners on the North Sea shore! Bailiffs began to sue them for payment of their debts, and ever since that time the bat has flown by night, for in no other way can he avoid his creditors. The cormorant, a solitary black figure, still broods beside the waves and dives into the sea, hoping to retrieve his shattered fortune, while the bramble has turned thief. Whenever a sheep goes by, he seizes a bit of the fleece, trying in this way to make up for the loss of the wool that went to the bottom of the Spanish Main instead of bringing him the gold of which he had dreamed.

BRIER ROSE

Retold from Grimm

(*Wonder Tale*)

In olden times there lived a king and queen, who lamented day by day that they had no children; and yet never a one was born. One day, as the queen was bathing and thinking of her wishes, a frog skipped out of the water and said to her: "Your wish shall be fulfilled. Before a year passes you shall have a daughter."

As the frog had said, so it happened, and a little girl was born who was so beautiful that the king almost lost his senses; but he ordered a great feast to be held, and invited to it not only his relatives, friends, and acquaintances, but also all the wise women who were kind and affectionate to children. There happened to be thirteen in his dominions, but since he had only twelve golden plates out of which they could eat, one had to stay at home. The feast was celebrated with all the magnificence possible, and, as soon as it was over, the wise women presented the infant with their wonderful gifts: one with virtue, another with beauty, a third with riches, and so on, so that the child had everything that is to be desired in the world. Just as eleven had given their presents, the thirteenth old lady stepped in suddenly. She was in a tremendous passion because she had not been invited, and, without greeting any one or looking at any one, she exclaimed loudly, "The princess shall prick herself with a spindle on her fifteenth birthday and shall die!" and without a word further she turned her back and left the hall. All were terrified, but the twelfth fairy, who had not yet given her wish, then stepped up. Because she could not take away the evil wish, but could only soften it, she said, "She shall not die, but shall fall into a sleep of a hundred years' duration."

The king, who naturally wished to protect his child from this misfortune, issued a decree commanding that every spindle in the kingdom should be burnt. Meanwhile all the gifts of the wise women were fulfilled, and the maiden became so beautiful, gentle, virtuous, and clever, that every one who saw her fell in love with her. It happened on the day when she was just fifteen years old that the queen and the king were not at home, and so she was left alone in the castle. The maiden looked about in every place, going through all the rooms and chambers just as she pleased, until she came at last to an old tower. Up the narrow winding staircase she tripped until she arrived at a door, in the lock of which was a rusty key. This she turned, and the door sprang open, and there in the little room sat an old woman with a spindle, spinning flax.

"Good day to you," said the princess, "what is this that you are doing here?"

"I am spinning," said the old woman, nodding her head.

"What thing is that which twists round so merrily?" inquired the maiden, and she took the spindle to try her hand at spinning. Scarcely had she done so when the prophecy was fulfilled, for she pricked her finger; and at the very same moment she fell back in a deep sleep upon a bed which stood near. This sleep extended over the whole palace. The king and queen, who had just come in, fell asleep in the hall, and all their courtiers with them; the horses in the stables, the doves upon the eaves, the flies upon the walls, and even the fire upon the hearth, all ceased to stir; the meat which was cooking ceased to frizzle; and the cook at the instant of pulling the hair of the kitchen boy lost his hold and began to snore, too. The wind also fell entirely, and not a leaf rustled on the trees round the castle.

Now around the palace a thick hedge of briers began growing, which every year grew higher and higher, till the castle was quite hidden from view, so that one could not even see the flag upon the tower. Then there went a legend through the land, of the beautiful maiden Brier Rose, for so was the sleeping princess named, and from time to time princes came, endeavoring to penetrate through the hedge into the castle; but it was not possible, for the thorns held them as if by hands, and the youths were unable to release themselves, and so perished miserably.

After the lapse of many years, there came another king's son into the country, and heard an old man tell the legend of the hedge of briers; how that behind it stood a castle where slept a wonderfully beauteous princess called Brier Rose, who had slumbered nearly a hundred years, and with her the queen and king and all their court. The old man further related what he had heard from his grandfather, that many princes had come and tried to penetrate the hedge, and had died a miserable death. But the youth was not to be daunted, and, however much the old man tried to dissuade him, he would not listen, but cried out, "I fear not, I will see this hedge of briers!"

Just at that time came the last day of the hundred years, when Brier Rose was to wake again. As the young prince approached the hedge, the thorns turned to fine large flowers, which of their own accord made a way for him to pass through, and again closed up behind him. In the courtyard he saw the horses and dogs lying fast asleep, and on the eaves were the doves with their heads beneath their wings. As soon as he went into the house, there were the flies asleep upon the wall, the cook still stood with his hands on the hair of the kitchen boy, and the maid stood at the board with the unplucked fowl in her hand. He went on, and in the hall he found the courtiers lying asleep, and above, by the throne, were the king and queen. He went on farther, and all was so quiet that he could hear himself breathe, until at last he came to the tower and opened the door of the little room where slept Brier Rose. There she lay, looking so beautiful that he could not turn away his eyes, and he bent over her and kissed her. Just as he did so she opened her eyes, awoke, and greeted him with smiles. Then they went down together, and immediately the king and queen awoke, and the whole court, and all stared at each other wonderingly. Now the horses in the stable got up and shook themselves; the dogs wagged their tails; the doves upon the eaves drew their heads from under their wings, looked around, and flew away; the flies upon the walls began to crawl; the fire began to burn brightly and to cook the meat; the meat began again to frizzle; the cook gave his lad a box upon the ear which made him call out; and the maid began to pluck the fowl furiously. The whole palace was once more in motion as if nothing had occurred, for the hundred years' sleep had made no change in any one.

By and by the wedding of the prince with Brier Rose was celebrated with great splendor, and to the end of their lives they lived happily and contented.

THE COAT OF ALL COLORS

Retold from Grimm

(*Thuringian Wonder Tale*)

There was once a king whose wife had golden hair and was altogether so beautiful that her equal was not to be found in the world. It happened that she fell ill, and when she felt she must soon die she called the king and said, "If you marry again after my death, take no one who is not as beautiful as I have been, nor one who has not golden hair like mine, and this you must promise me." After the king had promised she closed her eyes, and soon died.

For a long time the king would not be comforted and thought not of taking a second wife, but his councilors at last said that he must marry again. Then messengers were sent far and wide to seek a bride who should be as beautiful as the late queen, but there was no one to be found in the whole world so beautiful and with such golden hair. So the messengers returned home without accomplishing anything.

Now the king had a daughter who was just as beautiful as her dead mother. She had also the same golden hair, and, as she grew up, the king saw how like she was to his lost wife. He told his councilors that he wished to marry his daughter to his oldest councilor, and that she should be as queen. When the oldest councilor heard this he was delighted. But the daughter was frightened at the resolve of the king, and hoped yet to turn him from his intention. So she said to him, "Before I fulfill your wish I must first have three dresses: one as golden as the sun, another as silver as the moon, and a third as shining as the stars; further, I desire a cloak composed of thousands of skins and hides, and to which every beast in your kingdom must contribute a portion of his skin."

The princess thought this would be impossible to do, and so she should reclaim her father from his intention. But the king would not give it up, and the cleverest maidens in his kingdom had to weave the three dresses, one as golden as the sun, a second as silver as the moon, and a third as shining as the stars, while his huntsmen had to catch all the beasts in the whole kingdom and from each take a piece of skin wherewith a mantle of a thousand pieces was made. At length, when all was ready, the king let the mantle be fetched, and, spreading it before him, said, "Tomorrow shall the wedding be."

When the king's daughter now saw that there was no hope left of turning her father from his resolve, she determined to flee away. In the night, while all slept, she got up and took three of her treasures, a golden ring, a gold spinning wheel, and a gold reel; she put also in a nutshell the three dresses of the sun, moon, and stars, and putting on the mantle of all skins, she dyed her hands and face black with soot. Then, commending herself to God, she set off and traveled the whole night till she came to a large wood, where, feeling very tired, she took refuge in a hollow tree and went to sleep. The sun rose, and she still slept and slept on till it was again far into the morning. Then it happened that the king who owned this forest came to hunt in it. As soon as his dogs ran to the tree they snapped about it, barked, and growled, so that the king said to his huntsmen, "See what wild animal it is that is concealed there." The hunters obeyed his orders, and, when they returned, they said, "In that hollow lies a wonderful creature whose like we have never before seen; its skin is composed of a thousand different colors, but it lies quite quiet and asleep." The king said, "Try if you can catch it alive, and then bind it to the carriage, and we will take it with us."

As soon as the hunters caught hold of the maiden, she awoke full of terror, and called out to them, "I am a poor child forsaken by both father and mother! Pray pity me, and take me with you!" They named her "Allerleirauh," because of her mantle, and took her home with them to serve in the kitchen and rake out the ashes. They went to the royal palace, and there they showed her a little stable under the step where no daylight could enter, and told her she could live and sleep there. Afterwards she went into the kitchen, and there she had to carry water and wood to make the fire, to pluck the fowls, to peel the vegetables, to rake out the ashes, and to do all manner of dirty work.

Here, for a length of time, Allerleirauh lived wretchedly; but it happened once that a feast was held in the palace, and she asked the cook, "May I go and look on for a little while? I will place myself just outside the door." The cook said, "Yes, but in half an hour's time you must return and rake out the ashes."

Allerleirauh took an oil lamp, and, going to her stable, put off the gown of skins and washed the soot from her face and hands so that her real beauty was displayed. Then she opened her nut and took out the dress which shone as the sun, and as soon as she was ready she went up to the ball-room, where every one made way for her, supposing that she was certainly some princess. The king himself soon came up to her, and, taking her hand, danced with her, thinking the while in his heart that he had never seen any one like her. As soon as the dance was finished she disappeared, and nobody knew whither. The watchmen stationed at the gates were called and questioned, but they had not seen her.

She had run back to her stable and, having quickly taken off her dress, had again blackened her face and hands, put on the dress of all skins, and became "Allerleirauh" once more. As soon as she went into the kitchen to do her work in sweeping up the ashes, the cook said, "Let that be for once till the morning, and cook the king's supper for me instead, while I go upstairs to have a peep; but mind you do not let one of your hairs fall in, or you will get nothing to eat for the future."

So saying, he went away, and Allerleirauh cooked the king's supper, making some soup as good as she possibly could, and when it was ready she went into the stable, and fetched her gold ring, and laid it in the dish. When the dance was at an end, the king ordered his supper to be brought, which, when he had tasted, he thought he had never eaten anything so nice before. Just as he nearly finished it he saw a gold ring at the bottom, and, not being able to imagine how it came there, he commanded the cook to be brought before him. The cook was terrified when he heard this order, and said to Allerleirauh, "Are you certain you did not let a hair fall into the soup? For if it is so, you will catch a beating."

Then he came before the king, who asked who had cooked the supper, and he answered, "I did." But the king said, "That is not true; for it is of a much better kind and much better cooked than usual." Then the cook said, "I must confess that not I, but Allerleirauh, cooked it." So that the king commanded that she should be brought up.

When Allerleirauh came, the king asked, "Who are you?"

"I am a poor child, without father or mother," replied she.

"Why did you come to my palace?" then inquired the king.

"I am good for nothing else but to have the boots thrown at my head," said she.

The king asked again, "Where did you get this ring, then, which was in the soup?"

Allerleirauh said, "I know nothing of it." And, as she would say no more, she was at last sent away.

After a time there was another ball, and Allerleirauh asked the cook's permission to go again and look on, and he consented, and told her, "Return here in half an hour to cook the king again the same soup which he liked so much before."

Allerleirauh ran into the stable and, washing herself quickly, took out of the shell the dress which was silver as the moon, and put it on. Then she went up to the ball-room and appeared like a princess, and the king, stepping up to her, was very glad to see her again; and, as the dancing had just begun, they joined it. But as soon as it was over, his partner disappeared so quickly that the king did not notice where she went. She ran to her stable and changed her garments again, and then went into the kitchen to make the soup. While the cook was upstairs, she fetched the golden spinning wheel and put it in the tureen, so that the soup was served up with it. Afterwards it was brought before the king, who ate it, and found it tasted as good as the former; and the cook was called, who was obliged to confess again that Allerleirauh had made it. Allerleirauh was accordingly taken before the king, but she repeated what she had before said, that she was of no use but to have boots thrown at her, and that she knew nothing of the gold spinning wheel.

Not long afterwards a third feast was given by the king, at which everything went as before. The cook said to Allerleirauh when she asked leave to go, "You are certainly a witch, and always put something in the soup which makes it taste better than mine. Still, since you beg so hard, you shall go at the usual time." This time she put on the dress shining as the stars, and stepped with it into the ballroom. The king danced again with her, and thought he had never seen any maiden so beautiful, and while the dance went on he slipped the gold ring on to her finger without her perceiving it and told the musicians to prolong the time. When at last it ended, he would have kept fast hold of her hand, but she tore herself away, and sprang so quickly in among the people that she disappeared from his sight. Allerleirauh ran as well as she could back to her stable; but she had stayed over and above the half hour, and she had not time to pull off her beautiful dress, but was obliged to throw over it her cloak of skins. Neither did she quite finish the blacking of her skin, but left one finger white. Then she ran into the kitchen, cooked the soup for the king, and put in it the reel, while the cook stayed upstairs. Afterwards, when the king found the reel at the bottom of his soup, he summoned Allerleirauh, and perceived at once her white finger, and the ring which he had put on it during the dance. He took her by the hand and held her fast, and when she tried to force herself from him and run away, her cloak of skins fell partly off and the starry dress was displayed to view. The king then pulled the cloak wholly off, and down came her golden hair, and there she stood in all her beauty, and could no longer conceal herself. As soon, then, as the soot and ashes were washed off her face, she stood up and appeared more beautiful than any one could conceive possible on earth. But the king said to her, "You are my dear bride, and we will never separate from each other." Thereupon was the wedding celebrated, and they lived happily to the end of their lives.

THE POOR MAN AND THE RICH MAN

Retold from Grimm

(*Folk Tale — Ethics, teaching kindness*)

In olden times, when the good angels walked the earth in the form of men, it happened that one of them, while he was wandering about very tired, saw night coming upon him before he had found a shelter. But there stood on the road close by two houses opposite to one another, one of which was large and handsome, while the other appeared miserably poor. The former belonged to a rich man, and the other to a poor man, so that the angel thought he could lodge with the former, because it would be less burdensome to him than to the other to entertain a guest. Accordingly he knocked at the door, and the rich man, opening the window, asked the stranger what he sought. The angel replied, "I seek a night's lodging." Then the rich man scanned the stranger from head to foot, and perceiving that he wore ragged clothes, and seemed like one who had not much money in his pocket, he shook his head and said, "I cannot take you in; my rooms are full of herbs and seeds, and, should I shelter every one who knocks at my door, I might soon take the beggar's staff into my own hand. Seek a welcome elsewhere."

So saying, he shut his window to, and left the good angel, who immediately turned his back upon him and went over to the little house. Here he had scarcely knocked, when the door was opened and the poor man bade the wanderer welcome, and said, "Stop here this night with me; it is quite dark, and today you can go no farther." This reception pleased the angel much, and he walked in; and the wife of the poor man also bade him welcome and, holding out her hand, said, "Make yourself at home, and though it is not much that we have, we will give it to you with all our heart." Then she placed some potatoes at the fire, and while they roasted she milked her goat for something to drink with them. When the table was laid, the good angel sat down and ate with them, and the rude fare tasted good, because they who partook of it had happy faces. After they had finished, when bedtime came, the wife called the husband aside and said to him, "Let us sleep tonight on straw, my dear, that this poor wanderer may have our bed whereon to rest himself, for he has been walking all day long, and is doubtless very tired."

"With all my heart," replied her husband; "I will offer it to him;" and, going up to the angel, he begged him, if he pleased, to lie in their bed that he might rest his limbs thoroughly. The good angel at first refused to take the bed of his hosts, but at last he yielded to their entreaties and lay down, while they made a straw couch upon the ground. The next morning they arose early and cooked their guest a breakfast of the best that they had, and when the sun shone through the window he got up, too, and, after eating with them, prepared to set out again. When he stood in the doorway he turned round and said to his hosts, "Because you are so compassionate and pious, you may wish three times and I will grant, each time, what you desire."

The poor man replied, "Ah, what else can I wish than eternal happiness, and that we two, so long as we live, may have health and strength and our necessary daily bread? For the third thing I know not what to wish."

"Will you not wish for a new house in place of this old one?" asked the angel.

"Oh, yes!" said the man, "if I may keep on this spot, so would it be welcome."

Then the good angel fulfilled his wishes and changed their old house into a new one, and, giving them once more his blessing, went out of the house.

It was already broad daylight when the rich man arose and, looking out of his window, saw a handsome new house of red brick where formerly an old hut had stood. The sight made him open his eyes, and he called his wife up and asked, "Tell me what has happened; yesterday evening an old, miserable hut stood opposite, and today there is a fine new house! Run out and hear how this has happened!"

The wife went and asked the poor man, who related that the evening before a wanderer had come, seeking a night's lodging, and that in the morning he had taken his leave, and granted them three wishes — eternal happiness, health and food during their lives, and instead of their old hut, a fine new house. When he had finished his tale, the wife of the rich man ran home and told her husband all that had passed, and he exclaimed, "Ah! had I only known it! The stranger had been here before, and would have passed the night with us, but I sent him away."

"Hasten, then!" returned his wife. "Mount your horse, and perhaps you may overtake the man, and then you must ask three wishes for yourself also."

The rich man followed this advice, and soon overtook the angel. He spoke softly and glibly, begging that the angel would not take it ill that he had not let him in at first, for that he had gone to seek the key of the house door, and meanwhile he had gone away, but if the angel came back the same way he would be glad if he would call again. The angel promised that he would come on his return, and the rich man then asked if he might not wish thrice as his neighbor had been allowed. "Yes," said the angel, "you may certainly, but it will not be good for you, and it were better you did not wish."

But the rich man thought he might easily obtain something which would tend to his happiness, if he only knew that it would be fulfilled, and so the angel at length said, "Ride home, and the three wishes which you shall make shall be answered."

The rich man now had what he desired, and, as he rode homewards, began to consider what he should wish. While he thought he let his rein fall loose, and his horse presently began to jump, so that he was jerked about, and so much so that he could fix his mind on nothing. He patted his horse on the neck, and said, "Be quiet, Bess!" but it only began fresh friskings, so that at last he became savage, and cried quite impatiently, "I wish you might break your neck!" No sooner had he said so than down it fell upon the ground and never moved again, and thus the first wish was fulfilled. But the rich man, being covetous by nature, would not leave the saddle behind, and so, cutting it off, he slung it over his back and went onwards on foot. "You still have two wishes," thought he to himself, and so was comforted, but as he slowly passed over the sandy common the sun scorched him terribly, for it was midday, and he soon became vexed and passionate; moreover, the saddle hurt his back; and besides, he had not yet decided what to wish for. "If I should wish for all the treasures and riches in the world," said he to himself, "hereafter something or other will occur to me, I know beforehand; but I will so manage that nothing at all shall remain for me to wish for."

Many times he thought he knew what to wish, but soon it appeared too little. Then it came into his thoughts how well his wife was situated, sitting at home in a cool room, and appropriately dressed. This idea angered him uncommonly, and, without knowing it, he said aloud, "I wish she were sitting upon this saddle, and could not get off it, instead of its being slipping about on my back."

As soon as these words were out of his mouth, the saddle disappeared from his back, and he perceived that his second wish had passed its fulfillment. Now he became very hot, and began to run, intending to lock himself up in his room and consider there something great for his last wish. But when he arrived and opened the house door he found his wife sitting upon the saddle in the middle of the room, and crying and shrieking because she could not get off. So he said to her, "Be contented; I will wish for the riches in all the world, only keep sitting there."

But his wife shook her head, saying, "Of what use are all the riches of the world to me, if I sit upon this saddle? You have wished me on it, and you must also wish me off."

So, whether he liked it or not, he was forced to utter his third wish, that his wife might be freed from the saddle, and immediately it was done. Thus the rich man gained nothing from his wishes but vexation, trouble, scolding, and a lost horse; but the poor people lived contented and pious to their lives' end.

THE SILVER CONES

Adapted from Story by Johanna Spyri

(*Ethics — Geography*)

In the mountain land of Bohemia there lived in the long ago a miner with his wife and little daughter. They were happy in their hut in the forest, but after a time the father and mother died, and the child was left alone in the world. She had no money, and no aunts or cousins to take her in, and it seemed as if she would have to go hungry. But always there are kindly hearts among the poor, and one of the miners opened his house that she might have a home. He had six children of his own and little bread and meat to spare, but his good wife said, "We will divide what we have." So little Hilda became one of the family, and they grew to love her very much.

It was midwinter, and Christmas day not far away. The children thought of nothing but the coming of St. Nicholas, who they hoped would not forget them on the Holy Night, when every boy and girl in Bohemia expects a visit from the gift bringer. But when they spoke to the miner about it he shook his head and said, "Do not set your hearts upon his coming. Our hut is very small and stands so far in the forest that he may not be able to find it."

Gretchen, his little daughter, had a very different idea. She declared St. Nicholas could find a house in the dark if it were no bigger than an ant hill, and went to bed to dream of the toys and sweetmeats he would bring.

Day after day passed, and nearer, nearer came the season of Christ's birth. The children talked of him as they sat by the fire at night, as they picked up dead branches in the forest, and as they bedded the goats and shut them in, for Bohemian mountain folk are a toiling people, and even boys and girls must work.

At last the day before Christmas came, and in the afternoon little Hilda started out with her basket to get some cones. She wanted the fire to be brighter and more cheerful than ever that night, and perhaps if she met a servant from the castle, he might take some to feed the prince's fire, and give her a silver piece.

"And if he does," she thought as she trudged on her way, "I can buy something for the miner and his dear children."

Now, in that land of Bohemia, on the summit of a lofty mountain, a creature named Rübezahl made his home. He possessed all magic powers, and was so mighty that his sway extended to the very center of the earth. There he had chambers of gold and silver, and diamonds and jewels without number, and often gave of his treasures to those who were good enough to deserve them. He could change himself at will into any form. Now he was a bat flying in the night, now a country swain selling his wares at the fair, and now a woodman cutting down trees in the forest, because thus he was able to find out who was worthy and who unworthy, and to reward or punish them as they deserved.

Hilda had often heard of the strange ways of Rübezahl, and wondered if he would ever cross her path.

"I suppose not," she murmured, "because I am just a little girl."

As she came near the fir trees, a tiny white-haired man walked out of the shadow. He had a long white beard and a jolly red face, and looked as if he were the friend of children.

"What are you doing?" he called to her.

"I've come to gather cones," she replied; "some for our fire and some to sell, if the servant from the castle will only buy."

Then she told him of the miner's family, of how eager she was to get some money that she might buy a gift for his children, and of her hope that St. Nicholas would not forget them on the Holy Night.

The little old man seemed much interested, and when she finished her story he said, "The largest cones are on that tree. If you hope to sell, gather the best ones."

He pointed to a great, dark fir just beyond them, and then went back into the shadows of the forest.

Little Hilda thanked him and ran to the spot. She could see the cones like beehives on the branches, and just as she came under them there was such a downfall of beautiful brown things it frightened her and she began to run. But thinking of what she could do with such big ones, she went back, filled her basket, and started homeward.

It was very heavy, and the farther she went the heavier it grew.

"I'll have to ask little Gretchen to help me take it up the hill path to the castle," she thought. But by the time she reached the hut it had become such a load she could not move it, and the miner had to carry it in himself.

"They are lovely big ones and of a beautiful brown color," she said as the children crowded around to see.

But when they looked at the basket again, they saw no brown at all. Instead there was a gleam brighter than that of the moonbeams through the fir trees, for a wonderful thing had happened. In the twinkling of an eye every one of those cones had turned into shining silver, which sparkled and glistened so that they dazzled the eyes.

Then the little girl remembered the old man in the forest and told the miner about him.

He nodded his head in a knowing way and said, "Surely it was Rübezahl, and he has rewarded you for being sweet and gentle."

All of which seemed like a dream to little Hilda, but when she looked into the basket she knew it was true. And so knew all the other mountain folk, when the stars of the Holy Night shone out and the children went from door to door distributing silver cones. The good folk who gave her a home received so many that never again were they poor. They built a fine house with a porch and twenty windows, and were as rich as any one in Bohemia.

To make things lovelier still, St. Nicholas found the hut, just as Gretchen had said he would, and left some sweets and toys for the children. He laughed loud and long when he saw the shining cones, for he had heard all about it from Rübezahl himself.

This all happened very, very long ago, in the time so far away that even the oldest grandmother cannot remember the Holy Night when Hilda gave precious gifts to the miners; but the story has come down from the fathers and the fathers' fathers, and that is why, even to this day, the mountain folk of Bohemia still deck their Christmas trees with silvered cones.

THE FORGET-ME-NOT

Adapted from Version by Hoffman von Fallersleben

(*Thuringian Folk Tale — Helpful in Nature Study*)

In the beginning of things, when God the Father created every beast of the forest and every bird and tree and blossom, he gave each one a name, and the snowdrop, the lily, the pansy, the violet, and all the other flower sisterhood rejoiced and were glad, for each thought its own name the loveliest in the world. Everywhere in field and woodland there was happiness, and the blossoms lifted their faces toward heaven in gratitude, thanking the Gracious Giver.

But suddenly there was a sound of weeping. Somewhere in the meadow a flower had raised its voice in sorrow, and all the other flowers looked to see. At first they could not tell whence the sound came, then they beheld a tiny blossom, with petals the color of heaven and a heart the color of gold. It was sobbing bitterly, and the lily, looking down in pity, asked, "Why weepest thou?"

"Alas," came the reply, "I have forgotten my name."

Then — wonderful sound — the primrose and the violet and the pansy heard the voice of God the Father, for although the blossom was very tiny and half hidden by the grasses of the field, He heard and saw and knew.

"Forgotten your name?" He spake in tones that were

sweet and tender. "Then shalt thou be called 'Forget-me-not,' for that thou canst always remember."

"Forget-me-not," repeated the gorgeous rose and the modest violet, and the tiny one smiled through its tears and said, "Forget-me-not."

And ever since that day at creation time, when God the Father named every beast of the forest and every bird and flower and tree, the wee blossom whose petals are the color of heaven and whose heart is the color of gold, has been called "Forget-me-not."

THE LITTLE STEPMOTHER

(*Thuringian Folk Tale — Nature Study*)

Once upon a time, say the peasants of the Rhineland, a woodman lived with his wife and two daughters in a little hut in the forest. They were very poor, but what mattered that, since they were very happy?

They had five chairs, — one apiece, and one for company, — clean, sweet feather beds to keep them warm at night, a bit of soup to eat with their black bread, and once each year they went to the fair.

But after a time the mother died, and things were different. The father took another wife, who had two children of her own, and she was very unkind to her husband's little daughters. She forced them to do all the work, and if the poor woodman so much as opened his mouth to object, she beat him with her slipper. You will know how greedy she was when I tell you that she took two of the fine wood chairs for her own children and kept two for herself, and you remember there were only five in the hut. That left one for the husband and his daughters, and as the father was kind and good, he let them have it all to themselves and patiently stood while he ate his meals.

For a long time that greedy little stepmother ruled her

husband and his children with an iron hand, while her own daughters acted like spoiled princesses, until one night something happened. The hut and the family disappeared. Just how it came to pass, nobody knows, but the next morning the other woodmen found a little flower growing where the house had stood, and they knew that a fairy or witch or something had turned the family into the blossom which you may see almost any summer day. The greedy stepmother still sits on her two chairs, with her children on each side of her holding a chair apiece. The woodman's little daughters are crowded together on one, just as they were in the hut. And what of the poor henpecked husband, who did not dare to object to anything his spouse chose to do? Look in the center, right under her slipper, and you will find what most people say is the pistil. But the peasants of the Rhineland know better. It is the woodman, who once upon a time lived in the hut in the forest, and the flower you call the pansy is to them "The Little Stepmother."

THE RABBIT AND THE EASTER EGGS

(Bavarian Folk Tale)

Once, in the German land of Bavaria, there was a mother who was very poor. She was sad as Easter time drew near, for it was the custom in that land to give presents then just as we do at Christmas, and she had nothing for her children. She grieved about it day and night, and one day was so unhappy over it that she wept.

"Never fear," the old grandmother said, "the hens are laying well, and I know how to make beautiful dyes from moss and leaves. We can color some eggs for Hans and Annchen, and they will be happy."

This was a lovely thought to the poor mother, and she went to work. Soon she had beautiful red, blue, yellow, purple, and orange eggs, and when Easter morning came she and the grandmother hid them in a nest in the woods. It was a lovely spot, with a thick carpet of moss underfoot and the snowy blossoms of the wild plum overhead.

Then they all went to the tiny chapel that stood at the other side of the village, to listen to the music and hear the good pastor tell the story of Easter day, after which they walked home by the woodland path.

Little Hans and Annchen were running ahead of the others, and all at once they called, "Oh, Mother, Grandmother, come!"

The good mother said, "They must have found the eggs," and hurried to see.

Yes, there the children knelt, bending over the nest of eggs lovelier than they had ever seen.

"They are beautiful, Mother!" exclaimed Hans. "See, they look like hen's eggs, yet they are every color, like the rainbow. How did they get here in the woods?"

"I know," cried little Annchen. "A fairy bird laid them."

Just then a rabbit leaped out of some tall grass behind the nest, and hopped away into the forest.

The children screamed with delight. "The rabbit laid the eggs! The rabbit laid the eggs!" they shouted.

And ever since that time Bavarian children have played that rabbits lay Easter eggs.

THE EASTER EGGS

Adapted from Story by Canon Schmidt

(*Ethics*)

During the days of the Crusades a little village stood in the heart of a little valley. The people living there were very poor, but so good and gentle that despite their poverty they were happier than many of the great folk of the realm. They had none of the cares that trouble the rich. Their rude black huts, each with its tiny garden plot and bit of meadow land where they pastured the cow or goats, satisfied them because they knew nothing else, and they lived so simply and healthfully that there were men over a hundred years of age among them. Sometimes they burned charcoal for the iron works in the mountains and earned a few pennies, when they felt rich indeed, but if there was no money they did not complain. They ate their vegetables and black bread and drank their goat's milk in contentment.

One day, when the corn ears were yellowing, a little girl hurried down the mountain side where she had been tending goats. She ran to her home at the edge of the village, and called to her mother in the garden, "Oh, mamma, come quickly! A beautiful woman with two pretty children is waiting for me on the mountain. They are very tired and hungry, and she asked me for some bread and milk."

Kind hearts beat in the breasts of those village folk, and although they had little themselves, they were always ready to share their small store. Quickly the mother filled a jar with goat's milk and took some bread, butter, and cheese, and she and her husband followed the little daughter up the mountain side. After a while they came to a turn in the path, and saw a woman, very young and very beautiful, sitting on a rock under a beech tree. She was holding a little girl who was as lovely as herself, and beside them, on the ground, a tiny dark-eyed boy played with a bunch of thistles. Not far away an old man was unloading a mule and opening bundles as if preparing to camp for the night. Their clothing was of the costly kind that is worn only by the very rich, and it seemed strange that they should be asking food of the poor.

The village wife offered the bread, butter, and cheese she had brought with her, which the woman received with smiles and words of thanks. She kept nothing herself, but gave all to the old man and children, who ate the coarse peasant fare as if it tasted very good, and as she watched them tears streamed down her cheeks. She asked many questions about the valley, and finding that no one but charcoal burners lived there, and that strangers almost never came by, exclaimed, "I think God must have sent me here. I have been driven from home and am seeking a spot where we may rest in peace."

They went down to the valley together, and the peasant and his wife led the way to a vacant house, which the woman rented for her home. It was a very humble cottage, but she said it suited her, for it was new and clean, and from its little windows one could see out over the cabins and the garden plots to the tall, dark fir trees on the mountain slopes. She took one of the village girls for a servant, and the worn, unhappy look began to leave her face.

Early the next morning she called the maid Marie, gave her a silver piece, and said, "Go and get some eggs for breakfast."

The girl looked at her in surprise.

"Oh, madame!" she asked sorrowfully, "do you mean that I must take the eggs of the dear little birds that sing in the forest?"

"Of course not," her mistress replied, thinking her very silly, "I want hen's eggs, not bird's eggs."

But Marie looked more amazed than before.

"I don't know what you mean by 'hens,'" she said. "We have none of them here."

"You have no hens!" the woman exclaimed. "How can that be?"

Then she remembered that this was a village of poor peasants and that only the rich had chickens, because they had just been brought to Europe from Asia, and were very costly. So she bade the old man Kuno go to the city across the mountains and bring her everything she needed.

"And be sure not to forget the cock and hens," she called after him as he rode away.

Late that afternoon the man returned, and the woman met him at the door. "Have you brought the chickens?" she asked.

Nodding in reply, he set the cage on the ground.

By this time the village children had gathered around, and were greatly excited about the strange-looking birds. They laughed and clapped their hands, for they never had seen anything like them, and when Kuno turned them out of the cage and they walked around picking up the grain he threw to them, their joy knew no bounds. Then the cock flapped his wings and crowed and some of the hens cackled, and the children danced and screamed in delight. They stayed until it was dark, and early the next morning came again and brought their fathers and mothers to see the wonderful birds that sang such curious songs.

Summer passed and autumn came. The last apples fell from the trees, nuts dropped in the frost-painted forest, and the sharp winds of November blew down from the peaks, yet still the lovely stranger and her children stayed in the village. That was very strange, for the valley was entirely surrounded by rugged mountains, and was a rough, wild country in winter, when the tiny houses were almost buried in the snow. But they seemed happy there, and the people wondered much about it. They talked of it as they herded the goats on the slopes, as they burned charcoal in the shadow of the fir trees, and always would end by saying, "She is some great lady, for she speaks the language of court, and she and her children have costly clothes and many gold pieces."

But they found out nothing, for when they asked the children who their mother was they said, "She is mamma, and we are Blanche and Edmund."

So still they wondered and still they did not know. But they were glad she lived among them, because they had grown to love her very much. She was kind and charitable toward every one in the village. She gave food to the poor and took care of the sick, and the peasants repaid her with many kindnesses. They gave her game they killed in the forest, and when spring came and the snow melted, the village children roamed the woods for the earliest violets and cowslips, and brought them to her door.

These acts of kindness touched her, and the morning before Easter she thought, " I must do something to make them happy." But what could it be? She couldn't give them a feast, because, although she had plenty of money, it was impossible to get any meat in the village; and she couldn't give them presents, because there was no place to buy them. She had nothing but eggs, which she thought would be no treat at all. Then an idea came to her. Calling Marie, the maid, she told her of it and they merrily went to work.

They went into the woods and gathered roots, moss, and berries such as were used for dyeing in those days. They made cakes and custards. They colored eggs red, blue, green, orange, and lilac, and planned to give the people a grand surprise. Late in the afternoon little Blanche and Edmund went out through the village and stopped at every house, saying, "Mamma invites you, you and all your family, great and small, to a feast at our house tomorrow. Come after the mass."

Everybody accepted the invitation. They had never been to a real feast, and to go to one at the house of the lovely stranger would be fine indeed. They took out their best holiday attire, polished their shoe buckles until they shone, and made ready for a gala time, and on Easter morning a line of men, women, and children went from the chapel to the cottage of the lady.

She met them at the door and led them into the garden, where two long tables were spread. The parents were told to sit down, but she said to the children, "It is not time for you to eat yet. Go into the woods with Edmund and Blanche, and make little nests of moss. Put them under the trees, and be sure to remember where you left them."

They ran out laughing, and the parents sat down to the feast, and a splendid feast it seemed to them! There were eggs in the shell, fried eggs, eggs in milk, omelets, and sweet, yellow custards, and as they never had tasted eggs before, they thought them wonderfully delicious.

After a while the children came back for their share in the good things, and as soon as they had finished eating, the woman said, "Go out and look for your pretty nests."

A rush and a scramble and they were in the woods, and a moment later cries of delight and wonder were heard, for in each nest they found five lovely eggs of red, blue, green, purple, and orange. They came pell-mell to show them to their fathers and mothers, who discovered something written upon them.

It was a motto, and the villagers, who were too unlettered to read it, asked the lady to tell them what it meant. They smiled as they listened, as if believing in the truth of the words they heard:

In God's protecting goodness trust,
For He will aid the kind and just.

The afternoon passed joyously, and when the chapel bell rang out the Angelus, the villagers departed, and the woman stood in the doorway with a smile upon her face, watching them go to their homes. While she watched, a youth carrying a bundle came walking down the mountain path. He seemed very tired and sad, and tears came into his eyes as she called to him. He told her he was on his way to a village beyond to see his mother, who was old and sick, and that he had walked a long way without food.

"I have a little money," he said, "but must not spend it for myself, because it is needed at home."

Touched by his story, the woman took him into the house, where a good meal was set before him; and as he was about to start away, she gave him a gold piece and some eggs for his little brother and sister.

Refreshed by rest and food he strode on his way through the village, took the path that led to the other side of the mountains, and after a while came to the edge of a ravine. From that point the trail was narrow and dangerous, and he walked rapidly because he wanted to reach home before night.

But suddenly he stopped. Looking down to where a tiny stream wound through the gulch, he saw a horse. It was saddled and bridled, which seemed very strange to him.

"I wonder if some one has fallen and needs help," he murmured.

So, although he wanted to be on his way, he climbed down over the crags.

It was as he feared. A man was lying there, motionless as if dead. He was dressed in heavy armor, by which the lad knew he was some one rich and great.

Pulling off the helmet to use as a dipper, he ran to the river for water, and poured it over the drawn, white face.

The rider opened his eyes slowly, and when he saw the youth kneeling beside him said, "Thank God for sending you! I fell down over the cliffs, and thought I was to lie here and die. Oh, I am so weak and faint!" he sighed.

The peasant boy remembered the pretty eggs in his bundle that were intended for his little brother and sister at home. "But they would want me to give them to this poor fellow," he thought. So he shelled one and held it to the trembling lips.

The man ate it as if nearly starved, and another and another. Then, seeing the motto on the one that was still unbroken, he opened his eyes wide.

"Stop," he said as the boy was about to break it. "Let me have it as it is and I will give you a gold piece for it."

Then the peasant youth, who was stalwart and strong, helped him on to his horse, and led him to his own village, where the doctor said he must lie still for six weeks. He groaned as he heard those words, and exclaimed, "Six weeks, and my master waiting for word of her!"

But he was a soldier, and knew how to wait. He stayed patiently, and at the end of the time went on his way.

Meanwhile, back in the village in the valley, the beautiful stranger lived on with her children. She seemed very happy until one day the man Kuno went to the city across the mountain, and returned looking pale and worried.

"Madame," he said as she met him at the door, "I have bad news for you."

She turned white, as if some terrible thing had happened, took him into the house, and they talked together for a long time. Then Kuno left the cottage and hurried through the village to the house of the miller, who was also the mayor.

"My mistress wishes to speak to you," he said.

The man went back with him, and when they reached the house, the woman told a strange story.

"I am Rosalinde, daughter of the Duke of Burgundy," she said. "In my father's court were two knights, Hanno of Schraffeneck and Arno of Lindenburg, who were suitors for my hand. I chose Arno, and Hanno was furiously angry. He vowed he would have revenge, but I was happy with my husband, and did not fear him.

"All went well for a long time. Then the emperor summoned my husband to go on the Holy Wars to Palestine, and he rode away with the Crusaders, leaving me alone with the children. Hanno, too, was summoned to fight the Moslems, but he stayed behind, vowing that now he would have his revenge, and unless I married him he would put me into prison and kill my children.

"The castle of my lord was strong, but there was no one to defend it after he and his train went away, and Hanno brought many men and began a siege. My good Kuno, who knew a secret passage, aided me to escape and brought me across the mountains to your village, where I have felt safe. But today he saw Hanno in the city, asking people if a lady with two children and an old domestic had passed that way."

She stopped a moment as if she could not speak for tears, then went on sadly, "Kuno hid and was not seen, but I fear that when Hanno comes through the valley, the people will tell him I am here, and then he will put me in prison and kill my children."

The miller shook his head and spoke words of comfort.

"Have no fear, madame," he said. "The villagers will not tell that you are here, and if Hanno comes and tries to take you, we will defend you with our lives."

Then he went from house to house, telling the story of the Lady Rosalinde. Soon every one in the village knew it and the people swore to protect her at any cost, and the next day when Hanno came, they pretended to be so stupid that they didn't know what he was talking about.

"She has not been here," he said to his men. And they went away.

After that all was peaceful in the village, and the Lady Rosalinde was no longer afraid. Her children played with the charcoal burners' children, and every evening they went to the little chapel at the edge of the forest to pray for the safe return of the husband and father from Palestine.

One lovely evening in the month of May, they went to the church as usual, and when they came out, sat down on some rocks to watch the sun sink behind the mountain. A pilgrim came by, bending low over a staff, his long white hair reaching his shoulders and his beard flowing down over his breast. He noticed the children and spoke to them, and little Edmund said, "We have just been to church to pray for our dear papa."

The Lady Rosalinde was terribly frightened, for she thought he might be some one who would carry word to Hanno, but a moment later her fear turned to joy, for the pilgrim snatched off his beard and white hair, and a young, handsome knight stood before them. Little Blanche and Edmund screamed in delight, for they knew it was their father.

"How did you find us?" Lady Rosalinde asked.

"I found you, my dear Rosalinde, because you were good and charitable."

Then he told how he had returned from the Crusades to a ruined castle.

"I questioned the peasants around, who said Hanno had besieged it, and that you and the children had escaped. Then I led my train against him and took him prisoner, and sent out horsemen to find word of you. It seemed they would never come back, and when they did my heart almost broke, for although they had scoured the land they had no news. There was one, however, who did not return, and thinking he had been killed, I gave up hope. But six weeks later he came with a strange story, and gave me a colored egg, and imagine my joy, to find upon it in your own handwriting, the motto of my house:

"In God's protecting goodness trust,
For He will aid the kind and just."

Then, continuing the story, Lord Arno told how he had gone in the guise of a pilgrim to the home of the peasant from whom the cavalier received the egg, and learning that his wife and children were in the valley, had come seeking them.

Word that the lovely woman had been found by her husband soon traveled throughout the village, and the people, young and old, came to welcome him.

He was a true and valiant knight and thanked them for their kindness to his loved ones, for the Lady Rosalinde had told him of her stay in the valley, and of how good and gentle the peasants were.

"And now, my dear friends," he said, "to show you how grateful I am, I promise to give a fine, big cow to every family in the village. And every year at Easter time, my wife and I will send colored eggs to the children, not only to those of this valley, but to every boy and girl in the realm."

Then Lord Arno and his family departed, rebuilt their ruined castle, and lived happily there. But they never forgot the charcoal burners in the valley, and every year sent quantities of gay eggs to the children. As years passed the custom spread from country to country, until now colored eggs are given at Easter time to children in every Christian land.

PRINCE UNEXPECTED

From the Polish of Glinski

(Slavic Wonder Tale)

There were a king and a queen who had been married for three years, but had no children, at which they were both much distressed. Once upon a time the king found himself obliged to make a visit of inspection round his dominions; he took leave of his queen, set off, and was not at home for eight months.

Towards the end of the ninth month the king returned from his progress through his country, and was already hard by his capital city, when, as he journeyed over an uninhabited plain during the most scorching heat of summer, he felt such excessive thirst that he sent his servants round about to see if they could find water anywhere and let him know of it at once. The servants dispersed in various directions, sought in vain for a whole hour, and returned without success to the king.

The thirst-tormented king proceeded to traverse the whole plain far and wide himself, not believing that there was not a spring somewhere or other; on he rode, and on a level spot, on which there had not previously been any water, he espied a well with a new wooden fence round it, full to the brim with spring water, in the midst of which floated a silver cup with a golden handle. The king sprang from his horse and reached after the cup with his right hand; but the cup, just as if it were alive and had eyes, darted quickly on one side and floated again by itself. The king knelt down and began to try to catch it, now with his right hand, now with his left, but it moved and dodged away in such a manner that, not being able to seize it with one hand, he tried to catch it with both. But scarcely had he reached out with both hands when the cup dived like a fish, and floated again on the surface.

"Hang it!" thought the king, "I can't help myself with the cup, I'll manage without it." He then bent down to the water, which was as clear as crystal and as cold as ice, and began in his thirst to drink. Meanwhile his long beard, which reached down to his girdle, dipped into the water. When he had quenched his thirst and wished to get up again, something was holding his beard and would not let it go. He pulled once and again, but it was of no use; he cried out therefore in anger, "Who's there? Let go!"

"It's I, the subterranean king, immortal Bony, and I shall not let go till you give me that which you left unknowingly at home, and which you do not expect to find on your return."

The king looked into the depth of the well, and there was a huge head like a tub, with green eyes and a mouth from ear to ear; the creature was holding the king by the beard with extended claws like those of a crab, and was laughing mischievously.

The king thought that a thing of which he had not known

before starting, and which he did not expect on his return, could not be of great value; so he said to the apparition, "I give it."

The apparition burst with laughter and vanished with a flash of fire, and with it vanished also the well, the water, the wooden fence, and the cup; and the king was again on a hillock by a little wood kneeling on dry sand, and there was nothing more. The king got up, crossed himself, sprang on his horse, hastened to his attendants, and rode on.

In a week or maybe a fortnight the king arrived at his capital; the people came out in crowds to meet him; he went in procession to the great court of the palace and entered the corridor. In the corridor stood the queen awaiting him, and holding close to her bosom a cushion, on which lay a child, beautiful as the moon, kicking in swaddling clothes. The king recollected himself, sighed painfully, and said within himself: "This is what I left without knowing and found without expecting!" And bitterly, bitterly did he weep. All marveled, but nobody dared to ask the cause. The king, without saying a word, took his son in his arms, gazed long on his innocent face, carried him into the palace himself, laid him in the cradle, and, suppressing his sorrow, devoted himself to the government of his realm; but he was never again cheerful as formerly, since he was perpetually tormented by the thought that some day Bony would claim his son.

Meanwhile weeks, months, and years flowed on, and no one came for his son. The prince, named "Unexpected," grew and developed, and eventually became a handsome youth. The king also in course of time regained his usual cheerfulness, and forgot what had taken place; but alas! everybody did not forget so easily.

Once the prince, while hunting in a forest, became separated from his suite and found himself in a savage wilderness. Suddenly there appeared before him a hideous old man with green eyes, who said, "How do you do, Prince Unexpected? You have made me wait for you a long time."

"Who are you?"

"That you will find out hereafter, but now, when you return to your father, greet him from me, and tell him that I should be glad if he would close accounts with me, for if he doesn't soon get out of my debt of himself, he will repent it bitterly." After saying this the hideous old man disappeared, and the prince in amazement turned his horse, rode home, and told the king his adventure.

The king turned as pale as a sheet, and revealed the frightful secret to his son. "Do not weep, father!" replied the prince, "it is no great misfortune! I shall manage to force Bony to renounce the right over me, which he tricked you out of in so underhand a manner, but if in the course of a year I do not return, it will be a token that we shall see each other no more."

The prince prepared for his journey; the king gave him a suit of steel armor, a sword, and a horse, and the queen hung round his neck a cross of pure gold. At leave-taking they embraced affectionately, wept heartily, and the prince rode off.

On he rode one day, two days, three days, and at the end of the fourth day at the setting of the sun he came to the shore of the sea; and in the selfsame bay he espied twelve dresses, white as snow, though in the water, as far as the eye could reach, there was no living soul to be seen — only twelve white geese were swimming at a distance from the shore. Curious to know to whom they belonged, he took one of the dresses, let his horse loose in a meadow, concealed himself in a neighboring thicket, and waited to see what would come to pass. Thereupon the geese, after disporting themselves on the sea, swam to the shore. Eleven of them went to the dresses, each threw herself on the ground and became a beautiful damsel, dressed herself with speed, and flew away into the plain.

The twelfth goose, the last and prettiest of all, did not venture to come out on the shore, but only wistfully stretched out her neck, looking on all sides. On seeing the prince she called out with a human voice: "Prince Unexpected, give me my dress; I will be grateful to you in return." The prince hearkened to her, placed the dress on the grass, and modestly turned away in another direction.

The goose came out on the grass, changed herself into a damsel, dressed herself hastily, and stood before the prince; she was young and more beautiful than eye had seen or ear heard of. Blushing, she gave him her white hand, and, casting her eyes down, said with a pleasing voice: "I thank you, good prince, for hearkening to me. I am the youngest daughter of immortal Bony. He has twelve young daughters, and rules in the subterranean realm. My father, prince, has long been expecting you and is very angry. However, don't grieve, and don't be frightened, but do as I tell you. As soon as you see King Bony, fall at once on your knees, and paying no regard to his outcry, upbraiding, and threats, approach him boldly. What will happen afterwards you will learn, but now we must part."

On saying this the princess stamped on the ground with her little foot; the ground sprang open at once, and they descended into the subterranean realm, right into Bony's palace, which shone all underground brighter than our sun. The prince stepped boldly into the reception room. Bony was sitting on a golden throne with a glittering crown on his head; his eyes gleamed like two saucers of green glass and his hands were like the nippers of a crab. As soon as the prince espied him at a distance, he fell on his knees, and Bony yelled so horribly that the vaults of the subterranean dominion quaked; but the prince boldly moved on his knees towards the throne, and when he was only a few paces from it, the king smiled and said: "Thou hast marvelous luck in succeeding in making me smile; remain in our subterranean realm, but before thou becomest a true citizen thereof thou art bound to execute three commands of mine; but because it is late today, we will begin tomorrow; meanwhile go to thy room."

The prince slept comfortably in the room assigned to him, and early on the morrow Bony summoned him and said: "We will see, prince, what thou canst do. In the course of the following night build me a palace of pure marble; let the windows be of crystal, the roof of gold, an elegant garden round about it, and in the garden seats and fountains; if thou buildest it, thou wilt gain thyself my love; if not, I shall command thy head to be cut off."

The prince heard the command, returned to his apartment, and was sitting mournfully thinking of the death that threatened him, when outside at the window a bee came buzzing and said, "Let me in!" He opened the lattice, in flew the bee, and the princess, Bony's youngest daughter, appeared before the wondering prince.

"What are you thus thinking about, Prince Unexpected?"

"Alas! I am thinking that your father wishes to deprive me of life."

"Don't be afraid! Lie down to sleep, and when you get up tomorrow morning your palace will be ready."

So, too, it came to pass. At dawn the prince came out of his room and espied a more beautiful palace than he had ever seen, and Bony, when he saw it, wondered, and would not believe his own eyes.

"Well! thou hast won this time, and now thou hast my second command. I shall place my twelve daughters before thee tomorrow; if thou dost not guess which of them is the youngest, thou wilt place thy head beneath the ax."

"I unable to recognize the youngest princess!" said the prince in his room. "What difficulty can there be in that?"

"This," answered the princess, flying into the room in the shape of a bee, "that if I don't help you, you won't recognize me, for we are all so alike that even our father distinguishes us only by our dress."

"What am I to do?"

"What, indeed! That will be the youngest over whose right eye you espy a ladycow. Only look well. Adieu!"

On the morrow King Bony again summoned Prince Unexpected. The princesses stood in a row side by side, all dressed alike and with eyes cast down. The prince looked and marveled how alike all the princesses were; he went past them once, twice — he did not find the appointed token; the third time he saw a ladycow over the eyebrow of one, and cried out: "This is the youngest princess!"

"How the deuce have you guessed it?" said Bony angrily. "There must be some trickery here. I must deal with your lordship differently. In three hours you will come here again, and will show your cleverness in my presence. I shall light a straw, and you will stitch a pair of boots before it goes out, and if you don't do it you will perish."

The prince returned desponding and found the bee already in his apartment. "Why pensive again, prince?"

"How shouldn't I be pensive, when your father wants me to stitch him a pair of boots, for what sort of cobbler am I?"

"What else will you do?"

"What am I to do? I shan't stitch the boots, and I'm not afraid of death — one can die but once!"

"No, prince, you shall not die! I will endeavor to rescue you, and we will either escape together or perish together! We must flee — there's nothing else to be done."

Saying this, the princess spat on one of the window panes, and the spittle immediately froze. She then went out of the room with the prince, locked the door after her, and threw the key far away. Then, taking each other by the hands, they ascended rapidly, and in a moment found themselves on the very spot whence they had descended into the subterranean realm; there was the selfsame sea, the selfsame fresh meadow, and in the meadow cantered the prince's well-fed horse, who, as soon as he descried his rider, came galloping straight to him. The prince didn't stop long to think, but sprang on his horse, the princess seated herself behind him, and off they set as swift as an arrow.

King Bony at the appointed hour did not wait for Prince Unexpected, but sent to ask him why he did not appear. Finding the door locked, the servants knocked at it vigorously, and the spittle answered them from the middle of the room in the prince's voice, "Anon." The servants carried this answer to the king; he waited, waited, no prince; he therefore again sent the same servants, who heard the same answer: "Anon!" and carried what they had heard to the king.

"What's this? Does he mean to make fun of me?" shouted the king in wrath. "Go at once, break the door open, and conduct him to me!"

The servants hurried off, broke open the door, and rushed in. What, indeed? There was nobody there, and the spittle on the pane of glass was splitting with laughter at them. Bony all but burst with rage, and ordered them all to start off in pursuit of the prince, threatening them with death if they returned empty-handed. They sprang on horseback and hastened away after the prince and princess.

Meanwhile Prince Unexpected and the princess, Bony's daughter, were hurrying away on their spirited horse, and amidst their rapid flight heard "Tramp, tramp," behind them. The prince sprang from the horse, put his ear to the ground, and said, "They are pursuing us."

"Then," said the princess, "we have no time to lose." Instantly she transformed herself into a river, changed the prince into a bridge and the horse into a raven, and divided the grand highway beyond the bridge into three roads. Swiftly on the fresh track hastened the pursuers, came to the bridge, and stood stupefied; they saw the track up to the bridge, but beyond it disappeared, and the highway divided into three roads. There was nothing to be done but to return, and they came with naught. Bony shouted with rage, and cried out: "A bridge and a river! It was they. How was it that ye did not guess it? Back, and don't return without them!" The pursuers recommenced the pursuit.

"I hear 'Tramp, tramp!'" whispered the princess, Bony's daughter, affrightedly to Prince Unexpected, who sprang from the saddle, put his ear to the ground, and replied: "They are making haste, and are not far off."

That instant the princess and prince, and with them also their horse, became a gloomy forest, in which there were roads, byroads, and footpaths without number, and on one of them it seemed that two riders were hastening on a horse. Following the fresh track, the pursuers came up to the forest, and when they espied the fugitives in it, they hastened speedily after them. On and on hurried the pursuers, seeing continually before them a thick forest, a wide road, and the fugitives on it; now, now they thought to overtake them, when the fugitives and the thick forest suddenly vanished, and they found themselves at the selfsame place whence they had started in pursuit. They returned, therefore, again to Bony empty-handed.

"A horse, a horse! I'll go myself! they won't escape out of my hands!" yelled Bony, foaming at the mouth, and started in pursuit.

Again the princess said to Prince Unexpected: "Methinks they are pursuing us, and this time it is Bony, my father, himself, but the first church is the boundary of his dominion, and he cannot pursue us farther. Give me your golden cross."

The prince took off his affectionate mother's gift and gave it to the princess, and in a moment she was transformed into a church, he into the priest, and the horse into the bell; and that instant up came Bony.

"Monk!" Bony asked the priest, "hast thou not seen some travelers on horseback?"

"Only just now Prince Unexpected rode this way with the princess, Bony's daughter. They came into the church, performed their devotions, gave money for a mass for your good health, and ordered me to present their respects to you if you should ride this way."

Bony, too, returned empty-handed. But Prince Unexpected rode on with the princess, Bony's daughter, in no further fear of pursuit.

They rode gently on, when they saw before them a beautiful town, into which the prince felt an irresistible longing to go.

"Prince," said the princess, "don't go; my heart forebodes misfortune there."

"I'll ride there for only a short time, and look round the town, and we'll then proceed on our journey."

"It's easy enough to ride thither, but will it be as easy to return? Nevertheless, as you absolutely desire it, go, and I will remain here in the form of a white stone till you return; be circumspect, my beloved; the king, the queen, and the princess, their daughter, will come out to meet you, and with them will be a beautiful little boy — don't kiss him, for, if you do, you will forget me at once, and will never set eyes on me more in the world — I shall die of despair. I will wait for you here on the road for three days, and if on the third day you don't return, remember that I perish, and perish all through you." The prince took leave and rode to the town, and the princess transformed herself into a white stone and remained on the road.

One day passed, a second passed, the third also passed, and nothing was seen of the prince. Poor princess! He had not obeyed her counsel; in the town, the king, the queen, and the princess their daughter had come out to meet him, and with them walked a little boy, a curly-headed chatterbox, with eyes as bright as stars. The child rushed straight into the prince's arms, who was so captivated by the beauty of the lad that he forgot everything and kissed the child affectionately. That moment his memory was darkened, and he utterly forgot the princess, Bony's daughter.

The princess lay as a white stone by the wayside, one day, two days, and when the third day passed and the prince did not return from the town, she transformed herself into a cornflower, and sprang in among the rye by the roadside. "Here I shall stay by the roadside; maybe some passer-by will pull me up or trample me into the ground," said she, and tears like dewdrops glittered on the azure petals.

Just then an old man came along the road, espied the cornflower in the rye by the wayside, was captivated by its beauty, extracted it carefully from the ground, carried it into his dwelling, set it in a flowerpot, watered it, and began to tend it attentively. But — O marvel! — ever since the time that the cornflower was brought into his dwelling, all kinds of wonders began to happen in it. Scarcely was the old man awake, when everything in the house was already set in order, nowhere was the least atom of dust remaining. At noon he came home — dinner was all ready, the table set; he had but to sit down and eat as much as he wanted. The old man wondered and wondered, till at last terror took possession of him, and he betook himself for advice to an old witch of his acquaintance in the neighborhood.

"Do this," the witch advised him: "get up before the first morning dawn, before the cocks crow to announce daylight, and notice diligently what begins to stir first in the house, and that which does stir, cover with this napkin: what will happen further, you will see."

The old man did not close his eyes the whole night, and as soon as the first gleam appeared and things began to be visible in the house, he saw how the cornflower suddenly moved in the flowerpot, sprang out, and began to stir about the room; when simultaneously everything began to put itself in its place; the dust began to sweep itself clean away, and the fire kindled itself in the stove. The old man sprang cleverly out of his bed and placed the cloth on the flower as it endeavored to escape, when lo! the flower became a beautiful damsel — the princess, Bony's daughter.

"What have you done?" cried the princess. "Why have you brought life back to me? My betrothed, Prince Unexpected, has forgotten me, and therefore life has become distasteful to me."

"Your betrothed, Prince Unexpected, is going to be married today; the wedding feast is ready, and the guests are beginning to assemble."

The princess wept, but after a while dried her tears, dressed herself in frieze, and went into the town like a village girl. She came to the royal kitchen, where there was great noise and bustle. She went up to the clerk of the kitchen with humble and attractive grace, and said in a sweet voice: "Dear sir, do me one favor: allow me to make a wedding cake for Prince Unexpected."

Occupied with work, the first impulse of the clerk of the kitchen was to give the girl a rebuff; but when he looked at her, the words died on his lips and he answered kindly: "Ah, my beauty of beauties! do what you will; I will hand the prince your cake myself."

The cake was soon baked, and all the invited guests were sitting at table. The clerk of the kitchen himself placed a huge cake on a silver dish before the prince; but scarce had the prince made a cut in the side of it, when lo! an unheard-of marvel displayed itself in the presence of all. A gray tom-pigeon and a white hen-pigeon came out of the cake; the tom-pigeon walked along the table, and the hen-pigeon walked after him, cooing:

"Stay, stay, my pigeonet, oh stay!
Don't from thy true love flee away;
My faithless lover I pursue,
Prince Unexpected like unto,
Who Bony's daughter did betray."

Scarcely had Prince Unexpected heard this cooing of the pigeon, when he regained his lost recollection, bounced from the table, rushed to the door, and behind the door the princess, Bony's daughter, took him by the hand; they went together down the corridor, and before them stood a horse saddled and bridled.

Why delay? Prince Unexpected and the princess, Bony's daughter, sprang on the horse, started on the road, and at last arrived happily in the realm of Prince Unexpected's father. The king and the queen received them with joy and merriment, and did not wait long before they prepared them a magnificent wedding, the like of which eye never saw and ear never heard of.

THE GREEDY COBBLER

(*Welsh Folk Tale—Ethics, teaching contentment*)

Once upon a time a Welsh cobbler carrying a hazel wand was walking over London Bridge, and as he sauntered along he met an Englishman.

"Ah," the latter exclaimed, pointing to the wand the man of Cambria used as a cane, "where did you get it?"

"Where did I get it?" the Welshman repeated, amazed that any one should ask such a question. "Off of a hazel bush, to be sure."

But the stranger stared in big-eyed wonder and shook his head.

"There is only one hazel bush of that kind in all the world," he declared, "and under it a vast treasure is hidden. Lead me to the spot, and I will share it with you."

The Welshman smiled pleasantly, for he began to have visions of a luxurious, idle life. He hated to work, and was always grumbling because he had to hammer away at shoe lasts to make his living.

To be sure he would lead the Englishman to the spot, and once he had some gold in his possession, he'd do nothing but feast and ride in a coach and dance at the fair. So he said quite wearily, lest the stranger think he seemed too eager and change his mind, "It is a long way from here, in the Vale of Neath in my native Wales, and by my faith I have no desire to walk that distance."

But the Englishman coaxed, which was just what the Welshman wanted him to do. So they turned away from London Bridge and journeyed northward across mountains and valleys, until they came to Cambria.

After several days they came to Craig-i-Ddinas, in the lovely Vale of Neath. The Welshman led the way to the hazel bush, beside which he had often played when a boy, and the Englishman said, "In due time we will begin work."

When darkness was heavy enough to cover all trace of what they did, they dug up the bush, and the Englishman, who happened to be a wizard, pointed to a broad stone under the roots and said, "Below is the treasure. Do as I bid and you shall be rich."

And the Welshman began to feel very important, thinking how people would honor him when he lived in a great house and wore a velvet coat.

Then the cock crowed for dawn, and they knew they must hurry away before any of the peasants saw them. The Welshman did not wish his village cousins to know he was there, for they would question why he had come; so they found a vacant tinker's hut in which to rest until darkness made it safe for them to go to work again.

But the cobbler was too excited to sleep. The sight of

the broad, flat stone at the root of the hazel bush brought back to his mind a story he had often heard, one that the village grandmothers used to tell when he was a boy. Again and again he thought of it, the story of the treasure of King Arthur.

Historians state that when the ruler of Camelot was killed in the battle of Mount Badon, he was buried at Glastonbury, but the Welsh country folk say that is not true. They declare Merlin carried him straight to the lovely Vale of Neath, where he sleeps on his arms, with his Round Table Knights beside him and all the wealth of his realm piled at his feet. There he and his warriors will rest until the ringing of a warning bell, when the Black and Golden Eagles go to war. Then they will rise up and destroy every enemy of Cambria, when Britain will be governed with justice and peace will reign as long as the world endures. Could it be that the broad stone at the foot of the hazel tree covered the entrance to Arthur's cave? This the Welshman pondered until it was almost dark and time to go to work again.

Cautiously they left the hut and approached the spot, peering in every direction lest some one see and question them. Sturdily they pulled and tugged at the rock, and slowly, steadily moved it, until they found an opening like a door. Then the Englishman said in a low tone, "Behold King Arthur's cave! Follow me and obey."

The Welshman followed, and a wonderful sight met his eyes. Thousands of warriors slept in a circle on their arms, and in the midst of them, more splendid looking than any other, lay the King of Camelot, the mighty Arthur himself. His crown of gold was by his side, a pile of gold lay at his feet, and beyond the circle of his followers were a thousand steeds, all saddled and bridled as if ready for battle. Sometimes they champed as if eager for the war cry, sometimes they drooped their heads wearily.

Noticing a bell suspended just above the treasure heap, the cobbler pointed to it.

"Do not touch it," the Englishman warned. "But if by accident you do, and the warriors waken and ask if it is day, say, 'No, sleep thou on.' Otherwise a terrible fate will overtake you."

They helped themselves to the gold and left the cave, and each man went his way. The Welshman, having all the treasure he could carry, was no longer a poor cobbler who must spend his time bending over shoe lasts. He was richer than the mayor and could feast and ride in a coach, dance at the fair, and live like the lords of the land.

But riches made that cobbler greedy. He had far more gold than he needed, and the finest house in seven counties, but still he wanted more. He kept thinking of the gold piled high in Arthur's cave; so one day he journeyed back to the Vale of Neath and waited for nightfall.

Then, creeping to the place of the hazel bush, he moved the rock and went into the cave.

Ah, it was a goodly sight, those thousand warriors slumbering there beside the treasure heap and a thousand saddled chargers beyond! He would take all the gold he could carry, and very soon he would come back for more. But in his greed to increase his wealth he bumped against the bell, which clanged loudly. The warriors started up, asking if it was day, but the man was so dazzled by the pile of shining treasure that he did not have the answer ready. They leaped to their feet, called him a robber, beat him, and drove him from the cave.

Then what a change! He went limping homeward, to discover that all his wealth had disappeared and where his great house had stood was a miserable hut. He was as poor as ever, and unless he could get more gold out of the cave must go back to cobbling and never again ride in a coach. But try as he would, he could not find the place where the hazel bush had grown. Many a journey he made into the Vale of Neath, but never did he catch a glimpse of the broad, flat stone. He had to spend his days bending over shoe lasts instead of riding in a coach, and was a cripple as long as he lived.

THE STORY OF A SALMON

BY DAVID STARR JORDAN

(*Science*)

In the realm of the Northwest Wind, on the boundary line between the dark fir forests and the sunny plains, there stands a mountain — a great white cone two miles and a half in perpendicular height. On its lower mile the dense fir woods cover it with never changing green; on its next half mile a lighter green of grass and bushes gives place in winter to white; and on its uppermost mile the snows of the great ice age still linger in unspotted purity. The people of Washington Territory say that their mountain is the great "King-pin of the Universe," which shows that even in its own country Mount Tacoma is not without honor.

Flowing down from the southwest slope of Mount Tacoma is a cold, clear river, fed by the melting snows of the mountain. Madly it hastens down over white cascades and beds of shining sands, through birch woods and belts of dark firs, to mingle its waters at last with those of the great Columbia. This river is the Cowlitz; and on its bottom, not many years ago, there lay half buried in the sand a number of little orange-colored globules, each about as large as a pea. These were not much in themselves, but great in their possibilities. In the waters above them little suckers and chubs and prickly sculpins strained their mouths to draw these globules from the sand, and vicious-looking crawfishes picked them up with their blundering hands and examined them with their telescopic eyes. But one, at least, of the globules escaped their curiosity, else this story would not be worth telling. The sun shone down on it through the clear water, and the ripples of the Cowlitz said over it their incantations, and in it at last awoke a living being. It was a fish,—a curious little fellow, not half an inch long, with great, staring eyes, which made almost half his length, and with a body so transparent that he could not cast a shadow. He was a little salmon, a very little salmon; but the water was good, and there were flies and worms and little living creatures in abundance for him to eat, and he soon became a larger salmon. Then there were many more little salmon with him, some larger and some smaller, and they all had a merry time. Those who had been born soonest and had grown largest used to chase the others around and bite heads and swallow them whole; for, said they, "even young salmon are good eating." "Heads I win, tails you lose," was their motto. Thus, what was once two small salmon became united into a single larger one, and the process of "addition, division, and silence" still went on.

By and by, when all the salmon were too large to be swallowed, they began to grow restless. They saw that the water rushing by seemed to be in a great hurry to get somewhere, and it was somehow suggested that its hurry was caused by something good to eat at the other end of its course. Then they all started down the stream, salmon fashion,—which fashion is to get into the current, head upstream, and thus to drift backward as the river sweeps along.

At last they came to where the Cowlitz and the Columbia join, and they were almost lost for a time; for they could find no shores, and the bottom and the top of the water were so far apart. Here they saw other and far larger salmon in the deepest part of the current, turning neither to the right nor to the left, but swimming right on upstream just as rapidly as they could. And these great salmon would not stop for them, and would not lie and float with the current. They had no time to talk, even in the simple sign language by which fishes express their ideas, and no time to eat. They had important work before them, and the time was short. So they went on up the river, keeping their great purposes to themselves; and our little salmon and his friends from the Cowlitz drifted down the stream.

By and by the water began to change. It grew denser, and no longer flowed rapidly along; and twice a day it used to turn about and flow the other way. Then the shores disappeared, and the water began to have a different and peculiar flavor, — a flavor which seemed to the salmon much richer and more inspiring than the glacier water of their native Cowlitz. There were many curious things to see — crabs with hard shells and savage faces, but so good when crushed and swallowed! Then there were luscious squid swimming about; and, to a salmon, squid are like ripe peaches and cream. There were great companies of delicate sardines and herring, green and silvery, and it was such fun to chase and capture them! Those who eat sardines packed in oil by greasy fingers, and herrings dried in the smoke, can have little idea how satisfying it is to have a meal of them, plump and sleek and silvery, fresh from the sea.

Thus the salmon chased the herrings about, and had a merry time. Then they were chased in turn by great sea lions, — swimming monsters with huge half-human faces, long thin whiskers, and blundering ways. The sea lions like to bite out the throat of a salmon, with its precious stomach full of luscious sardines, and then to leave the rest of the fish to shift for itself. And the seals and the herrings scattered the salmon about, till at last the hero of our story found himself quite alone, with none of his own kind near him. But that did not trouble him much, and he went on his own way, getting his dinner when he was hungry, which was all the time, and then eating a little between meals for his stomach's sake.

So it went on for three long years; and at the end of this time our little fish had grown to be a great, fine salmon of twenty-two pounds' weight, shining like a new tin pan, and with rows of the loveliest round black spots on his head and back and tail. One day, as he was swimming about, idly chasing a big sculpin with a head so thorny that he never was swallowed by anybody, all of a sudden the salmon noticed a change in the water around him.

Spring had come again, and the south-lying snowdrifts on the Cascade Mountains once more felt that the "earth was wheeling sunwards." The cold snow waters ran down from the mountains and into the Columbia River, and made a freshet on the river. The high water went far out into the sea, and out in the sea our salmon felt it on his gills. He remembered how the cold water used to feel in the Cowlitz when he was a little fish. In a blundering, fishy fashion he thought about it; he wondered whether the little eddy looked as it used to look and whether caddis worms and young mosquitoes were really as sweet and tender as he used to think they were. Then he thought some other things; but as the salmon's mind is located in the optic lobes of his brain, and ours is in a different place, we cannot be quite certain what his thoughts really were.

What our salmon did, we know. He did what every grown salmon in the ocean does when he feels the glacier water once more upon his gills. He became a changed being. He spurned the blandishment of soft-shelled crabs. The pleasures of the table and of the chase, heretofore his only delights, lost their charms for him. He turned his course straight toward the direction whence the cold water came, and for the rest of his life never tasted a mouthful of food. He moved on toward the river mouth, at first playfully, as though he were not really certain whether he meant anything after all. Afterward, when he struck the full current of the Columbia, he plunged straight forward with an unflinching determination that had in it something of the heroic. When he had passed the rough water at the bar, he was not alone. His old neighbors of the Cowlitz, and many more from the Clackamas and the Spokane and Des Chutes and Kootanie, — a great army of salmon, — were with him. In front were thousands pressing on, and behind them were thousands more, all moved by a common impulse which urged them up the Columbia.

They were all swimming bravely along where the current was deepest, when suddenly the foremost felt something tickling like a cobweb about their noses and under their chins. They changed their course a little to brush it off and it touched their fins as well. Then they tried to slip down with the current, and thus leave it behind. But, no! the thing, whatever it was, although its touch was soft, refused to let go, and held them like a fetter. The more they struggled, the tighter became its grasp, and the whole foremost rank of the salmon felt it together; for it was a great gill net, a quarter of a mile long, stretched squarely across the mouth of the river.

By and by men came in boats, and hauled up the gill net and the helpless salmon that had become entangled in it. They threw the fishes into a pile in the bottom of the boat, and the others saw them no more. We that live outside the water know better what befalls them, and we can tell the story which the salmon could not.

All along the banks of the Columbia River, from its mouth to nearly thirty miles away, there is a succession of large buildings, looking like great barns or warehouses, built on piles in the river, high enough to be out of the reach of floods. There are thirty of these buildings, and they are called "canneries." Each cannery has about forty boats, and with each boat are two men and a long gill net. These nets fill the whole river as with a nest of cobwebs from April to July, and to each cannery nearly a thousand great salmon are brought every day. These salmon are thrown in a pile on the floor; and Wing Hop, the big Chinaman, takes them one after another on the table, and with a great knife dexterously cuts off the head, the tail, and the fins; then with a sudden thrust he removes the intestines and the eggs. The body goes into a tank of water; and the head is dropped into a box on a flatboat, and goes down the river to be made into salmon oil. Next the body is brought to another table; and Quong Sang, with a machine like a feed cutter, cuts it into pieces each just as long as a one-pound can. Then Ah Sam, with a butcher knife, cuts these pieces into strips just as wide as the can. Next Wan Lee, the "China boy," brings down a hundred cans from the loft where the tinners are making them, and into each can puts a spoonful of salt. It takes just six salmon to fill a hundred cans. Then twenty Chinamen put the pieces of meat into the cans, fitting in little strips to make them exactly full. Ten more solder up the cans, and ten more put the cans into boiling water till the meat is thoroughly cooked, and five more punch a little hole in the head of each can to let out the air. Then they solder them up again, and little girls paste on them bright-colored labels showing merry little cupids riding the happy salmon up to the cannery door, with Mount Tacoma and Cape Disappointment in the background; and a legend underneath says that this is "Booth's" or "Badollet's Best," or "Hume's," or "Clark's," or "Kinney's Superfine Salt Water Salmon." Then the cans are placed in cases, forty-eight in a case, and five hundred thousand cases are put up every year. Great ships come to Astoria, and are loaded with them; and they carry them away to London and San Francisco and Liverpool and New York and Sydney and Valparaiso; and the man at the corner grocery sells them at twenty cents a can.

All this time our salmon is going up the river, eluding one net as by a miracle, and soon having need of more miracles to escape the rest; passing by Astoria on a fortunate day, — which was Sunday, the day on which no man may fish if he expects to sell what he catches, — till finally he came to where nets were few, and, at last, to where they ceased altogether. But there he found that scarcely any of his companions were with him; for the nets cease when there are no more salmon to be caught in them. So he went on, day and night, where the water was deepest, stopping not to feed or loiter on the way, till at last he came to a wild gorge, where the great river became an angry torrent, rushing wildly over a huge staircase of rocks. But our hero did not falter; and summoning all his forces, he plunged into the Cascades. The current caught him and dashed him against the rocks. A whole row of silvery scales came off and glistened in the water like sparks of fire, and a place on his side became black and red, which for a salmon is the same as being black and blue for other people. His comrades tried to go up with him; and one lost his eye, one his tail, and one had his lower jaw pushed back into his head like the joint of a telescope. Again he tried to surmount the Cascades; and at last he succeeded, and an Indian on the rocks above was waiting to receive him. But the Indian with his spear was less skillful than he was wont to be, and our hero escaped, losing only a part of one of his fins; and with him came one other, and henceforth these two pursued their journey together.

Now a gradual change took place in the looks of our salmon. In the sea he was plump and round and silvery, with delicate teeth in a symmetrical mouth. Now his silvery color disappeared, his skin grew slimy, and the scales sank into it: his back grew black, and his sides turned red, — not a healthy red, but a sort of hectic flush. He grew poor; and his back, formerly as straight as need be, now developed an unpleasant hump at the shoulders. His eyes — like those of all enthusiasts who forsake eating and sleeping for some loftier aim — became dark and sunken. His symmetrical jaws grew longer and longer, and projected from his mouth, giving him a savage and wolfish appearance, quite at variance with his real disposition. For all the desires and ambitions of his nature had become centered into one. We may not know what this one was, but we know that it was a strong one; for it had led him on and on, — past the nets and horrors of Astoria; past the dangerous Cascades, past the spears of Indians; through the terrible flume of the Dalles, where the mighty river is compressed between huge rocks into a channel narrower than a village street; on past the meadows of Umatilla and the wheat fields of Walla Walla; on to where the great Snake River and the Columbia join; on up the Snake River and its eastern branch, till at last he reached the foot of the Bitter Root Mountains in the Territory of Idaho, nearly a thousand miles from the ocean which he had left in April. With him still was the other salmon which had come with him through the Cascades, handsomer and smaller than he, and, like him, growing poor and ragged and tired.

At last, one October afternoon, our finny travelers came together to a little clear brook, with a bottom of fine gravel, over which the water was but a few inches deep. Our fish painfully worked his way to it; for his tail was all frayed out, his muscles were sore, and his skin covered with unsightly blotches. But his sunken eyes saw a ripple in the stream, and under it a bed of little pebbles and sand. So there in the sand he scooped out with his tail a smooth round place, and his companion came and filled it with orange-colored eggs. Then our salmon came back again; and softly covering the eggs, the work of their lives was done, and, in the old salmon fashion, they drifted tail foremost down the stream.

They drifted on together for a night and a day, but they never came to the sea. For the salmon has but one life to live, and it ascends the river but once. The rest lies with its children. And when the April sunshine fell on the globules in the gravel, these were awakened into life. With the early autumn rains, the little fishes were large enough to begin their wanderings. They dropped down the current in the old salmon fashion. And thus they came into the great river and drifted away to the sea.

THE PIGEONS OF VENICE

(*History*)

In one of the upland valleys of Italy, shut away from the rest of the world by the high, white peaks men call the Dolomites, there lived, about five hundred years ago, a little boy named Leonardo. He dwelt in a tiny hut with his black-eyed peasant mother, fed the pigeons and milked the goats each day, and in the evening, the pleasant summer evening that spread rainbow-colored draperies over the Dolomite peaks, he lay in the shadows under the plum tree, thinking about his brother Vittorio, who was a soldier down in the great city of Venice.

"I wish brother would come home," he said to his mother one morning as they ate their breakfast of macaroni and mountain bread, "because he always tells such wonderful things about the city. Some day I mean to go there and be a soldier, too."

His dark eyes gleamed as he spoke, and he sat very

straight in his heavy oaken chair, as of course a soldier ought to do.

Everybody knows that wishes do not always come true, but sometimes they do, and when that happens the whole world seems brighter and lovelier than it seemed before. The next afternoon, as Leonardo was turning the goats into their inclosure, he gave a shout so joyous that even Armando the weaver, in his shop at the other end of the village, heard and ran to see what it meant. He soon found out, for he saw Leonardo hurrying toward a man who was moving along the highway. Vittorio, the soldier brother, was coming home, coming back to the mountain village with many a tale of the splendid city beside the Adriatic, and perhaps with a goody that would taste very sweet after the coarse fare of weeks and months.

Far into the night the brothers sat and talked together, talked of palaces and gliding gondolas, of great lords and ladies, of soldiers moving in splendid uniforms about the Piazza of St. Mark. They talked of Carnival time too, of the merry pranks the people played on each other, of the procession on the water and the presents given to the Doge.

"And sometimes," Vittorio exclaimed proudly, "they are very splendid. Sometimes they are of gold and silver, and of silk stuffs brought from the Indies."

Leonardo sat silent for a minute. He knew little of present giving, for in the mountains where he lived there was no money to spend on such things. But always when he made his mother a garland of flowers on her birthday, she seemed so happy about it that he thought it must be very lovely to bestow gifts. So he said softly, "I should like to send a present to the Doge. It would seem like doing something for Venice. But I have nothing to give."

"Wait until you are a man and can be a soldier," the big brother answered. "Then you will be doing much."

The next morning he was up at daybreak. Vittorio had

only two days' leave, which meant that he must start back at noon, and his mother had promised that Leonardo might go with him to the edge of the village if he finished his tasks in time. So he milked the goats before there was a bit of stirring about the hut, and led the geese from their pen to crop the green grass on the hillside. Then he cut some grass and threw it to the old horse that was their most prized possession, and by the time his brother came from the hut he called to him, "I have only to feed the pigeons yet."

Vittorio smiled and stood watching as the boy whistled to the birds.

The gentle creatures flew up at Leonardo's call, and as he scattered crumbs to them, he thought again of the great carnival at Venice and the gifts that would be made to the Doge. He wished that he too might join that throng of givers, but he possessed nothing but his pigeons, and a bird would seem a very poor present to offer a ruler. But he happened to think that the schoolmaster had once told him that it is not the cost or the beauty of an offering that makes it precious, but the good will of the giver, and that a beggar's portion may be a lovelier gift than that of a prince. The schoolmaster was very wise. He could both read and write, which only a few could do in that day, so anything that he said must be true; and the memory of the words brought an idea to Leonardo that made the boy's eyes dance.

"Vittorio," he exclaimed suddenly, "I have thought of something."

Vittorio wondered what excited his brother so.

"Well?" he asked as he walked near.

"Will you take a pair of pigeons back to the city with you?"

"A pair of pigeons," the soldier repeated. "Why?"

"I want to send a present to the Doge, and I have nothing else," he answered. "But the birds are so gentle I am sure he will like them. They are fine carriers, too."

Vittorio smiled. Being in the army of the Doge, he was pleased that his brother showed such loyalty to the master he served. It meant that he would probably grow up to be a good soldier, and in those days nothing was considered finer than that. So he answered pleasantly: "Of course I will, Leonardo, if you are sure you can give up your pets. I will ask my captain, who knows the Doge well, to take them to him and say that they are the gift of a mountain boy."

Leonardo's eyes sparkled with delight. It seemed a glorious thing that he too might give with the rich and great; so he selected the handsomest pair in the covey, birds of a soft gray, with shadings of blue and purple along their delicate wings, and he and Vittorio made a rude cage in which to carry them to the city.

Then they walked together to the edge of the village, and Leonardo watched his brother go along the road that wound down to the low country. He waved good-by until Vittorio passed from sight, then went back to the hut, happy in the thought that he was doing something for Venice.

Many months passed. It was September when Vittorio went away, and now the blossom time had come and hills were bright with touches of summer. All through that long period Leonardo wondered much about the pigeons, but no word came from his brother; for letters went only by courier in those days, and poor folk could not pay for the carrying. But he was sure the birds had reached the Doge, for Vittorio had promised and a soldier never broke his word.

Then one day in the autumn, when the brightness on the mountains had faded to bronze and gray, and squirrels were stocking their houses as nuts dropped in the woods, Vittorio came back. He looked older and graver than the year before, and some worrying thing seemed on his mind.

"It is just to say good-by," he said, as the gray-haired mother stroked his hands and Leonardo looked at him with loving eyes. "The war has begun, and we soldiers of Venice must sail away to Candia for the fighting."

Leonardo's eyes grew wide, and tears came into them as he exclaimed, "If only I were old enough to go with you and help serve our glorious city of St. Mark!"

The big man laid his hand lovingly on the dark head.

"Never mind, brother," he said. "You have already done much. I gave your birds to my captain, who took them to the Doge, and the Doge is proud of them because they are splendid carriers. So Dandolo, our general, will take them along with the army to bring back news of the war. And now good-by. When the fighting is over, I will come again."

He mounted his horse and rode away, and two pairs of dewy eyes looked after him as he went.

The days that followed seemed very long to the two who waited in the highlands. They knew that the army had gone, and that away on the eastern island perhaps the fighting had begun. But what of the fate of the Venetian hosts, and what of the son and brother who had sailed under the standard of the Lion? As to that they could only hope and wonder.

Slowly, slowly dragged the days, but no word came back.

One morning, while Leonardo and his mother prayed and waited in the mountain cabin, down in Venice in the splendid Palace of the Doges, the Council of Ten sat and pondered. They talked much about the absent army, wondering if victory or defeat had been its share, and while they wondered there came a fluttering of soft gray wings.

"Pigeons!" some one called. "See, they are carriers!"

The dignified assemblage broke up in excitement, for they knew the tiny birds were messengers, and the men hurried to read the missives fastened to their crimson feet.

"They come from Dandolo," said one of the nobles, "bringing news of the war."

"From Candia!" another exclaimed. "It cannot be that they have flown so far!"

But it was true, for upon reading they learned that the Venetian army had been victorious and the soldiers would soon sail home in triumph. The tiny birds had flown all the long leagues across the sea to carry the glad news to the waiting people.

Up in the hut in the Italian highlands Leonardo and his mother still watched and wondered, when one evening a few days later Armando, the village weaver, came by on his way home from the city. He was greatly excited and called to them as he stopped at the door.

"Rejoice," he said, "for the war is over!"

"How do you know?" the mother asked. "Are the soldiers back?"

"No. But the pigeons brought the word, and every one is glad."

"Pigeons!" exclaimed Leonardo. "My pigeons! Then after all I did something for Venice."

And he spoke the truth. So much did the message mean to the anxious people, that the lawmakers said they would always keep the birds, they and their young and their children's young. And although hundreds of years have passed since then, still the gray-winged creatures fly about St. Mark's Square, and the people love and feed them. For they know they are descended from the pair sent to the Doge by a mountain boy, Leonardo's pigeons, that long ago flew across the wide seas, bringing word of the victory of the Venetian hosts.

THE COMING OF THE WONDER TREE

Retold from an Arabian Legend

(Geography — Nature Study)

Abi Ben Ahmed was a chief of Araby, and there was no sweeter child in the land than his little daughter Zuleika. She was fair to look upon, with eyes slender as an almond and soft as a gazelle's, and the goodness of her heart was known to every one in the tribe. Lowly slave and mighty sheik alike loved her, and when she was with her father he forgot all his trouble.

One evening when the sun was dropping low over the desert, Zuleika sat in front of the tent waiting for a chance to have her supper. Her father was eating just then, for by the laws of Arabian politeness women and children must wait for meals until their lords and masters have finished. She was hungry, yet she did not mind the delay, because she knew nothing else, and when you think all the world does things as you do, your way does not seem hard. So she watched the color flame across the western sky, hummed snatches of song, and made pictures in the sand with her fingers.

Suddenly, away to the south, a yellow cloud seemed to rise out of the desert. It moved nearer, and as Zuleika watched it her dark eyes began to sparkle. She knew what it meant and it made her glad.

"Father," she called, "some one is riding this way."

Abi Ben Ahmed left his supper and came from the tent to see. The Arab is fond of his food and very loth to leave it, but when strangers almost never come by it is worth going without a meal to see them.

"Yes," he agreed, as his piercing eyes scanned the southern horizon, "some one is traveling across the desert."

Zuleika danced with delight. Only once or twice since she

could remember had any one come to the camp, for it was in the very heart of El Nedjed, and there was little traveling in those far-off days. Long before, when she was a tiny girl, a traveler had come that way, and while he lingered at camp, told of the blue Persian Gulf beyond the Oman shore, and of the music of its plashing waves. No word has such a magical sound to the Arab as "water," and to hear of lakes and rivers of it is like some exquisite fairy tale.

"It is a desert of water more beautiful than the land," he said in the soft, sweet tongue of the East. "Houris dwell there, and often when the moon is shining they come out and sport upon the sands."

The tale fascinated her at the time, and had always stayed in her memory. That is why she was happy to see a stranger approaching. She thought he might tell her of the lovely realm beyond.

As the cloud rolled nearer they saw a rider on a milk-white steed. Abi Ben Ahmed called to his men to come and welcome the stranger, for an Arab who lets even one slave stay away when a guest arrives, is lacking in courtesy. So they advanced, stalwart, dark-skinned men, whose turbaned heads were bowed almost to the ground as they gave the low salaam of the East, while the chief spoke words of welcome to his camp.

Very swarthy was the rider, and of proud demeanor that proclaimed him a person of much consequence, and as he returned Ben Abi's salute he spoke with dignity befitting his bearing.

"I bring greeting from the sheik Ben Nedi," he announced. "He rides this way tomorrow."

The chief replied, "Mighty is Ben Nedi, and a man of high esteem among his people. He shall have welcome and all that Arab hospitality can offer."

Then, leading the way, Ben Ahmed took the stranger to

the tent, where camel's milk and dried goat's flesh were set before him.

Zuleika, on the sand without, could hear their words, but the joyous light was no longer in her eyes. Her face was drawn in wrinkles, and her lip quivered as if she were about to cry. She knew that the man expected on the morrow was not only a powerful chieftain, but a teacher and prophet as well, and that according to the Arab custom every person in camp, even to the lowliest slave, would lay gifts before him. For it is believed by the desert people that to do so brings a blessing. But Zuleika, although she was a chieftain's daughter, had nothing to offer, for the wealth of Arab rulers is in their flocks and lands, and the poorest child of the West has more treasures than had this little princess of the desert.

"If I had my baby camel I could give that," she thought as she listened to the murmurs in the women's tent and knew that all was excitement there over the coming of the stranger.

But the camel she had loved and petted had died a few weeks before, and she had nothing else.

"Do not grieve," her mother said when she saw tears in the big almond eyes and asked the reason they were there. "The law of giving does not apply to children, and the sheik Ben Nedi, who is as wise as he is powerful, knows that sometimes empty hands give most of all. The blessing comes of having the great desire, not through the treasure that is offered."

But Zuleika did grieve, and the world seemed very dark. And after she went to bed she thought about it until she grew so restless she could not lie quietly. So she crept outside and sat on the ground.

It was midnight, and Abi Ben Ahmed and the stranger slept in the tent. The slaves, both men and women, were sleeping too, and nothing broke the stillness of the desert night save an occasional breeze that shifted the loose sand, or a stirring among the animals just beyond. She sat there for a minute, then stole out across the waste. Past the camel keep she went, hurrying through the silver of the moonlight until she came to a rock that rose out of the desert like a grizzled head facing westward. It was her favorite spot, for her mother had told her that a lovely houri (fairy) once made her haunt there, and she hoped she might come back and do wonderful things for her as she was said to have done in the long ago. So she climbed up and looked across the desert.

Away to the west, glowing more brightly than any other in the sky, was the star that according to Arab teaching shines always over Mecca, the city of the Prophet. The sight of it made her grieve more than ever over the thought of her empty hands, and she began to cry.

Then, with a sound of wonderful music, a white creature rose out of the sands. Her beauty was more radiant than any of which Zuleika had ever dreamed, and jewels of many colors glistened in her hair. Her smile was wonderfully sweet, and the girl knew it must be the good fairy returned to her old haunt.

"Why do you weep?" she asked.

Zuleika answered with a low salaam, "The prophet comes tomorrow, and I have nothing to offer him because the baby camel I would have given is dead."

"But you have a gift more precious than the others," the fairy spoke.

The little girl was amazed.

"I!" she exclaimed. "Why, I have nothing!"

"Ah, but you have," came the low reply. "The desire in the heart. That is the only thing worth giving, and that you have. But you shall have still another. Come here in the morning at sunrise, and you will find it on the sands."

The radiant creature glided away in the light, that dimmed as she went, and in a moment Zuleika could see only the desert and her father's camp beyond the rock.

Creeping down, she went back to the tent to bed. But the beauty of the shining creature was in her eyes and brain, and she could not sleep. Eagerly she waited for the coming of morning, and as soon as she heard a stirring beyond the tents, and knew that Hassan, the camel keeper, was looking after the animals, she bounded out of bed and down to the place of rock. Her mother saw her go, but thought nothing about it, for it was the time of gray dawn when every Arab looks in prayer toward Mecca, and she was probably going to the fairy rock for her devotions. But Zuleika thought of something besides her prayers.

When she came to the spot she stared around, wondering if it could be the place she had visited in the night. Then only a glittering waste stretched far as the eye could reach. Now there was a tree, straight and branchless almost to the crown, where from beneath wide-spreading leaves hung bunches of pulpy fruit. Nothing like it had been seen on the desert before.

Wild with delight, she rushed back to camp and told of the wonder.

"A tree on the desert!" her father exclaimed. "It cannot be."

Nor could she make him believe so strange a thing had happened until she led him to the spot. But there it stood, with head held high like an Arab sheik, and when he tasted of the fruit he found it good.

In the late afternoon of the following day the caravan of the sheik Ben Nedi came to the camp of Abi Ben Ahmed. The women within the tents received him with singing, and the men with low salaams. Then the gifts were brought: the finest camels of the herd, turban cloth enough for all the men of his train, and silk, a portion of her mother's marriage dower worth the price of many camels. It had been brought by ship across the sea and by caravan over the desert, and was rainbow-hued and fine, such as is woven only in the Vale of Cashmere. The great man received them with gratitude, and spoke words of praise for the tribe of Ben Ahmed. "Surely nothing more splendid can be set before a sheik," he said.

But the chief smiled and answered, "Not so, O mighty prophet! Zuleika's gift, the finest of all, is yonder on the desert."

Then he led the way to the place of rock and pointed to the wonder tree that had sprung up in the night. Ben Nedi found the fruit cooling and sweet, and as he listened to the story, he stood with dewy eyes.

"The gift of a child's tears!" he exclaimed. "Yes, that is most precious of all. The Arab will bless the day it came to be."

And the prophecy was fulfilled. It still grows in the depths of the desert, the wonder tree of the East that men call the date palm, and the Arab blesses it whenever he rides that way. He knows that for a thousand years and more it has been the salvation of the solitary wanderer across the wastes, and that as long as it lifts its stately head above the sands he will have food from its fruit, clothing from its fiber, and shelter from the noonday heat.

THE GIFT OF THE GNOMES

THE SWISS LEGEND OF THE ALP HORN

(*Geography — Ethics*)

In the days of long ago a chamois hunter, caught in a storm on the mountains, took refuge in a deserted hut. The floor was so wet and cold that to stay there was almost as bad as being out in the rain and hail, and so he climbed into the loft and lay down on a pile of straw.

Just how long he slept he did not know, but after a while he was awakened by the tinkle of bells and the lowing of many cattle. That seemed very strange, for it was almost winter, and Swiss herdsmen drive their flocks to the valley early in the autumn. Yet as he looked out through the tiny window he saw herds on every alp, herds hundreds strong, cropping luxuriant grass that grew out of the snow.

Then he heard a noise below in the hut, and peeping down through a knot hole, saw three strange-looking little men. They were warming themselves beside a fire that blazed on the hearth, and by their long green cloaks and red caps he knew that they were gnomes of the Alps.

They were bustling about and seemed to be making cheese. One of them stirred the milk in a big silver kettle, one scurried in and out of the hut bringing fresh milk to add to that which was already cooking, and one fed the fire with moss and dry branches, which piled up out of the earth.

After a while one of the gnomes poured something into the kettle, the second one brought out three golden bowls, and the third blew a blast on a horn that was seven times as large as himself.

Then the hunter heard the sound of cattle lowing nearer and nearer, as if they were drawn by the music of the horn, and a moment later a voice called out, "Come down from the loft, Moni, and taste of the good things in the bowls."

This amazed him, for he was sure they had not seen him, and how could they know his name? But he crept down from his straw pile, as he was bid, and into the room.

"Choose whichever you please," the little man said, "and besides the drink in the bowl you will receive a gift that goes with the liquid of your choice."

The golden bowls stood side by side on the floor, and each one contained a different-colored liquid. One was red, like the wine of Geneva, one yellow as the honey of Zurich, and the third was white like goat's milk. Moni looked from one to the other, deciding which to take. He was hungry from his long tramp over the crags in the storm and needed milk far more than honey or wine, so he chose that bowl and drank greedily.

Then the little gnomes began to dance.

"Ah," the cheese maker shouted, "you have won the Alp horn!"

"Yes," another exclaimed, "and it is a precious gift. You can make other horns like it, and teach the people how to call their herds, which will not stray away and be lost as happens now. Thus the herdsmen will become very prosperous."

"But remember, if you wish to be happy, you must give up chamois hunting, and never again kill a harmless wild creature."

The gnomes disappeared, and with them went the cattle, the kettle, and the shining bowls. But the horn lay where the little man had dropped it, and as the hunter looked at it he found it was pure silver. Catching it up, he ran down the mountain side to the hut where his sweetheart lived. He told her the story and showed her the Alp horn, and she was very happy; for she never had wanted him to be a chamois hunter, as the life was full of danger, and she loved the poor little animals that he killed. Now he would tend flocks as she did, and they would be happy in the life of herding.

At first the hunter thought he could not change his ways, for he loved to roam over the mountains and bound from crag to crag in pursuit of the fleet-footed creatures, but the promise of the gnomes and the pleas of Heidi persuaded him, and he gathered a herd and tended it all summer.

He made an Alp horn like the one he had received in the hut and gave it to the maiden, and sometimes as they tended their cattle on different sides of the valley, they would call across to each other, and they were happy and contented — until, one evening, he forgot the warning of the gnomes and shot a chamois.

Then he raised his horn to call good night to his sweetheart. But she did not answer. He blew blast after blast, but only the echoes came back, instead of the sound of the voice he knew and loved. Darkness fell and stars flashed like diamonds above the snowy Jungfrau, and still he called and sought her, but found no trace. The next morning, as he moved with his herd, a boy told him of a strange happening.

"Last night at sunset time I was watching my goats," he said, "and saw a girl standing on the mountain side above her cattle. She smiled as the wine color of the Alpine glow crept down toward Chamounix, and throwing back her head, sang one of our herd songs. Suddenly she disappeared, but she could not have fallen, and just then an arrow whizzed through the air and fell on the spot where she had been standing."

He took the arrow out of his peasant blouse and showed it to the hunter, who recognized it as his own, the one he had shot at the chamois.

Then Moni remembered the words of the gnomes, and knew that because he had forgotten their warning he had lost Heidi. He burned his arrows and sorrowfully went back to herding, never again to shoot a wild creature of the hills. By day he followed the cattle, and by night made Alp horns, always thinking of his sweetheart. But he never saw her again. Some of the herdsmen say that she fled in grief because he broke his word to her, and some declare that the gnomes carried her away to an ice palace in a crevasse. But nobody knows. They know only that from that time forth he tended flocks and made Alp horns, until every herdsman in the mountains had one, and because they could keep the cattle from straying and getting lost, they became more prosperous than they had ever dreamed of being.

Since then every peak and valley in Switzerland has resounded to the notes of the Alp horn. Throughout the summer time they are heard around the lakes of Zug and Geneva, and the cattle follow them as the children of Hamelin town followed the music of the piper. They echo along the Jungfrau as the shepherds behind Interlaken call their flocks together, and their weird sweet blasts mingle with the songs of herd girls as they yodel to each other across the ravines. Travelers from every land smile at the sound of them, for one of the charms of going to Switzerland is in hearing the Alp horns; but very few of these strangers know that the mountain people say the reason the sound is so magical to the cattle is because in the beginning the horn came from the gnomes.

THE DUTY THAT WASN'T PAID

(*Biography — Music — Ethics*)

More than a hundred years ago a man and his two children were journeying from their home in Salzburg to Vienna. They traveled by the Danube boat, and Marianne, the sister, stood by the rail tossing pebbles into the water and watching the turbulent river swallow them up. Her dress was worn almost threadbare, but her face was so sweet and her eyes were so large and bright that she looked pretty for all her shabbiness.

Just behind her on the deck her father and brother were talking. "If we make some money in the city you'll buy sister a new dress, won't you, Father?" little Wolfgang asked.

Marianne whirled and started toward him. She knew that was sure to make her father sad, and she called, "Don't coax, Wolfgang. My dress will do very well until we can afford to buy another, and a new one will seem all the nicer because of my having worn this one so long."

Her brother turned his big, earnest eyes upon her, and answered, "But, Marianne, I know you want one. I heard you wish for it by the evening star, and last night you put it in your prayer."

Father Mozart turned from them with a sad look on his face, and walked up and down the deck, wishing very much he could do what Wolfgang asked. But he was just a poor orchestra conductor with an income so small he had to stretch it hard to provide food and shelter for his family. Marianne must wear the shabby frock until better times began, which he hoped would be soon. They were to give some concerts in the Austrian capital, and maybe in that rich, music-loving city would earn enough to make them more comfortable than they had been before. But until then they must not spend a penny save what was needed for food and shelter, because the customs fee on the harp they carried must be paid, and that would reduce their little fund to a very small amount.

Wolfgang, too, thought about it as the boat crept in and out between the hills, and wondered much if there was no way in which Marianne might have the dress before they played in Vienna. His old teacher in Salzburg had often told him that there is a way out of every difficulty if one is clever enough to think of it, and there must be out of this. But although he tried and tried he could not find one. His own suit was bright and new, for his birthday was just past and it had been his uncle's gift. But Marianne was a very shabby little girl, and he knew she was unhappy even though she was brave and sweet about it.

They were gliding past the ruins of the castle that once,

men said, had been the prison of Richard the First, England's Lion-Hearted King, when his enemies took him captive on his return from the holy wars. Wolfgang thought of the many brave things that soldier ruler had done during the Crusades, for often in the twilight time at Salzburg, as they waited for the father to come from his work, the mother told his tale, and of how the faithful servant Blondel found him at last by singing a song he knew the master loved.

"He was very brave and wise, too," the boy thought as he looked at the crumbling pile. "He would have found a way for Marianne to have a new dress if she had been his sister."

Was it the prayer being answered, or just the fulfillment of the wish made by the evening star? For while he thought, an idea came into his head. It was a good idea, it seemed to him, so good that it made him smile. If it worked out, and he believed it would, Marianne might have the dress she wanted so much, because then his father would have more money to spend.

Just to the south they could see the great spire of St. Stephens, a tall, gray finger against the sky, which told that Vienna was not far away. As it grew nearer and nearer, looming up bigger and plainer before them, Wolfgang thought more and more of his idea, until when they reached the mooring his eyes were dancing and his cheeks were aflame. His father believed the thought of seeing the great capital had excited him, but that was not it at all. He had a secret plan and could hardly wait until he knew whether or not it would work out.

The journey was ended and the people were going ashore. "Please loosen the cover, Father," he said as Leopold Mozart carried the harp toward the customs gate.

"Ah, you are proud of it!" the man answered with a smile.

Wolfgang did not reply, thinking what a poor guesser his father was. He watched him as he set the instrument down and undid the wrapping, bringing the polished frame and glistening strings into full view. Then he went over and took his place beside the harp as the customs officer drew near, and Marianne came and stood beside him. She had forgotten all about her shabby dress in her eagerness to find out how much duty they would have to pay.

"What have you to declare?" the man asked.

"Only a harp," Leopold Mozart answered, as he laid his hand on their one treasure.

"It is a beautiful instrument and valuable," the official said as he looked at it, and named as the price of the duty an amount so big as to cut their little hoard almost in half.

Father Mozart's face grew very serious, and the merriment went out of Marianne's eyes. But Wolfgang did not worry at all. He still had that idea in his mind, and believed it would work out.

Leopold Mozart reached into his pocket for the little sack containing his savings, but it was not necessary to open it, for just as he was about to do so Wolfgang started to play. The customs officer turned with a start and listened, and the people gathered there forgot all about duty charges as they crowded around the little musician. His tiny hands swept the strings as if his fingers had some magic power, and the melody they made was sweeter than any ever heard on that old wharf. For five minutes, ten, he kept at it, and there was not a whisper or a murmur, only a sort of breathless surprise that one so young could play so wonderfully.

"What!" one exclaimed as he finished, "a lad of his age to perform like that!"

"Yes," the father answered with a smile, "he does well at the harp."

"Amazing," the officer murmured, "'tis amazing! I've heard many a good harpist in my day, but never anything sweeter than that. Play some more, boy," he said.

Wolfgang smiled. The idea was working out, and he was very glad. Already he had visions of a happy sister in a handsome new gown, and turning again to the instrument, he played even more beautifully than before, for the gladness that crept into his heart was creeping also into the music.

For some minutes he picked the strings, while the people listened as if held in a spell, until the father said, "We must go now, for it is getting late, and we have yet to find lodgings in the city." And he handed the money to the officer.

But the man shook his head. "No," he said, and his eyes were very tender as he spoke. "A boy who can give as much pleasure as that deserves something. Keep the money and buy a present for him."

As Wolfgang heard the words he gave a bound. "Father," he exclaimed, with sparkling eyes, "buy the dress for Marianne. You can do it now, since you have saved the customs money."

The officer looked at him in amazement. "He is a wonderful lad, truly," he exclaimed, "and as kind as he is wonderful!"

"Yes," came the low reply. "He has wanted nothing so much as a new dress for his sister, and now he is happy because he thinks she will get it."

And she did get it, too, a beautiful one of soft, bright red, all trimmed with shining buttons. Wolfgang danced with delight when he saw it, and there was no happier child in all that great capital.

They gave many concerts there, some before the royal family; and Maria Theresa, the empress, became greatly attached to both brother and sister, gave them handsome clothes and beautiful gifts, and forgot all about affairs of state while Wolfgang played. She called him the "little sorcerer," and agreed with the customs officer that he was a wonderful child.

Then, after some weeks, they went back to the home in Salzburg, where the boy kept on at his music, doing such marvelous things that his fame traveled far. He grew to be the great master, Mozart, at whose glorious music the world still wonders, and he was a generous and sweet-souled man, just as he was a big-hearted and thoughtful child. Many lovely acts are told of him, but none that shows his kindness and tenderness in a more delightful way than when as a boy on the Vienna wharf he charmed the customs officer and all others who heard, and Marianne had the dress for which she had wished by the evening star with the duty money that wasn't paid.

WILHELMINA'S WOODEN SHOES

(*Biography — Art Teaching*)

It was summer time, and a boy named Rembrandt van Rijn was lying on top of the ramparts that walled in the city of Leyden, his eyes fixed on the yellow highroad that stretched away toward The Hague. It was good to be there in the shadow of the mill sails, for the trees beyond were beautifully green, and he loved to watch the market folk coming and going, loved to see strangers journeying from far away and to dream of the time when he, too, would fare forth to see the world. Instead of being a miller like his father and living always beside the Leyden ramparts, he would go to Amsterdam, where ships sailed in from the Indies, and perhaps he would board one of those wonderful craft and journey over leagues of ocean to distant realms of the East. The thought brought a smile to his face and a deeper blue to his eyes, and he whistled a strain from an old Dutch song of rejoicing.

Suddenly he started up in surprise, for a familiar figure

was coming along the Rhine road. It looked like his Uncle Peter, but that seemed impossible, for it was Saturday morning, and his uncle was an industrious merchant who was never known to leave his shop on business days. Then as the man hurried through the great gate that opened into the city, Rembrandt saw that it was his Uncle Peter; and his surprise changed to alarm, for he believed his uncle's coming would mean trouble for him.

The day before, in the Latin school, he had drawn pictures on his cousin Wilhelmina's wooden shoes and had been caught. She was quite willing to have them decorated, and laughed merrily at sight of the ducks and chickens and spotted pigs marching from heel to toe; but Mynheer Speelburg, the teacher, had a very different idea. He considered that it was defacing property, and wasting one's time as well. Although Wilhelmina declared it was all her fault, Rembrandt was severely scolded, and the master sent a note home to his uncle. Now the uncle was probably coming to tell the boy's father about it, and the thought sent all the brightness out of the day.

The merchant did not notice Rembrandt until he had passed the ramparts and a cawing crow caused him to turn and see the boy on top of the wall. Then he looked up and smiled, which did not seem like anger, and yet — what else could have taken him from the shop on Saturday morning?

"I've come to have a talk with your mother," he said as he stopped a moment.

Rembrandt climbed down to go with him, hoping that something besides the shoes had brought him, but the man shook his head.

"No, stay where you are," he said. "I want to see your mother alone."

Again the uneasy feeling surged over the lad. After all, it must be those wooden shoes, and he felt very uncomfortable; and a little later, when both mother and uncle came from the house and hurried to the mill, he wished very much that he never had seen pigs and fowls — most of all that he had not drawn them on his cousin's shoes. Then his father called to him, and although he wanted to creep away and hide, he went on the run.

"Here's the young rascal," the uncle said as the boy went in at the broad, low door. Rembrandt noticed that he held one of Wilhelmina's shoes, and his heart sank. But a moment later he was as much amazed as he had been alarmed, for his mother spoke pleasantly and asked, "Would you really like to be a painter?"

"A painter?" he answered quickly. "More than anything else in the world."

Then his father smiled, too, which seemed strange indeed, for he had declared that his son never should become an artist. Often Rembrandt had dreamed of being one, and when he spoke to his mother about it the idea seemed to please her. But the sturdy Dutch miller shook his head and announced that his boy must become a syndic, one of the wise lawgivers of Holland, or else a miller like himself. So, instead of being allowed to spend his days drawing the pictures that were constantly running through his fancy, Rembrandt had been sent to the Latin school to do sums and conjugations. It seemed impossible that the miller could have changed his mind; but he had changed it, for he said, "Very well. We will see about it."

Then, while the mill sails whirred above them, and the voices of passing market folk came in through the open window, the merchant uncle told what seemed to Rembrandt a wonderful story.

"This morning, as I was opening the shop," he began, "Speelburg, the schoolmaster, came to talk about the pictures on Wilhelmina's shoes. He urged me not to be too hard on the lad because he had thought much about it during the night and had come to believe that perhaps Rembrandt cannot help drawing. He is a wise man, this Speelburg, and told me much of how the young masters Giotto, Cimabue, and Raphael had made pictures on stones, sand, and anything that would hold a drawing, and that their parents could no more prevent it than they could keep water from running downhill. He thinks our Rembrandt may be like them, and so he offered to tend the shop for me if I would come and ask you, his father, to let him study with Master Swannenburg."

Those words were music to Rembrandt's ears, for Swannenburg was the master painter of Leyden.

An hour later, miller and merchant went through the old White Gate into the city, and Rembrandt trudged along beside them, carrying a roll of paper. As they hurried along the highway his eyes gleamed, for it seemed to him like a dream come true, and the stern Dutch schoolmaster began to appear in the guise of a fairy godfather. He did not see the market folk they passed on the way, did not hear the murmur of the Rhine sweeping seaward just beyond them, for the thought that he might become a painter had crowded out all other things.

Very soon they reached the workshop of the artist, and knew what the great man thought of the sketches, for as he looked them over he murmured, "H'm, h'm! Pretty good! The old woman's head is too small for her body, and a pig never had legs as crooked as that; but he will learn, and if he is willing to work I'll gladly take him as a pupil."

So Rembrandt went into the studio of the painter, for his father had come to believe that he was intended for neither a syndic nor a miller. He was so eager to learn that he worked with all his might, and his progress amazed his teacher, who, although he knew he had talent, had not dreamed he could advance so rapidly. Before two years were gone his pictures were better than those of Swannenburg himself, who said sadly one day, "I am no longer the master painter of Leyden."

But that artist had a great, good heart, and he was so glad to see the boy's progress that he helped him all he could.

Now it happened, about the time the work of the miller's son was causing Leyden folk to open their eyes, that Jan Lievens, who was a successful painter in Amsterdam, came home to visit his parents, who were neighbors of Rembrandt's family. He was greatly excited over the work of his young friend and exclaimed, "You must go back to Amsterdam with me, for the best masters of Holland are there, and you must study with them."

The idea seemed good to the miller, who was very proud of the progress of his son; so to Amsterdam young Rembrandt went, where he progressed as amazingly as he had done in the studio of Swannenburg. The great harbor city fascinated him, and he loved to roam along its splendid streets watching the people hurrying to and fro or idling in groups on the corners, laughing and chatting in their merry Dutch way; loved to go to the docks where ships came in from the Indies, and to see the sunrise and sunset painting marvelous-hued pictures on the waves of the wild North Sea. Then he would go back to the studio and work, picturing the men and women he saw on his rambles, the mill by the old White Gate, and the market folk he used to watch from the Leyden ramparts. His paintings delighted the great of Amsterdam just as the pigs and chickens he drew on Wilhelmina's shoes had delighted the boys and girls in the Latin school, and he became rich and famous. He lived in a palace fine enough for a prince, and could have bought whole cargoes of those ships that sailed in from the Indies; and his wealth seemed all the more glorious because he had earned it with the labor of his hand and brain. He married a great and gracious lady, and as his children drove through the streets in their fine carriage the people would say, "See, the son and daughter of Rembrandt van Rijn, the wonderful painter."

But all his good fortune and all the honors heaped upon him did not make him selfish and overbearing. He never forgot or ceased to love his native Leyden. He lived in the harbor city because it fascinated him and was a better place for an artist than his childhood town, but he never tired of going back to the old home or lost interest in the pigs and cows and the market folk on the Rhine road. Sometimes on these visits he would lie on the ramparts just as he had done when a boy, and strangers journeying to and from The Hague had no idea that the grave-eyed man dreaming there in the shadow of the mill sails was the famous painter of Amsterdam.

Then, one day he died, and they laid him to rest in the harbor city where for so many years he had lived and worked. The people of Leyden asked to have him taken back there, and those who know how he loved it wish it had been done; for it would be pleasant to think of him sleeping in the shadow of the mill sails, and perhaps if he could have been asked he would have wanted it, too.

Years passed, but instead of dimming the glory of Rembrandt's name they brightened it. After his death his works became priceless, and the world still prizes them just as Amsterdam prized them two hundred years ago. To own a canvas by this king of Dutch painters is to be rich and envied, for it requires a great deal of money to buy one of his paintings. Even the crude drawings of his boyhood are now treasured by princes, and one of the most prized possessions of a great museum in Holland is a pair of wooden shoes. They are brown and clumsy and covered with marks, half of which have been worn away by the staining finger of Time; but a fortune could not buy them, because ever so long ago they were worn by little Wilhelmina van Rijn to the Latin school of Leyden, and were decorated by the hand of a mill boy, and who would not be proud to own them? That mill boy became the immortal Flemish painter, Rembrandt, whose work will be treasured as long as the world loves beautiful things.

THE LADY OF STAVOREN

Retold from a Dutch Legend

(*Geography — Ethics*)

There was once, in Holland, a great and beautiful city called Stavoren. It stood beside the sea, and many of the inhabitants were proud and rich. They had houses stately enough for royal palaces. They had gold and silver plate and diamonds without number, and great oaken chests filled with money. Their vessels sailed to the farthest parts of the ocean and brought back treasures from every land, and as the wealth of the people increased their selfishness increased, until they thought of nothing but their good fortune and had no pity for the poor.

Richest of all the rich folk in the city was a stately, beautiful woman. There was no home in Stavoren as princely as hers, there were no jewels as gorgeous or silks and velvets as lustrous as those she possessed, and when she drove through the streets in her gold-blazoned carriage her splendor dazzled the eyes of all who saw. But she was as selfish as she was rich and powerful, and always she pondered in her mind the question, "How can I become richer still?"

One day she summoned the captain of her largest vessel and said, "Make ready to sail at once."

"Yes, madame," the officer replied, "but where shall I go and upon what mission?"

"Where you go you must decide for yourself, for I care

nothing about that. But you must bring back the most precious cargo in all the world."

The man looked at her in surprise.

"That shall I gladly do, madame," he said, "if you will but tell me what you wish. Is it to be gold and silver, diamonds and jewels, or rare laces, tapestries, and velvets?"

The rich woman tossed her head and replied haughtily, "There is but one thing in the world more precious than all others, and what it is you must find out. I have given my orders. Go now and fulfill them."

The captain was greatly troubled, for he feared the anger of his mistress. She was so powerful that she could have him thrown into prison or even put to death if she chose, and as he walked down the street from the house he thought, "What is the most precious thing in all the world?"

Sometimes he thought it was one thing and sometimes another, but when he reached the shipyard he had not decided. He called to the officers and sailors standing there, told them of the woman's strange order, and said sadly, "But, alas! I know not what it may be. If any among you can tell, let him speak."

Every one thought a minute, then came a chorus of suggestions. One officer suggested gold, another silver, and another precious stones, but the captain was not sure which was right. He must not decide too quickly, for to make a mistake would be a terrible thing.

Silently listening the sailors stood, for according to the law of the city they must not open their lips until the officers had had their say. Then one of the group, a slender, blue-eyed fellow, who seemed no more than a boy, said, "No, my captain! The most precious thing in the world is neither gold and silver, pearls and diamonds, nor costly laces and velvets. It is wheat, for without it we could have no bread, and without bread we cannot live."

Some of the officers laughed at this idea, for common

sailors were not supposed to know much. But the captain quieted them, saying, "He is right. We will sail away and bring back a cargo of wheat."

So they sailed out of the harbor, and across the Baltic to Dantzic. There they bought a great cargo of wheat, the largest that had ever been started out to sea, and the captain, delighted with the purchase, turned the ship's prow back toward Stavoren town.

He could hardly wait to get to his mistress and tell her what a wise and wonderful choice he had made. She frowned when she saw him, displeased that he had returned so soon.

"You must have flown like a pigeon," she said. "Have you brought me the cargo I ordered?"

"Yes, madame," he replied, bowing low before her. "I have the finest cargo of wheat that ever went out of a port."

The woman screamed in anger. "Wheat!" she yelled. "A cargo of wheat! I told you to bring me the most precious thing in the world, and do you mean to say that you have brought a common, cheap thing like wheat?"

The captain was terribly frightened, but he did not regret his selection. He believed in the value of his cargo, and tried to lead the woman to see that he had made a wise purchase.

"Pardon, madame," he spoke. "Wheat is not cheap and common. It is in truth the most precious thing in the world, for without it we could have no bread, and without bread we could not live."

But he could not convince his mistress. She tossed her head and wrung her hands in anger and exclaimed, "Wheat! Wheat! Go to the port and throw your precious cargo of wheat into the sea."

The captain was horrified.

"Madame!" he exclaimed, "surely you do not command me to do that! Wheat is precious. If you will not have it yourself, give it to the poor and hungry, of whom there are many in Stavoren."

But she drove him from the house, saying, "Do as I bid you. In a few minutes I shall come myself to see if you have carried out my order."

Sadly the man went down the street, wondering how one so rich and beautiful could be so hard and unkind. But he had no thought of executing the order. Instead, he told all the poor he met, and dispatched messengers to tell others, that his mistress had refused to accept the cargo of wheat and perhaps, if they came to the port and asked her, she would give it to them.

A little later the great lady of Stavoren drove in her gold-emblazoned carriage to the shipyard, where a group of men, women, and children had joined the sailors and stood looking at the splendid vessel piled high with the best wheat that ever came out of Dantzic. But when she saw them her anger increased.

"Have you carried out my orders?" she said to the captain, as he came in answer to her summons and stood beside the carriage.

"No, madame, not yet," he replied.

"Then," the woman commanded, "do it at once. Throw the cargo of wheat into the sea. I want to see, myself."

But the captain shook his head. "See these poor people," he said, pointing to the hollow-eyed men, women, and children who were standing there. "Give them the wheat, for they are hungry."

But the haughty woman silenced him and commanded, "Throw it into the sea!"

Then the captain seemed afraid no longer. He stood straight and fearless before her and declared, "Never, madame!"

But she shouted word to the officers, who dared not disobey, and amid the cries and pleas of the poor, the cargo that would have meant bread for thousands, was thrown into the sea.

The woman watched the waters swallow it up and smiled heartlessly. Then she called to the people, "Did you see it go into the waves?"

"Yes, madame," they answered sadly.

"Yes, madame," repeated the captain, "and a day will come when you will regret what you have done. A day will come when you will be hungry, and no one will pity and help you."

The mistress looked at him in amazement. Then she laughed loudly. "I, go hungry," she exclaimed, "I, the richest of all the rich of Stavoren! It is impossible!"

Then she took a diamond ring, held it up for the people to see, and tossed it into the ocean. "When that ring returns into my hand," she said, "I shall believe what the captain has said." And she drove away in her splendid carriage, and boasted to the citizens of what she had done.

The next day one of her servants came running to her in wild excitement. "Madame," she cried, "the cook has found this in the stomach of a fish he is preparing for dinner." And she held up the diamond ring the woman had tossed into the sea the day before.

The great lady of Stavoren opened her eyes wide and wider. She was amazed and frightened, for she remembered the captain's words. "Can it be," she thought, "that they are to come true?"

It proved to be just as she feared, for that same afternoon she received word of the destruction of all her ships, of the loss of all her houses and lands, of the pillaging of her chests of gold. She was no longer the richest woman in Stavoren, but was as poor as any beggar. She went from house to house, begging for food as pitifully as the people at the port had begged her for wheat, but no one helped her, and at last she died from cold and hunger.

The other rich folk of Stavoren still lived on in the old selfish way. They drove through the streets in sumptuous carriages. They wore costly clothing and jewels, they danced and feasted and sailed their vessels out across the seas, forgetful of every one but themselves. There were still many poor in the city, but they neither thought nor cared about them. They believed themselves to be so great and powerful that nothing could harm them, and they refused to listen to advice.

After a while the port of Stavoren became blocked by a great sandbank. It rose just at the spot where the lady's cargo had been thrown into the sea, and was covered with wheat. Ships could no longer go in and out. Commerce was ruined, and because there were no vessels to unload, the poor lost the only way they had of making a living. They begged the rich people to help them dig the bar away, but they refused. They had enough to eat and plenty of gold, so what cared they for the distress of the laborers?

Then something else happened. One night as they feasted, a man came running into the banquet hall. "I have found two fish in my well," he said. "The dike is broken. Protect the city! Protect the houses of the poor that are close to the sea wall and will be swept away."

But one of the great folk said haughtily, "Let the beggars take care of themselves. The sea cannot harm us. We must finish the banquet." They turned away from him and went on with their revelry, but only for a short time. A few hours later the entire dike gave away, and the ocean rolled in and covered the houses, — not only the huts of the poor which were in the low quarter of the city, but even the palaces of the rich who had declared they could not be harmed. The great perished as well as the humble, and the waves of the Zuider Zee rolled where the banquet laughter had sounded.

It rolls there still. The sailors say that sometimes when the weather is fine and the sea is smooth as glass, they see spires and domes and stately columns far down under the water. They declare, too, that often strange, weird music like the sound of distant bells falls upon their ears, and then they look and listen and nod to each other, for they think of the palaces and chimes of Stavoren, once the fairest city of the Netherlands, submerged hundreds of years ago while the poor cried for help and the mighty danced.

THE LUCK BOAT OF LAKE GENEVA

A Swiss Legend

(Geography)

The Alpine herdsmen say that in the marvelous long ago an enchanted boat was seen gliding up and down the blue waters of Lake Geneva. Neither oars nor sails were needed to speed it over the waves, for it was drawn by singing swans and carried a fairy crew. A radiant creature in a robe whiter than goat's milk stood on the prow, her gleaming hair rippling down over the hem of her garment. She bore a golden basket of rare fruits and flowers, and although she scattered the contents with lavish hand upon the sprites at her feet, it was never empty. Sometimes the vessel touched the shore, and then the soil around that spot produced as never soil produced before or since, and if any peasant was so fortunate as to catch a glimpse of the boat, he and his children became rich beyond want and were blessed and happy to the end of their days.

For hundreds of years the magic ship sailed the lake, and as it touched the shore frequently and numbers of peasants saw it, there was wonderful prosperity in Old Helvetia.

But a great misfortune befell the country and the glad, abundant days became but a memory. A steamboat was brought to Geneva, and it plowed, a screaming, snorting monster, across the waters. The noise terrified the gentle swans, and with one wild cry they flew away. Never again did the peasants catch a glimpse of the white-robed fairy and the shining sprites. Never again did the music of the snowy pilots gladden their ears.

The Luck Boat disappeared, and with it went prosperity from the land of Geneva. But marvelous things like that are never forgotten. Those who had seen the fairy craft in their youth told the story to their sons and daughters, who passed it on to their children and their children's children, and although the mountain folk of today have never beheld it, they know just how it looked. They have pictured it so often in their minds, that their artists have pictured it on paper, and so it has become the custom for the peasants around Lake Geneva to send "Luck cards" to their friends on New Year's Day. These are gay, colored postals containing a likeness of the Luck Boat, and to those of whom a peasant is fondest he sends as many as he can afford, because to receive them is supposed to bring good fortune, just as a glimpse of the swan-drawn vessel was said to do in the marvelous long ago.

WHY THE JAPANESE LOVE THE STORK

A Japanese Legend

(Geography)

Ages ago, in the Japanese city of Nagasaki, there lived a young and handsome noble named Vasobiove. Life seemed very beautiful to him. He loved the blossoms that are so sweet and abundant in his native Saikaido, loved the racing and the wrestling matches, the sunset on the purple Gulf of Sinabara, the evening festivals with the dances of the geisha girls, and his only sorrow was the thought that he could not live forever.

"Alas, to have to leave this beautiful world!" he often sighed.

At which his old father would say, "Fear not, my son. By the time you are threescore years and ten you will think differently."

But the young noble would shake his head and reply, "Nay, nay, I want to live always, always."

One day an aged pilgrim came into Nagasaki and rested on a stone outside Vasobiove's garden. The owner was walking under the tulip trees, and seeing the sad-looking man in the sun and dust of the road, called and bade him come into the shade of his park.

Leaning heavily upon his staff, the wanderer came and sat down beside the fountain, and the young noble asked him many a question of lands and men he had seen.

"Is it throughout the world as here in Japan," he questioned, "that people must die even while they yearn to live?"

The aged pilgrim nodded.

"Yea," he answered, "in all the lands through which I have journeyed. But men have told me that there is a region where death never comes."

The young noble leaned forward eagerly. "Where is it," he questioned, "ah, where? Tell me, for I mean to go to that land."

The pilgrim shook his head, saying, "That you cannot do, my son. It is in the Happy Islands of Everlasting Life, but although mortals have seen them in the distance, never has one succeeded in entering there."

"But I must, I will reach that land!" Vasobiove exclaimed.

His father, who was old and wise, begged him not to go.

"You will perish on the way," he said sorrowfully. "But even if you reach and enter the islands, you will not be happy. That which is best for us is given to us, and after a long life, death is good."

But Vasobiove shook his head and objected, "No, no! I go to the Everlasting Islands." And the next day he set out from Nagasaki in a boat.

Straight southward he journeyed and eastward. Storms raged and tropic heat beat fiercely on his head, but he pressed onward, and at last, in spite of wave and tempest, reached the green shore of Horaisan. It was the land no mortal had ever entered, the Happy Islands of Everlasting Life.

Vasobiove's cup of joy was full. There was no sorrow there, no birth or death, no tempest and black weather or flight of time — nothing but dancing, music, splendid men and beautiful women, with enchanted flowers of unfading beauty in the groves and gardens, and always iridescent reaches of the sea beyond. There were wrestling matches, such as were not dreamed of in Nagasaki, long days filled with feasting, and long nights of dance and song.

Vasobiove smiled the smile of the contented.

"At last!" he said. "It is good to know that I shall live forever."

Two hundred years he spent in the eternal mirth of Horaisan, and then, somehow, he longed for other things. The music he had loved grew wearisome, the never ending dance became hateful to his eyes.

He wanted to return to Nagasaki, but there was no way. The boat that had carried him to the islands had long since fallen into decay, and it was impossible to get another. He must stay forever and ever in the land of dance and song, and the thought became hideous.

Then he heard a weird cry. Looking behind him, he saw a giant stork settling on the bank of a lake to catch some of the rainbow fish within.

A happy thought came to him. No, he would not dwell eternally in Horaisan. He would go back to Nagasaki.

Catching the bird, he tamed it, and one morning while the islanders reveled and the sea was as many colored as the enchanted blossoms in the gardens, he flew away, borne by the giant stork back to the sweet land of Saikaido, back to the shining Gulf of Sinabara, and his native Nagasaki. He would live as his fathers had lived, he would die when his time came, and never again would he pine for a land where all was revelry and beauty and song.

Ever since that time the Japanese have loved the stork. They picture it upon their royal banners and upon the walls of their houses, and give it the freedom of their gardens. Whenever a youth becomes dissatisfied and yearns for a land where delights are never ending, they tell him the story of the man who went to the Everlasting Islands, show a picture of the stork that carried him back to Nagasaki, and say,

"Even as it was with Vasobiove, so would it be with you."

WHY GRIZZLY BEAR GOES ON ALL FOURS

A Shasta Legend. Adapted from Bancroft

(*Indian Folk Tale — Geography — Ethics*)

Ages ago, before there were any mountains or valleys or rivers flowing seaward, Great Spirit lived up in the sky, higher than the most distant star. All about him were snow heaps and white cloud billows, so thick he could not see through them, and he wondered what lay beyond.

"I will make a hole and see," he said.

So, taking a sharp rock, he bored an opening through the cloud floor and looked below. A strange sight met his eyes. There lay the world, but a very different world from the one we know. It was flat like a table, with no hills or valleys, or rivers, or growing things, and Great Spirit said, "I will build a teepee there, and then I shall make it better."

The snow heaps lying around him made him think of a

good way of building a wigwam; so he pushed some down through the floor window, working day and night through many, many moons, until he had the pyramid white men call Mount Shasta. He built a fire and lived in the teepee, and then he walked abroad.

It was a fine land for a home, but lonely and too flat. He wanted mountains and valleys; so he created them. Then he wanted living and growing things about him; so he said, "I will make men and animals too."

He dug holes in the ground with his fingers, some large, some small, and when he breathed into them, trees of many sizes and kinds rose out of the earth. Then he stripped leaves from the branches and scattered them about, and they became men. He caused snow from the mountain sides to melt and flow in streams, and now, instead of the flat, brown vastness, there were uplands and lowlands, green fields and snowy peaks, and rivers running seaward, and other leaves stripped from the branches and torn into bits became fishes that swim.

"Now I shall make beasts of every kind," he said, and as he spoke he smote down a mighty tree. He broke it into pieces, some large, some small, which he turned into animals of various sizes and varying strength. Grizzly Bear he created from the heaviest part of the trunk, and the bear stood before him, on his hind legs, straight and powerful like a young hunter, stronger than any other creature of the earth.

It pleased Great Spirit to have living creatures around him, and he did not go back to the cloud world, but stayed in the teepee. The Indians knew he was inside, because often they saw the smoke from his flaming coals curl far above the peaks.

Many, many moons he dwelt there and grew so lonely that he sent for Little Daughter. She came and lived with him, made his moccasins and tended his fire, and was happy.

One day there was a mighty storm. The wind raged fiercely, sending the smoke back through the smoke hole into Great Spirit's face. He did not like that, and bade Little Daughter go up to command the wind to stop.

She did as she was told, and put her head out through the hole to call to the wind. But never having beheld the world before, she grew very curious at the strange sights that met her eyes, and leaned out far, far, to see all she could.

Suddenly she fell, and the wind carried her to the land of the Grizzly Bear. Little Daughter did not want to stay there and begged to be taken back to the teepee of her father.

"Let her stay here and work for me," Mother Grizzly growled, and Young Grizzly agreed, saying, "Yes, let her work."

So they would neither go with her nor let her try to find the way herself.

Great Spirit knew Little Daughter was in the land of the Grizzly Bear, and he went to take her home. When she told him how she had begged to go back, but was forced to stay and work, he was very angry.

"I shall punish you," he said to the bears. "Never again shall you walk upright like a man; always you must go on all fours."

Taking Little Daughter, he went back to the snow teepee, and they lived there for ages and ages, always keeping the fire burning, and always the Indians saw the smoke come out through the smoke hole.

At last the white men came, and as Great Spirit did not like the palefaces, he went away and the fire died out. But the teepee they call Mount Shasta is still there, although smoke no longer curls above it, and Grizzly Bear still goes on all fours, never standing upright except when he is fighting.

THE LUCK BOY OF TOY VALLEY

(*Geography — Ethics — Manual Training*)

In a chalet high up among the Austrian mountains, blue-eyed Franz was very unhappy because his mother and brother Johan were going to Vienna and he had to stay at home with his old grandfather. He bit his lips to keep back the tears as he watched the packing of the box that was to carry their clothing. Then his mother tried to comfort him.

"Never mind, lad," she said. "I'll send you a present from Vienna, and we'll call it a 'luck gift' and hope it will bring good luck. If it does you'll be a luck boy."

He smiled even if he did feel sad. He had often heard of luck children, for among the Tyrolean peasants there were many stories of those who had been led by fairies to have such wonderful good fortune that ever afterward they were spoken of as the elf-aided, or "Glücks Kinder," and it was so delightful to think about being one of them that he forgot his sorrow. Of course it would be very fine to travel down to Vienna and go into the service of a rich noble there, as his mother and brother were to do, but it would be still better to be a "Glücks Kind," and such things sometimes did happen. So he did not feel sad any more, but whistled and sang and helped with the packing.

Early next morning the post chaise rattled up to the door, and Johan and the mother drove away. Franz watched them go down the winding white road, calling after them in sweet Tyrolean words of endearment until they were out of sight. Then he went back into the hut and began to sandpaper some blocks that his grandfather needed for his work. The old man was a maker of picture frames, all carved and decorated with likenesses of mountain flowers, and these, when sent to Innsbruck and Vienna, brought the money that gave him his living. The figures were too fine and difficult for Franz to carve, but he could lend a hand at fetching blocks and sandpapering. He worked with a vim, for Tyrolean boys think it a disgrace to shirk, but all the while his thoughts were on the luck gift.

"I wonder what it will be?" he said to his grandfather. They took turns at guessing, until it was time to feed the goats and house the chickens for the night.

A week later the man who had driven Johan and his mother away came by on his return from Vienna, and Franz fairly flew out to get his gift.

"It is something very big," he called to the old frame maker as he took a bulging bag. "See, it is stuffed full!" And he expected to find something very wonderful.

But when he opened it, he thought it wasn't wonderful at all. There was a blue velvet jacket, trimmed with gold braid and fastened with glittering buttons, such as Tyrolean boys wore in those days, and in one of the pockets he found a shining knife.

"Well, of all things!" he exclaimed as he held them up for his grandfather to see. "It's a splendid jacket, and the knife is a beauty, but I don't see where the luck part comes in."

But Hals Berner was old and wise, and a knowing smile played over his wrinkled face as he spoke. "It won't be the first time luck has hidden in a knife," he said, as he bent over his carving.

Franz did not know what he meant. He had always had a knife, for being of a carver's family he was taught to whittle when he was a very little fellow, and he had become remarkably skillful for one of his years. But no wonderful good fortune had come to him, and he was very sure that although each of the presents was nice, neither would bring luck, and he sent that word to Johan. But the brother wrote back from the city, "It will surely turn out to be a luck gift, Franz. Just wait and see." And still the boy wondered.

Winter came and icy winds blew down from the peaks.

There was no word from Vienna now, for the valley was shut in by a glittering wall, and travel over the snow-drifted passes was impossible. There were other boys in the village, but each had his work indoors, and there was little time to play, so Franz had no chance for games. He helped his grandfather part of the day and sometimes whittled for his own amusement. It was a lonely life there in the hut, with just the old frame maker, who was often too busy to talk, so Franz was glad to do something to keep him busy. Now he made rings and tops and then just fantastic sticks or blocks.

One day, as he whittled, his grandfather said, "Why don't you make an animal, Franz?"

The boy looked up in surprise. "I don't think I can," he answered.

"Not unless you try," came the reply. "But if you do that you may surprise yourself."

Franz hated to have any one think he was afraid to make an attempt, so he exclaimed, "I wonder if I could make a sheep?"

"Begin and see," the old man advised.

The boy went to work. At first it was discouraging. After many minutes of whittling there was little to suggest what he had in mind. But then, with an occasional turn of the knife by the frame maker, and now and then a bit of advice, the boy began to see that a sheep would grow out of the block, and when it did he felt like a hero who has won a battle.

"It wasn't a bit hard, was it, lad?" Hals Berner asked when it was finished.

And Franz agreed that it was not.

That was the beginning, and every day thereafter Franz worked at his whittling, and animal after animal grew under his knife. He was so busy he did not have time to be lonely, and had quite forgotten how sad he had felt over having to stay at home. It was such fun to see the figures come out of the wood and feel that he had made them. Of course they were crude, and not half so handsome as those his grandfather could have made; but any one could tell what they were, and that was worth a great deal.

By spring he had a whole menagerie, and when his mother came home she found he had been a busy boy, and a happy one as well.

"All made with the luck knife," Johan said as he looked over the work.

"So grandfather says," Franz answered. "It's a splendid knife, but I don't see yet where the luck comes in."

And again the knowing smile went over the old man's face.

One day soon afterward his mother had word from the man who had been her employer in Vienna that his little son was not well, and he was sending him to regain his health in the mountain air. A week later the child arrived with his nurse, and the first thing that attracted his attention was Franz's menagerie.

"Oh! oh!" he exclaimed, "dogs, cats, sheep, goats, lions, elephants, and all made of wood! I want them."

"He means that he wants to buy them," his nurse explained. "Will you sell them, Franz?"

For a minute the boy hesitated. That menagerie had meant many months of whittling, and he loved every animal in it, and if Johan hadn't interrupted, probably he would have refused.

"Why, Franz," the brother exclaimed, "it begins to look like a luck knife after all."

That put a thought into his mind that caused him to answer, "Yes, take them. I can make some more."

So, when the child went back to Vienna he took a wooden menagerie from the Tyrolean mountains. Other Viennese children, seeing it, wanted to possess one, and orders began to pour in to Franz, far more than he could fill. Then other villagers took up the work, until all over the valley people were making animals and toys.

The work grew to be a big industry, and toys from the Grödner Thal were sent all over Germany, and even to the lands beyond. One generation after another went on with the work, and although it is two hundred years since Franz began it, the craft continues there to this day. At Christmas time shops in every land are filled with toys from the Tyrolean mountains, and although they do not know the story, thousands of children have been happier because of a peasant boy's whittling.

So out of the bag sent back from Vienna there came in truth a luck gift, and it wasn't the fine jacket either, but the knife with which Franz whittled his first sheep. The boy had found out that luck doesn't mean something sent by fairies, but the doing a thing so well that it brings a rich reward, and although he lived to be a very old man, he never got over being grateful that his mother made him stay behind when she and Johan went to the city.

The little valley among the Austrian Alps is still called Grödner Thal on the maps, but because of the animals and toys that have come out of it, it is almost as well known by another name. If you are good guessers you can surely tell what it is, especially if you know that the peasants still speak of the lad who made the first menagerie there as the Luck Boy of Toy Valley.

THE EMPEROR'S VISION[1]

Adapted from the Swedish of Selma Lagerlöf

(Medieval Legend — Ethics)

When Augustus was Emperor of Rome and Herod was King of Jerusalem, a great and holy night sank down over the earth. It was the darkest night that any one had seen,

[1]From Lagerlöf's *Christ Legends.* Copyright, 1908, by Henry Holt & Co.

and one could not find the way on the most familiar road. How could it be otherwise, since all the stars stayed at home in their houses and the fair moon hid her face?

The silence was as profound as the darkness. The rivers stood still in their courses, the wind did not stir, and even the aspen leaves had ceased to quiver. Everything was as motionless as if turned to stone, and the grass was afraid to grow, lest it disturb the holy night.

There was no cruelty or wickedness. Wild beasts did not seek their prey, but lay in the forest depths and wondered; serpents did not sting or dogs bark, and no false key could have picked a lock, no knife could have drawn a drop of blood.

In Rome, the mighty city, a group of people came from the Emperor's palace at the Palatine and took the path across the Forum which led to the Capitol. During the day the senators had asked the Emperor if he had any objection to their erecting a temple in his honor on Rome's sacred hill, but he had given no answer. He did not know if it would be agreeable to the gods for him to own a temple next to theirs, and he wanted to ascertain their will in the matter by offering a sacrifice. Therefore he and his trusted friends were on their way to the Capitol.

Augustus let them carry his litter, for he was old and the stairs leading to the Capitol were long. He held in his hands the cage of doves for the sacrifice. No priests or soldiers accompanied him, only his nearest friends. Torch bearers walked in front of him to light the ways through the black darkness, and behind him followed slaves who carried the tripod, knives, and charcoal for the sacred fire. He chatted gayly with his followers, and all were so interested in the conversation that they did not notice the stillness over the earth. Only when they reached the highest point on Capitol Hill did they realize that something unusual was taking place.

There they saw a most remarkable thing. An old woman,

so bent and twisted that at first they thought it must be a distorted olive tree, was standing on the very edge of the cliff, and they knew her to be the sibyl who had lived as many years as the sand grains by the sea.

"Why does she come from her cave tonight?" they whispered. "What does she foretell for the Emperor and the Empire?"

She stood there as if she had gone up on the hillside that she might see what was happening far away, and the night was so dark, so dark!

Then Augustus and his retinue remarked how profound was the stillness. They could not hear even Tiber's hollow murmur, and they feared some disaster was impending. But no one cared to show that he was afraid. They told Augustus it was a good omen, and counseled him to hurry with the sacrifice.

The sibyl seemed not to notice the Emperor's train moving up to the Capitol. In fact, she did not see them. She was in a distant land making her way over something higher than grass tufts. She was walking among great flocks of sleeping sheep.

Then she saw a shepherd's fire. It burned in the middle of the field, and she groped her way to it. The shepherds lay asleep in its glow, and beside them were the long, spiked sticks with which they defended their flocks from wild beasts. Jackals with glittering eyes and bushy tails stole up toward the blaze, but the men did not hurl the sticks at them. The dogs continued to sleep, the sheep did not flee, and the beasts of prey lay down to rest beside human beings.

Only this the sibyl saw. She did not know that a sacrificial fire was being kindled behind her. She did not see the Roman Emperor take a dove from the cage to use as an offering. She was in the far hills of Galilee, among slumbering shepherds and sheep.

Then, wonderful sight, a company of angels singing gloriously flew back and forth above the wide plain. They moved in long, swaying lines like migratory birds. Some held lutes in their hands, some zithers and harps, and their songs rang out as merry as child laughter, as carefree as lark trills. The shepherds wakened, marveling at what they heard and saw, then rose up to go to the mountain city to tell of the miracle.

Behind the sibyl, on the summit of Capitol Hill, still stood the train of Augustus. But he did not make the sacrifice. Although he exerted his full strength to hold the dove's frail body, it flung itself free and disappeared into the night.

And the shepherds, what of them?

They groped their way forward on a narrow, winding path. Suddenly, in the light up there on the mountain, a great heavenly body kindled, and the city beneath it glittered like silver in the starlight.

All the fluttering angel throngs hastened thither, shouting for joy, and the shepherds hurried so that they almost ran. Upon reaching the city, they found the angels had assembled over a stable near the gate. It was a wretched structure with a roof of straw, and a naked cliff for a wall. But over it hung the star, and thither flocked more and more angels. Some seated themselves on the roof or alighted on the steep mountain wall back of the house, others poised themselves in air on outspread pinions, while high up, high up, the sky was illuminated by creatures with wings as white as pearl.

The instant the star kindled over the mountain city all nature awoke. Trees swayed, the Tiber began to murmur, stars twinkled, and the moon stood out of the sky and lighted the world. Out of the clouds a dove circled down and alighted on the shoulders of Augustus.

The Emperor was proud and happy, and his friends and slaves fell at his feet.

"Hail, Cæsar!" they cried. "Thou art the god who shall be worshiped on Capitol Hill!"

This cry of homage was so loud that the sibyl heard it and roused from her vision. She turned from her place at the edge of the cliff and came down among the people, so twisted, so shriveled, so terrifying in her tangled hair and marks of age, that they fell back in awe. With one hand she clutched the hand of the Emperor, with the other she pointed toward the east.

"Look!" she commanded.

The vaulted heavens opened before his eyes, and his glance traveled slowly to the distant Orient. He saw a lowly stable behind a steep rock wall and shepherds kneeling in an open doorway. He saw a young mother with a child upon her knees, resting on a bundle of straw.

The sibyl's big, knotty fingers pointed toward the Babe.

"Hail, Cæsar!" she cried in a burst of scornful laughter. "There is the God who shall be worshiped on Capitol Hill!"

Augustus shrank back from her as from a maniac. But upon the sibyl fell the mighty spirit of prophecy. Her dim eyes began to burn, her hands were stretched toward heaven, her voice rang out with such resonance and power that it must have been heard throughout the world. And she uttered words which she seemed to be reading among the stars.

"Upon Capitol Hill shall the Redeemer of the world be worshiped — Christ, but not frail mortals."

When she had said this she strode past the terror-stricken men and disappeared down the mountain.

On the following day Augustus forbade the people to raise a temple to him on Capitol Hill. In place of it he built a sanctuary to the new-born God-Child, and called it *Heaven's Altar* — Ara Cœli.

THE SHEPHERD WHO TURNED BACK

Retold from a Syrian Legend

(*Ethics*)

This is a story they tell in Palestine when the Christmas stars shine out and Syrian children sit, cross-legged and big-eyed, in front of the old grandfather, listening to his tales by the light of the charcoal fire, while the moon flings its veil across the jagged Hebron Hills and the far, high peaks out Moab way are white as wool.

On the wonderful night when the star in the east proclaimed glad tidings to the Magi, and these three wise ones started away from their pleasant homes on a long and perilous journey, marvelous things are said to have happened in every quarter of the earth. Away in imperial Rome, the Emperor Augustus, straight and proud in his litter, was borne up the long stairway leading to Capitol Hill to invoke his gods on the spot where the people were to erect a temple to him. But suddenly the darkness broke away and he beheld a manger in a distant land and a Babe wrapped in swaddling clothes, and as the voices of his subjects shouted, "Hail, Cæsar, thou art the god who shall be worshiped on Capitol Hill!" instead of feeling great and exalted like a sovereign he felt very small and humble, for he knew that One just born was mightier than Cæsar, and would rule not only Rome, but all the earth.

And on that same night, where the mountains break southward from Bethlehem to form the high plateau of Bêt Sahûr, there were shepherds guarding their white-fleeced charges — six in all, five of whom slept by the gate of the sheepfold while one walked up and down, starting whenever he heard a stirring among the flocks and going in the direction of the sound to make sure that all was well.

Sometimes he added wood to the fire, for the night was

cold and a wind from the white peaks eastward brought numbness to his hands, and sometimes he stood and looked over the scene he knew so well — the pools of Solomon, shimmering darkly under the moon, and the broad vales of Boaz, bare and lifeless now, but yellow with ripened grain and gay with reapers' songs in harvest time. As a child he had played there with his brothers, as a boy he had roamed up and down the ravines, and now, alone in the darkness, it gladdened him to live again those days in memory.

Midnight drew near, yet he had no desire to sleep. The world was very silent, very still, for the wind had died away, and the Ilwa, in its rocky bed below, seemed to rest instead of surging Jordan-ward. Into the hoot of the owls came a note of unwonted tenderness, and even the cries of the jackals, that always made the night watch hideous and sent terror to the hearts of the herders, softened to a sound like a song. The man felt the calm and it soothed him, and although he had followed the flocks all day long and the hills were steep and jagged, he knew no weariness, but a strange sense of peace and delight, and as he looked at his companions wrapped in their rough skin coats and dreaming beside the embers, he wondered if they felt in sleep a sensation as exquisite as the one he experienced awaking.

"How bright the heavens are tonight!" he thought as he looked up to where a golden haze began to gleam around the crescent of the moon. Billions of stars glittered in the purple spaces, and directly over the center of the fold was a cluster large and brilliant that he had not seen before.

It grew warmer, too, and instead of the sting of winter that had kept the men close by the fire after darkness fell, a balm came into the air, a softness like that of May. Never had he dreamed there could be such a winter night, and almost he felt tempted to rouse his companions that they too might enjoy it.

But suddenly he stiffened and stood watching, cold with

fear. A glory came, and across the sky, which flamed as if on fire, floated a white-winged heavenly host singing the glad tidings of the Messiah come. The flocks started up and ran wildly about the fold. The sleeping shepherds wakened and crouched on the ground, half dazed with fear.

The bright ones flew about the heavens. They moved in shining columns down from the heights and fluttered above the fold, whiter than the sheep, then glided across to the rugged cliffs, and sat there as if on couches of down. And ever as they marched or floated or poised on glittering pinions ready for another flight, they blended their voices in a triumphal chorus as if all the hosts of heaven had descended to make melody among the Judean hills.

"What is it?" one of the shepherds asked in a voice that shook.

Then, like an answering message, came a jubilant anthem, "Fear not, for unto you is born this day in the city of David, a Saviour which is Christ the Lord."

As if a soothing hand had touched their fleeces, the sheep settled to rest again; the fear left the hearts of the shepherds, and in a radiance which dimmed and paled as they went, the shining ones floated upward out of sight, singing, "Glory to God in the Highest, Peace on Earth, Good Will to Men."

For several minutes the keepers of the flocks stood silent, too bewildered either to think or to speak. Then, by the peace among the sheep and the perfect calm of the night, they realized a marvelous thing had happened, and one of the herders lifted his voice.

"Didst hear?" he spoke in tones of reverence. "They say the Christ is born."

"Aye," a companion answered, "in the city of David, which is Bethlehem. Let us go and seek him." And his comrades, speaking agreement, said they would journey there together.

Now, when subjects go into the presence of a loved sovereign, they bear with them tokens of loyalty and affection. Those who are rich give priceless gifts, and those who are poor offer the best out of their scanty possessions and the fullness of their hearts. And so these herders of Bêt Sahûr, having nothing but their flocks, each chose the lamb he prized most, and cradling it tenderly in his firm, warm arms, left the sheepfold and started for the town.

Down over the cliffs they hurried, along perilous slopes and across chasms that seemed like great black mouths agape; yet they did not fear, for a light from above showed the path as plain as noontide and there was no danger of falling. From one rock to another they proceeded, from ledge to ledge they made their way, and soon were well down into the ravine, from the bottom of which the road led to the town. Directly above, so close that had they looked up they could have counted some of them, the sheep lay white and shining under the stars; but the thoughts of the shepherds were on Bethlehem, which, straight ahead, still showed a few flickering tapers, and not on the flocks behind.

Ben Ezra, he who had stood on the night watch, was the most stalwart of the six, and he it was who led the descent to the valley.

"Ah," he exclaimed when at last their feet struck the white firmness of the road, "from here on the way is smooth and easy. Let us hasten, brethren, and soon we shall be there."

And as he spoke he smoothed the fleece of the warm, white bundle he carried, which bleated softly at his caress.

Just then was heard the cry of a lamb.

The shepherds stopped and listened, for having spent their lives among the flocks, they knew the helplessness of the sheep, and although rugged, fierce-looking men, their hearts were tender toward the weak and appealing. The bleat of a ram or ewe never failed to call them from their meals by day or their rest by night; and now other thoughts left their minds, and they remembered only their charges alone on the hill. Then, thinking of the glory in the sky and the word of the heavenly host that the Christ was born in Bethlehem, one of them said, "Come. Methinks all is well. Did we not feel on the hills that God would take care of the sheep? Let us on to Bethlehem and seek the King."

But another of the number, he who stood sentinel while his comrades slept, shook his head and demurred.

"Nay," he said. "Take my lamb and say 'tis the gift of Ben Ezra, but I must go back. It is my night on the watch, and a good shepherd is not deaf to the cry of a sheep."

He gave his tiny white burden into the keeping of one of his companions and turning, hurried back to the cliffs, while the others went ahead to Bethlehem. He knew it would take much longer to make the climb than it had taken for the descent, and a fear seized him that perhaps jackals had broken upon the flock and he might reach the fold too late to save the sheep. But as he moved forward the mounting of the first cliff seemed no task at all. Hands invisible seemed to lift him up the mountain way, and he reached the sheepfold easily and quickly.

A great relief came. The flocks lay silent, stirring only when a lamb or ewe moved a white leg and turned as it slept, but there was no sign or sound of danger, not even the howl of a jackal away on the mountain side or the moving shadow of a panther creeping stealthily upon the fold. Then he knew that in truth God was watching over the sheep, and that the lamb had probably cried out in wonder, even as he and his brethren might have done.

Secure in the thought that the flock was safe, he started down the mountain toward Bethlehem, musing upon the strange things that had come to pass that night. His comrades were far ahead, and he knew he could not overtake them. Perhaps already they had reached the town and found the place of the Child, while he yet had a long way to go. But his feet sped over the spaces and he swung lightly along, the shaggy skin of his shepherd's cloak flapping as he went. He was not sorry he had gone back, even though it meant he must journey alone, for there was a peace in his heart that could not have been there had he gone ahead hearing the cry of a lamb.

At last he reached Bethlehem and asked one of the soldiers who guarded the gate, "Where is it that the Christ is born?"

"The Christ?" the man repeated like one dazed. "He is not in Bethlehem. Better get you back to the hills, which is the place of shepherds."

Ben Ezra stood firm.

"He must be here," he insisted, "for so sang the angels at Bêt Sahûr, saying, 'In the city of David,' which is Bethlehem."

Whereupon some of the guardsmen smiled and pointed to their heads, and some laughed jeeringly.

There was one, however, a tall, gentle-faced archer, who smiled and spoke kindly, "They say a man child has come to the stable beyond the khan, where Joseph ben David the Nazarene and his wife have taken shelter. You might try there."

The shepherd nodded and thanked him, his dark eyes moistily tender and in his face a light that silenced the mockers.

"Thither will I go," he exclaimed, and hurried on his way, bowing his head reverently as he came in sight of the place.

Now it happened when Ben Ezra reached the stable where Joseph ben David was abiding because of the multitude in the khan, that he found the Child lying in a manger, and the other shepherds who had gone before knelt beside Him, looking into His gentle eyes and marveling. Around them on the ground, softly bleating as if they too understood the marvel and rejoiced in it, were the lambs the men had brought as offerings to the Babe; and some of the townsfolk too were there, murmuring in awed tones and looking on the scene in wide-eyed wonder. No one noticed the herder who entered late, or saw him fall on his knees beside the manger. But as his sturdy head drooped low, the Child lifted His tiny hand as if in blessing and smiled down on Ben Ezra's upturned face; and then the keepers of the sheep knew that thus God had chosen to reward him who had not been deaf to the cry of a lamb.

For many a year after that time, the Syrian herders say, Ben Ezra tended his sheep on the hills. Through summer and winter he abode in the pasture place, his only respite from toil being the rare visits he made to the village where his wife and wee ones dwelt; but he never was weary, and his flocks never went astray. To his children and his children's children he told the story of how he went back to the hills that night and how he was rewarded, bidding them to be ever mindful of the fact that he who is tender to the sheep serves well a higher Master. And as years rolled into decades and centuries passed away, all the herders of Judea came to know the story and to shape their lives by it, so that to this day the Syrian shepherds have remained men of tender heart and simple faith. And when strangers visit the land and wonder at the gentleness of the keepers of the flocks, some old grandfather or brown-eyed boy is ever ready to explain what it is that has kept them sweet and serene, and tells the story of Ben Ezra, the shepherd who on the wonderful night went back to the hills, and so came late to Bethlehem.

THE PET RAVEN

A Legend of the Rhine

(*Geography — Ethics*)

One autumn morning a thousand years ago, a boy and a girl stood in a forest path beside the Rhine. His great eyes, brown and full of feeling, looked wistfully into the face of the golden-haired maiden, while his clumsy hands stroked tenderly the glossy feathers of a young raven.

"Father says it is a poor gift to offer a princess," he said as he held the bird toward her, "but I have nothing else. Will you please take it?"

Blue-eyed Willeswind smiled. She was the petted child of a baron and accustomed to receiving gifts, but something about this boy's earnestness touched her in an unusual way. He was only a forester's son, with but little to break the monotony of his life of toil, and it seemed wonderful that he should be willing to part with his only treasure.

"I cannot take your only pet, Rupert," she said kindly, "but it is good of you to offer it."

Disappointment crept into the boy's dark eyes.

"Oh, please," he pleaded. "I want you to have it, because you bound up my foot with healing herbs when I tore it on the brambles in the wood. Please take it."

The girl answered with a smile that made her face very lovely, "Of course I shall take it, and I will keep it always because you gave it to me." Reaching over, she took the fluttering creature from the big dark hands, and stroked it gently as it quivered at the strange touch. Then she made her way back to the castle over a carpet of fallen leaves, while Rupert the forester's son hurried to the hunting lodge, happy in the thought that he had made a gift to her who had been kind to him.

"She will keep it and feed it and be glad I did not forget," he thought as he fed the falcons that evening, while up in the castle court Willeswind was busy with her pet.

"See how glossy its feathers are!" she said as her brother Othmar came near. "Rupert gave it to me, and I promised to keep it always."

The young squire laughed. "A raven is sure to be a bother," he said. "Better let it fly into the woods."

Willeswind shook her golden head. "No, no," she exclaimed, "I like it. Your horses and hounds and falcons are far more bother than one raven, yet you would not think of being without them."

Othmar mounted his horse and rode out to his archery practice, thinking how soon his sister would tire of the bird. But she did not tire of it. It was different from any pet she had ever owned, and she cared for it and trained it.

Seven years passed, and the brother had grown from a squire to a knight, and upon the death of his father the baron, became lord of the castle. Willeswind too had changed from the slender maid who stood under the November trees with Rupert the forester's son. She was now the stateliest of all the great ladies on the Rhine. But her hair was still the color of sun-kissed straw, and her eyes the same sympathetic ones, as blue as wood gentians. Rupert was tall and stalwart, one of the sturdiest vassals of Castle Stolzenfels, and although Willeswind seldom saw him, she remembered him kindly because he had given her the pet raven which she still kept and loved. She spent many hours teaching it tricks, and the bird was so clever that it learned rapidly. Sometimes it flew into the forest and came back with flowers and leaves for its mistress. Sometimes it winged its way across the river and brought sprigs of the sweet wild berries growing there.

Everything was bright about the castle, for the young master and mistress were kind to those who served them, and there were no happier vassals along the Rhine than theirs.

One day in springtime, when the elder flowers were creamiest and swallows were teaching their nestlings to fly, a stranger came riding along the river. Past the postern gate his armored steed dashed, and straight he sat in his saddle as he called to Lord Othmar.

"I bring a challenge from the great lord who is my master," he spoke defiantly as the young knight moved forth to meet him. With flashing eyes he tossed his gauntlet to the ground.

A murmur went among the vassals who stood by. To throw down a gauntlet was to invite war, and all waited for the master to act. But the silence was only for a minute. Then came a shouting and clashing of arms, for with defiance in his face Othmar picked up the glove and flung it back at the rider. That meant war, which in those days was believed to be a glorious thing.

The strange knight rode away along the Rhine shore as rapidly as he had come, while in the great courtyard of Castle Stolzenfels began the marshaling of vassals and preparation for fighting. The women burnished arms and gave all the aid they could, while the Lady Willeswind moved here and there, making suggestions where they were needed. All night long the sound of clanging armor was heard, and the next morning, when the men of Castle Stolzenfels went out of the castle gate to meet the enemy, Rupert the forester's son marched at the head of the vassals.

Willeswind stood at the tower window and watched them go along the winding river road, thinking sadly of the days and nights of danger into which they went. Perhaps they would not return. Perhaps, too, some robber band might pillage the castle while they were away, for all the able-bodied men had gone to battle, and in those days many brigand hordes ravaged the Rhine valley, which the handful of old men at Stolzenfels would not be able to hold back. But she was brave, and although danger threatened, she faced it as a baron's daughter should.

Autumn came, with swallows and martins flying southward, and still the battling raged away in the northland, sometimes with victory for Othmar and his men, sometimes with defeat, but always with dread for the anxious hearts of those who waited at home.

One night the wind raged like a mad thing, whipping the Rhine into foam. As the castle mistress sat in the great hall among the women, a servant entered, saying that a pilgrim stood at the outer gate, begging shelter from the night and storm.

"He is white and bent," the man explained. "Shall I let him come inside?"

Willeswind's heart was big and tender. "Yes, let him come," she said.

A moment later he followed the servant through the hall to the sleeping quarters, a hobbling figure leaning heavily on a staff. Willeswind pitied him as he went by, but thought his face seemed hard and cruel.

A few days later she sat alone with her maid, in that same great hall, looking happier than she had looked for many weeks. "A courier came by with word from Othmar," she said. "He sends greetings, says the worst of the fighting is over, and soon they will be home. I feel quite safe again."

Suddenly the door was violently thrust open. The maid screamed and Willeswind turned pale, for a man in heavy armor strode into the room. She knew he was one of the dreaded robber barons who terrorized the Rhine valley, and knew too, as she looked into his savage face, that it was the same man who, in the guise of a pilgrim, had sought shelter there a few nights before.

"I have come to take you with me," he said in a voice of thunder, "for I mean you to be my wife."

Willeswind shuddered. She knew how wicked and cruel he was, and that it was her great wealth he craved, for Stolzenfels was one of the richest estates on the river. "That can never be, sir," she answered haughtily. "So go back whence you came."

He looked at her with an evil smile. "You give me a blithe refusal now," he exclaimed, "but in three days I will come again and it will be sad for you if I get not a different answer."

The robber chief strode out, and Willeswind and the trembling maid looked at each other in terror.

"My lady," the woman spoke, as soon as the outer gate clanged and they knew the man was beyond hearing, "you must get away from here."

"Yes," answered the mistress, "I must leave Stolzenfels and seek refuge at some other castle."

So that same afternoon a little cavalcade wended its way through the woods, over the carpet of leaves that late autumn had whipped from the trees. It was Willeswind and her attendants, bound for the home of another baron, where she would be protected until the return of Othmar and his men. Beside her rode Hulda the maid, and on her shoulder sat the pet raven.

But they did not go far. Suddenly from behind some thickly growing brush a band of horsemen appeared. One rider, taller and heavier than the others, called out orders to his men.

"To my castle!" he shouted.

Willeswind knew well they were the tones of the robber baron, and that she was now a prisoner in his power.

Sad indeed was her heart as the men turned her horse's head away from her road to safety, and tears came into her blue eyes as she caught a glimpse of the Stolzenfels towers.

"Oh, my home," she murmured, "when shall I see you again?"

On they went through the forest, along that part of the river whose gray cliffs she had known since childhood, then into unfamiliar country as they neared the castle of the robber chief.

"If only they will let us stay together," she murmured to Hulda as they drew rein at the gate.

They rode in through the courtyard, and then, dismounting, the baron led the two women up a winding stairway to the tower.

"Here you may stay," he said savagely, "and decide what to do."

Then, striding out, he bolted the heavy door.

They looked around. The windows were covered with an iron grating, and there was no possible way of escape.

"We cannot get away," said Hulda, "so let us make the best of it and find something to eat, for I am hungry."

But there was no food about the place, and they realized then that he meant to starve Willeswind into obeying him.

But suddenly a bright thought came to her, and she smiled. "He cannot do it, though, for I have my raven." And stroking its glossy wings she said, "Berries, pet, berries."

Her hours of training had been well spent. For as if it understood, the bird spread its shining wings and flew out between the grating. After a while it returned with a sprig of crimson berries, the fragrant, juicy Rhine buds, and laid them in its mistress' lap.

Many trips it made during the days that followed, and the woodland fruit kept the women from starvation, for it contained both nourishment and water.

So, instead of growing weak and wan, they kept their strength, and the baron could not understand how, with neither food nor water, Willeswind remained strong and well, and as defiant as ever. But to Willeswind and Hulda it was no mystery, and they were full of gratitude to the raven.

One morning Hulda stood by the window, looking out over the woods at the sunlight on the river. Suddenly she gave an excited cry. "Some horsemen are riding up the Rhine road!" she exclaimed. "They are coming this way."

Willeswind flew to the casement and watched as they drew near. Straight along the forest path they advanced, so close that the watchers could see their faces.

"Oh!" cried the lady of Stolzenfels. "It is Othmar and his men. The war is over and they are coming home."

She called loudly, waving her handkerchief between the grating, and Othmar saw and heard. "We are up here, prisoners in the tower!" she shouted, as he galloped nearer.

And a minute later the Stolzenfels men were battering at the castle gate.

"For your mistress, comrades!" called Rupert the forester's son, as he led the charge.

The robber baron knew the Stolzenfels force was too strong for him to hold out against, for with right on their side they had even greater strength. He surrendered, and the captives were freed.

The Stolzenfels towers never looked as fair to their owners, as when on the return they beheld them through the trees. It was a joyful homecoming to both lord and vassal, and to the raven, for he flew in and out of its windows as if overcome with gladness. Othmar watched its joyous flight with a smile.

"We will always keep the bird," he said, "for it saved you from the baron's power."

And they did keep it until it died. Then, in memory of its service, they placed its stone image on the castle gate and carved its likeness on the Stolzenfels shield.

Centuries passed. The robber bands that had been the terror of the Rhine valley became a part of the past, and Castle Stolzenfels fell into decay, for hundreds of years being one of the noblest ruins on the river. Then the German emperor restored it. He rebuilt the crumbling towers and bastions where bats made their nests, furnished it after the fashion of long ago, and today it is a favorite summer home of the imperial family. And still on the outer gate a stone raven stands, and to all who know the Rhine stories it speaks eloquently of that olden time when knights were bold, and of a gratitude offering made by the forester's son to the daughter of the castle.

JUSSIEU AND THE HELIOTROPE

(*Science — Nature Study*)

In the year of Our Lord 1735, Joseph de Jussieu, the famous botanist, came into the presence of Louis the Fifteenth and besought him to give his royal sanction to a mission that was considered very wonderful in those days.

"I would go to South America to study the plant life there," he said, "and mayhap I may discover something that will bring glory to France."

The king looked with favor upon the venture, and a little later the botanist and his attendants sailed out of the port of Havre, toward the distant land of the Andes.

Many months they were on the way, now tossing on the high seas at the mercy of wind and wave, now threading a perilous path through the selvas. At last they ascended the snow-capped Cordilleras, examining every tree and plant they found.

"We will take back seeds of every rare specimen," Jussieu said, "and great will be the rejoicing in France."

One day, as the botanist and his men made their way from a deep ravine up a sunny slope, they smelled something wonderfully fragrant.

"Such a powerful odor must come from a gigantic, gorgeous flower," the naturalist said. And they searched eagerly, each man anxious to discover the prize. But the only gorgeous flower they found was a clump of flaming peonies, which, although regally beautiful, were devoid of fragrance.

Then one of the men stumbled upon a plant bearing clusters of tiny purple blossoms. The odor was very heavy around it, and he knew he had found the perfume giver.

"Ah!" he exclaimed in disappointment, "it is not half so stately as our fleur-de-lis."

Jussieu came and examined it with great interest, and

although it was a small, unpretentious flower, thought it a precious find. He noticed that the most perfect blossoms were on the sunny side of the plant, and that they seemed to reach the sun. He named it "heliotrope," from Greek words meaning "to turn toward the sun," and when he returned to France took with him some of the seeds, which were planted in the royal garden.

The princesses, who were always looking for something novel, became greatly excited about the purple blossoms from the Andes. They called it the flower of love, and no bouquet was deemed fit to offer a court lady that did not contain at least a sprig of it. Being greatly in demand, it was very costly. People speculated in it, and for a time fortunes were won and lost, as during the tulip craze in Holland.

Then, after a while, when all the florists grew quantities of heliotrope, it became so common that it went out of favor as the court flower. But it was just as popular as ever, because it had lost none of its grace and fragrance. It grew in the gardens of the people, and there was no peasant too poor to own a plant.

So the dainty heliotrope that is still the favorite of the gardens is a traveled and storied flower. It grew on the slope of the Andes. It crossed the broad seas and was planted in a royal garden. It gladdened the peasants and townsfolk of Lorraine and Brittany and Provence, and still it scatters its fragrance and reaches out its petals toward the sun.

THE FALL OF LONDON BRIDGE

(History)

Almost everybody, whether he be ten or seventy-five, has played the good old game of London Bridge, but not everybody knows that once upon a time the bridge really did fall down.

It was nine hundred years ago — before William the Conqueror was born, and the United States had not even been thought of. Up in the cold, white northland lived a race of fearless vikings, and down in pleasant England reigned a weak, unable king. His name was Ethelred, and because he was always behind time with his plans and his work, people called him the Unready, and in the day in which he lived it was a very serious thing for a king to be unready.

Ever since the Danes had discovered what a fair land England was, they had wanted to take it. They came with their armies in King Alfred's time. They returned again during the reign of his sons, and when young Ethelred ascended the throne and word went forth of how unable and unready he was, their boats brought a mighty army and surrounded the island. Danish soldiers camped on the broad English moorlands, Danish songs echoed through the woods of Kent and Surrey and sounded in the streets of London town. The invaders were in full possession of the city. They held the royal castle, and their generals slept in King Ethelred's beds, while he had to take a bunk wherever he could find one. They were bold, brave, and strong. They had leaders who knew not the meaning of fear and were always ready, and it seemed that this time they would take the kingdom.

Yet they didn't take it after all, for there were other brave, bold men who came to Ethelred's aid.

Twenty ships sailed down from the seas of Norway, twenty goodly vessels bearing blue and crimson sails, for the boy king Olaf, who dwelt in the far north country, had heard of the plight of Ethelred the Unready and said to his men, "Let us go and fight for him as we fight for our own land."

At these words the soldiers cheered and bent to the oars, and thus they went to England.

In from the sea they came and up the broad green Thames

toward London town. The people along the river despaired at sight of their standard, for they thought another army was coming to attack them. But the sorrow turned to rejoicing when King Ethelred met them just below the city, and Olaf said, in loud, clear tones, "I have brought my soldiers to fight for thee."

Then there rang out such a blast of welcome as never English war horns sounded before or since.

Olaf lost no time. The men of the north country fought for the love of fighting, and he was eager to hurl his army against the Danes.

"First we will take the fort they have built to command the Thames," he exclaimed. "Then we will drive them from the city."

King Ethelred shook his head.

"It will not be easy to do that," he said. "Thrice already my army has tried it, but the Danish soldiers are thick on London Bridge. We cannot get near enough to attack the fort, because whenever the ships start up the river arrows and spears and stones come down upon them and they are driven back."

King Olaf stood thinking and did not answer. Finally he said, "Then we must tear down the bridge."

Ethelred looked at him as if he thought him crazy. "Tear down the bridge!" he repeated in amazement. "That is impossible. London Bridge is strong, and neither of us has an army of giants."

Young Olaf looked at him and smiled, thinking how little this man knew of warfare.

"Do as I bid you," he said, "and you shall see it fall."

Ethelred had little faith in the viking's words, but he was in so terrible a plight that he was willing to do anything that might pull him out of it. Who wouldn't be, with a Danish general sleeping in his bed?

King Olaf gave some orders to his men. Then he said to

Ethelred, "Bring your ships alongside mine, and we will get them ready."

He ordered the men to make broad, flat roofs for every vessel, for he knew they could not tear down London Bridge unless protected from the spears and arrows of the Danes. The enemy had seized so much of King Ethelred's lumber that he hadn't half enough to make the roofs, so they tore down houses that the command might be carried out.

Finally everything was ready, and the fleet of England and the fleet of Norway moved side by side up the Thames. The Danish soldiers laughed as they saw the queer-looking vessels coming toward them, thinking what fun it would be to drive back the boats of Ethelred the Unready, as they had done several times before. But the Danes didn't know as much as they thought they knew, and although their spears and arrows flew fast, the lumbering warships came on.

Then the soldiers on the bridge shot their bows and threw their javelins as they had not done before. They hurled great rocks down upon the vessels, damaging some of them so much that they had to turn back. But they did not harm or frighten Olaf the viking. He called to his men and cheered them on, and nearer, nearer these good ships came, until they were close to the piles of London Bridge.

Then they stopped a moment, still under the rain of stones and spears and arrows, and the Danish soldiers wondered what it meant. They could not see the thick, strong cables that were wound around the heavy supports of the bridge. They could not see the soldiers of Olaf lash the other ends fast to the vessels. But a moment later they understood all they had not seen. The ships turned with a sudden spurt. The Danish soldiers felt a mighty tug and pull. The roofed warships darted down the river, and then was heard the fall of London Bridge.

How joyfully the men of England shouted, for now they could push ahead and attack the fort. They took it too, and drove the enemy out of the city. Danish warriors no longer slept under satin covers in the castle of King Ethelred. Danish songs no longer resounded through the woods of Kent and Surrey and across the broad, sea-lapped moorlands. The soldiers routed the Danes and drove them out of the country, and Olaf the boy viking sailed back to his far, white northland, rejoicing in the thought that he had saved his kingdom to Ethelred, which he could not have done but for the fall of London Bridge.

HOW THEY CAME TO HAVE KITE DAY IN CHINA

Retold from a Chinese Folk Tale

(Physical Education)

In the lovely province of Kwang Tung, a sage named Ng Chew lived in the far-off time. He not only was versed in the lore of past and present, but knew future events as well, and used his knowledge and his power to benefit mankind.

One night in a vision he saw that a pestilence was about to sweep over the valley in which he lived, and his first thought was that he must save his people. He went from house to house telling the news and bidding every one flee with him to the mountains, and a few hours after he started on his mission the homes in the lowlands were deserted.

Up on the heights the people were safe in the crisp, clean air. But after many days had passed they wanted to return to their homes. They thought of the growth in the rice fields and of the approaching harvest time. "We have been here long enough," they declared. "By this time the danger is over and we ought to go back." But the wise Ng Chew knew it was not safe to return, and urged them to stay. There were a few who would not listen to his words. They started back to the lowlands, and Ng Chew wondered how he could keep the others on the mountain. Then a happy thought crossed his mind. He set everybody to making and flying kites, and soon had them so interested that they were glad to stay.

Days afterward, when he knew the danger was past, he led them back to the valley. Then they realized what a blessed thing he had done in keeping them on the mountain, for all who had refused to stay there with him had died of the pestilence.

The people's hearts were filled with gratitude toward the man who had saved them.

"We will honor Ng Chew as long as he lives," they said. "When his birthday comes we will all fly kites."

This they did. Each year, on the birthday of Ng Chew, they left the rice fields and spent the day flying kites.

The word spread beyond the little valley and from province to province, until all over the land kite flying marked the birthday of the sage of Kwang Tung. The wise man died and centuries passed, but still the Chinese keep Kite Day, honoring him who in the long ago led his people to safety in the mountains.

THE STORY OF A STONE

By David Starr Jordan

(*Science*)

Once on a time, a great many years ago, so many, many years that one grows very tired in trying to think how long ago it was; in those old days when the great Northwest consisted of a few ragged and treeless hills, full of copper and quartz, bordered by a dreary waste of sand flats, over which the Gulf of Mexico rolled its warm and turbid waters as far north as Escanaba and Eau Claire; in the days when Marquette Harbor opened out towards Baffin's Bay, and the Northern Ocean washed the crest of Mount Washington and wrote its name upon the Pictured Rocks; when the tide of the Pacific, hemmed in by no snow-capped Sierras, came rushing through the Golden Gate between the Ozarks and the north peninsula of Michigan, and swept over Plymouth Rock and surged up against Bunker Hill; in the days when it would have been fun to study geography, for there were no capitals, nor any products, and all the towns were seaports — in fact, an immensely long time ago there lived somewhere in the northeastern part of the state of Wisconsin, not far from the city of Oconto, a little jellyfish. It was a curious little fellow, about the shape of half an apple, and the size of a pin's head; and it floated around in the water, and ate little things, and opened and shut its umbrella pretty much as the jellyfishes do now on a sunny day off Nahant Beach when the tide is coming in. It had a great many little feelers that hung down all around like so many little snakes; so it was named Medusa, after a queer woman who lived a long while ago, when all sorts of stories were true. She wore snakes instead of hair, and used to turn people into stone images if they dared to make faces at her. So this little Medusa floated around, and opened and shut her umbrella for a good while, — a month or two, perhaps; we don't know how long. Then one morning, down among the seaweeds, she laid a whole lot of tiny eggs, transparent as crab-apple jelly, and smaller than the dewdrop on the end of a pine leaf. That was the last thing she did; then she died, and our story henceforth concerns only one of those little eggs.

One day the sun shone down into the water — the same sun that shines over the Oconto sawmills now — and touched these eggs with life; and a little fellow whom we will call Favosites, because that was his name, woke up inside the egg, and came out into the world. He was only a little piece of floating jelly, shaped like a cartridge pointed at both ends, or like a grain of barley, although very much smaller. He had a great number of little paddles on his sides. These kept flapping all the time, so that he was constantly in motion. And at night all these little paddles shone with a rich green light, to show him the way through the water. It would have done you good to see them some night when all the little fellows had their lamps burning at once, and every wave as it rose and fell was all aglow with Nature's fireworks, which do not burn the fingers and leave no smell of sulphur.

So the little Favosites kept scudding along in the water, dodging from one side to the other to avoid the ugly creatures that tried to eat him. There were crabs and clams of a fashion neither you nor I shall ever see alive. There were huge animals with great eyes, savage jaws like the beak of a snapping turtle and surrounded by long feelers. They sat in the end of a long, round shell, shaped like a length of stove pipe, and glowered like an owl in a hollow log; and there were smaller ones that looked like lobsters in a dinner horn. But none of these caught the little fellow, else I should not have had this story to tell.

At last, having paddled about long enough, Favosites thought of settling in life. So he looked around till he found a flat bit of shell that just suited him. Then he sat down upon it and grew fast, like old Holger Danske in the Danish myth, or Frederick Barbarossa in the German one. He did not go to sleep, however, but proceeded to make himself a home. He had no head, but between his shoulders he made an opening which would serve him for mouth and stomach. Then he put a whole row of feelers out, and commenced catching little worms and floating eggs and bits of jelly and bits of lime, — everything he could get, — and cramming them into his mouth. He had a great many curious ways, but the funniest of them all was what he did with the bits of lime. He kept taking them in, and tried to wall himself up inside with them, as a person would "stone a well," or as though a man should swallow pebbles and stow them away in his feet and all around under the skin, till he had filled himself all full with them, as the man filled Jim Smiley's frog.

Little Favosites became lonesome all alone in the bottom of that old ocean among so many outlandish neighbors. So one night, when he was fast asleep and dreaming as only a coral animal can dream, there sprouted out from his side, somewhere near where his sixth rib might have been if he had had any ribs, another little Favosites; and this one very soon began to eat worms and to wall himself up as if for dear life. Then from these two another and another little bud came out, and other little Favosites were formed. They all kept growing up higher and cramming themselves fuller and fuller of stone, till at last there were so many and they were so crowded together that there was not room for them to grow round, and so they had to become six-sided like the cells of a honeycomb. Once in a while some one in the company would feel jealous because the others got more of the worms, or would feel uneasy at sitting still so long and swallowing lime. Such a one would secede from the little union without even saying "good-by," and would put on the airs of the grandmother Medusa, and would sail around in the water, opening and shutting its umbrella, at last laying more eggs, which for all we know may have hatched out into more Favosites.

So the old Favosites died, or ran away, or were walled up by the younger ones, and new ones filled their places, and the colony thrived for a long while, until it had accumulated a large stock of lime.

But one day there came a freshet in the Menominee River, or in some other river, and piles of dirt and sand and mud were brought down, and all the little Favosites' mouths were filled with it. This they did not like, and so they died; but we know that the rock house they were building was not spoiled, for we have it here. But it was tumbled about a good deal in the dirt, and the rolling pebbles knocked the corners off, and the mud worked into the cracks, and its beautiful color was destroyed. There it lay in the mud for ages, till the earth gave a great, long heave that raised Wisconsin out of the ocean, and the mud around our little Favosites packed and dried into hard rock and closed it in. So it became part of the dry land, and lay embedded in the rocks for centuries and centuries, while the old-fashioned ferns grew above it, and whispered to it strange stories of what was going on above ground in the land where things were living.

Then the time of the first fishes came, and the other animals looked in wonder at them, as the Indians looked on Columbus. Some of them were like the little gar-pike of our river here, only much larger, — big as a stove pipe, and with a crust as hard as a turtle's. Then there were sharks, of strange forms, and some of them had teeth like bowie knives, with tempers to match. And the time of the old fishes came and went, and many more times came and went, but still Favosites lay in the ground at Oconto.

Then came the long, hot, wet summer, when the mists hung over the earth so thick that you might have had to cut your way through them with a knife; and great ferns and rushes, big as an oak and tall as a steeple, grew in the swamps of Indiana and Illinois. Their green plumes were so long and so densely interwoven that the Man in the Moon might have fancied that the earth was feathering out. Then all about, huge reptiles, with jaws like the gates of doom and teeth like cross-cut saws, and little reptiles with wings like bats, crawled, and swam, and flew.

But the ferns died, and the reptiles died, and the rush trees fell in the swamps, and the Illinois and the Sangamon and the Wabash and all the other rivers covered them up. They stewed away under layers of clay and sand, till at last they turned into coal and wept bitter tears of petroleum. But all this while Favosites lay in the rocks in Wisconsin.

Then the mists cleared away, and the sun shone, and the grass began to grow, and strange animals came from somewhere or nowhere to feed upon it. There were queer little striped horses, with three or four hoofs on each foot, and no bigger than a Newfoundland dog, but as smart as ever you saw. There were great hairy elephants, with teeth like sticks of wood. There were hogs with noses so long that they could sit on their hind legs and root. And there were many still stranger creatures which no man ever saw alive. But still Favosites lay in the ground and waited.

And the long, long summer passed by, and the autumn, and the Indian summer. At last the winter came, and it snowed and snowed, and it was so cold that the snow did not go off till the Fourth of July. Then it snowed and snowed till the snow did not go off at all. And then it became so cold that it snowed all the time, till the snow covered the animals, and then the trees, and then the mountains. Then it would thaw a little, and streams of water would run over the snow. Then it would freeze again, and the snow would pack into solid ice. So it went on snowing and thawing and freezing, till nothing but snowbanks could be seen in Wisconsin, and most of Indiana was fit only for a skating rink. And the animals and plants which could get away, all went south to live, and the others died and were frozen into the snow.

So it went on for a great many years. I dare not tell you how long, for you might not believe me. Then the spring came, the south winds blew, and the snow began to thaw. Then the ice came sliding down from the mountains and hills and from the north toward the south. It went on, tearing up rocks, little and big, from the size of a chip to the size of a house, crushing forests as you would crush an eggshell, and wiping out rivers as you would wipe out a chalk mark. So it came pushing, grinding, thundering along, — not very fast, you understand, but with tremendous force, like a plow drawn by a million oxen, for a thousand feet of ice is very heavy. And the ice plow scraped over Oconto, and little Favosites was torn from the place where he had lain so long; but by good fortune he happened to fall into a crevice of the ice where he was not much crowded, else he would have been ground to powder and I should not have had this story to tell. And the ice melted as it slid along, and it made great torrents of water, which, as they swept onward, covered the land with clay and pebbles. At last the ice came to a great swamp overgrown with tamarack and balsam. It melted here; and all the rocks and stones and dirt it had carried — little Favosites and all — were dumped into one great heap.

It was a very long time after, and man had been created, and America had been discovered, and the War of the Revolution and the Civil War had all been fought to the end, and a great many things had happened, when one day a farmer living near Grand Chute, in Outagamie County, Wisconsin, was plowing up his clover field to sow to winter wheat. He picked up in the furrow a curious little bit of "petrified honeycomb," a good deal worn and dirty, but still showing plainly the honey cells and the bee bread. Then he put it into his pocket and carried it home, and gave it to his boy Charley to take to the teacher and hear what he would say about it. And this is what he said.

LIST OF STORIES BY MONTHS FOR EACH GRADE

LIST OF STORIES BY MONTHS FOR EACH GRADE

First Grade

September

Bryant, Sara Cone: The Gingerbread Man, The Whale and the Elephant (*Stories to Tell to Children*).

Coe, Fanny E.: Three Billy Goats Gruff (*First Book of Stories for the Story-Teller*).

Heber, Elizabeth: Coming and Going (*A Child's Story Garden*).

Holbrook, Florence: How Flax Was Given to Men (*Book of Nature Myths*).

Lindsay, Maud: Dust under the Rug, Giant Energy and Fairy Skill (*Mother Stories*).

Perrault, Charles: Red Riding Hood (*Fairy Tales from Perrault*).

Sly, W. R.: Boots and His Brothers (*World Stories Retold*).

October

Arnold, Sarah L.: Columbus, the Boy of Genoa (*Stepping Stones to Literature — Book 3*).

Bailey, C. S.: Bobby Squirrel's Busy Day (*Story-Telling Time*).

Bryant, Sara Cone: Little Jackal and the Camel (*Stories to Tell to Children*).

Coe, Fanny E.: The Boy and the Wolf, The Sun and the Wind (*First Book of Stories for the Story-Teller*).

Dillingham, E. T.: A Hallowe'en Story ("*Tell It Again*" *Stories*).

Grierson, E. W.: The Smith and the Fairies (*Book of Celtic Stories*).

Lang, Andrew: The Witch (*Yellow Fairy Book*).

Potter, Beatrix: Squirrel Nutkin, Bunny Cottontail (*Squirrel Nutkin*).

Poulsson, Emilie: The Thrifty Squirrels (*In the Child's World*).

Rhys, Ernest: The Witch That Was a Hare (*English Fairy Book*).

November

Bailey, C. S.: The Kid Who Would Not Go (*Firelight Stories*).

Chadwick, Mara L. Pratt-: Stories of the Pilgrim Babies (*Stories of Colonial Children*).

Coe, Fanny E.: Jack the Giant Killer, Tom Thumb (*First Book of Stories for the Story-Teller*).

DILLINGHAM, E. T., and EMERSON, A. P.: Gretchen and the Magic Fiddle (*"Tell It Again" Stories*).

KEYES, ANGELA M.: Lazy Jack (*Stories and Story-Telling*).

OLCOTT, F. J.: The Ears of Wheat (*Good Stories for Great Holidays*).

POULSSON, EMILIE: The Chestnut Boys, The Crane Express (*In the Child World*).

WHITE, ELIZA O.: A Thanksgiving Dinner (*When Molly Was Six*).

A Thanksgiving at Hollywood, Grandmother's Thanksgiving Story (*Half a Hundred Stories*).

December

BAILEY, C. S., and LEWIS, C. M.: The Legend of the Christmas Tree (*For the Children's Hour*).

BRYANT, SARA CONE: The Golden Cobwebs (*How to Tell Stories to Children*).

COE, FANNY E.: St. Christopher (*First Book of Stories for the Story-Teller*).

DILLINGHAM, E. T., and EMERSON, A. P.: Santa Claus' Helpers, The Story of the Man in the Moon, The Kitten That Wanted to Be a Christmas Present, A Christmas Legend (*"Tell It Again" Stories*).

LINDSAY, MAUD: The Christmas Cake (*More Mother Stories*).

OLCOTT, F. J.: The Stranger Child (*Good Stories for Great Holidays*).

SLY, W. R.: The Christmas Gift, The Wise Men and the Star, The Shepherds and the Angels (*World Stories Retold*).

January

ÆSOP: The Bear and the Fowls (ADAMS: *Fables and Rhymes*).

ALDEN, R. M.: The Forest Full of Friends (*Why the Chimes Rang*).

BAILEY, C. S.: The Travels of a Fox (*For the Story-Teller*).

LINDSAY, MAUD: Mrs. Tabby Gray (*Mother Stories*).

MACDONNELL, ANNE: Peter, the Stone Cutter (*Italian Fairy Book*).

POULSSON, EMILIE: An All the Year Round Story, The Fairies' New Year's Gift (*In the Child World*).

RICHARDS, L. E.: The Pig Brother (*The Pig Brother*).

SLY, W. R.: The Golden Goose, The Baby Brother in the Basket Boat, The Flood and the Rainbow (*World Stories Retold*).

SLOSSON, MRS. A. T.: The Horse That Believed He'd Get There (*Story-Telling Library*).

SOUTHEY, ROBERT: The Three Bears.

February

Dillingham, E. T., and Emerson, A. P.: Elaine's Valentine (*"Tell It Again" Stories*).

Gross, H.: Lincoln and the Pig (*Lincoln's Own Stories*).

Lang, Andrew: East o' the Sun and West o' the Moon (*Blue Story Book*).

Lindsay, Maud: Story of Gretchen.

Nixon-Roulet, Mary F.: The Sake Waterfall (*Japanese Folk Stories*).

Sly, W. R.: The Children's Friend, The Boy Who Lived in Church (*World Stories Retold*).

White, Eliza O.: A Sunday Valentine (*When Molly Was Six*).

Wiggin, K. D., and Smith, N. A.: Little George Washington (*The Story Hour*); Three Little Pigs (*Tales of Laughter*).

Williston, Teresa P.: The Stolen Charm (*Japanese Fairy Tales*).

Wiltse, Sara: Jack and the Beanstalk (*Hero Folk of Ancient Britain*).

March

Alden, R. M.: The Boy Who Discovered Spring (*Why the Chimes Rang*).

Asbjørnsen, P. C.: Little Fred and His Fiddle (*Fairy Tales from the Far North*).

Bailey, C. S.: Why the Bear Sleeps All Winter (*Firelight Stories*).

Bryant, Sara Cone: The Jackal and the Alligator, Little Jack Roll-a-Round (*How to Tell Stories to Children*).

Grimm, Jacob: The Queen Bee, The Elves and the Shoemaker (*German Household Tales*).

Hall, I. F., and Lennox, E. D.: Easter Lily (*Red Letter Days*).

Holbrook, Florence: Why the Sea Is Salt (*Book of Nature Myths*).

Jacobs, Joseph: The Cat and the Mouse (*English Fairy Tales*).

Kipling, Rudyard: The Elephant's Child, How the Rhinoceros Got His Skin (*Just So Stories*).

Poulsson, Emilie: A Wise Old Horse (*In the Child World*).

The Pink Knight (*Dumpy Books for Children*).

April

Andersen, Hans Christian: The Wild Swans (*Wonder Stories*).

Bailey, C. S.: The Little Old Woman Who Went to the North Wind (*Firelight Stories*).

BRYANT, SARA CONE: Why the Morning Glory Climbs, Why the Evergreen Trees Keep Their Leaves (*How to Tell Stories to Children*).

BRYCE, C. T.: The Little Slipper Orchid (*That's Why Stories*).

HOLBROOK, FLORENCE: The First Humming Bird (*Book of Nature Myths*).

JACOBS, JOSEPH: Mr. Vinegar (*English Fairy Tales*).

JOHNSON, CLIFTON: The Travels of a Fox (*Oak Tree Stories*).

LINDSAY, MAUD: The Little Gray Pony (*Mother Stories*).

OLCOTT, F. J.: The Loveliest Rose in the World (*Good Stories for Great Holidays*).

SETON, ERNEST THOMPSON: Raggylug (BRYANT: *How to Tell Stories to Children*).

May

ALDEN, R. M.: King's Garden (*Why the Chimes Rang*).

ASBJØRNSEN, P. C.: Paper Tom (*The Fairy World*).

BAILEY, C. S., and LEWIS, C. M.: Hans and the Wonderful Flower, The Legend of the Dandelion (*For the Children's Hour*).

BLAKEWELL, E. S.: The Elder Tree Mother (*True Fairy Stories*).

BRYCE, C. T.: The Mountain Ash (*That's Why Stories*).

JUDD, M. C.: How the Water Lily Came (*Wigwam Stories*).

KEYES, ANGELA M.: The Two Brothers (*Stories and Story-Telling*).

LINDSAY, MAUD: The Closing Door (*Mother Stories*).

WIGGIN, K. D., and SMITH, N. A.: Pancake (*Tales of Laughter*).

A Story of the Flag (*Our Holidays Retold from St. Nicholas*).

June

BRYANT, SARA CONE: The Little Pink Rose (*How to Tell Stories to Children*); Another Little Red Hen, The Blackberry Bush, The Whale and the Elephant, The Jackal and the Camel (*Stories to Tell to Children*).

CABOT, ELLA L.: Hans, the Shepherd Boy (*Ethics for Children*).

DILLINGHAM, E. T., and EMERSON, A. P.: The First Flag of the United States (*Tell It Again*).

HALL, I. F., and LENNOX, E. D.: Flag Day (*Red Letter Days*).

SLY, W. R.: The Boy with His Lunch (*World Stories Retold*).

SECOND GRADE

September

ÆSOP: The Ant and the Grasshopper (ADAMS: *Fables and Rhymes*).
ANDERSEN, H. C.: The Flax (*Wonder Tales*).
BJÖRNSON, BJÖRNSTJERNE: Oeyvind and Marit (KEYES: *Stories and Story-Telling*).
BRYANT, SARA CONE: The Sailor Man (*How to Tell Stories to Children*).
GRIMM, JACOB: The Town Musicians, The Wolf and the Seven Little Goats (*German Household Tales*).
HOLBROOK, F. E.: How Flax Was Given to Man (*Book of Nature Myths*).
O'GRADY, ALICE: The Old Woman Who Lived in a Vinegar Bottle (*The Story-Teller's Book*).
SLY, W. R.: How a Happy Home Was Lost, The First Two Brothers (*World Stories Retold*).

October

BALDWIN, JAMES: Wondering Jack (*Second Fairy Reader*).
BRYANT, SARA CONE: The Cat and the Parrot (*Best Stories to Tell to Children*.)
BRYCE, C. T.: The Raven (*That's Why Stories*).
CABOT, ELLA L.: The Squirrel's Devotion (*Ethics for Children*).
GRIMM, JACOB: Brier Rose (*German Household Tales*).
JACOBS, JOSEPH: Tom Tit Tot (*English Fairy Tales*).
KIPLING, RUDYARD: The Cat That Walked by Himself (*Just So Stories*).
SLY, W. R.: The Ladder That Reached to Heaven, The Slave Boy Who Became a Prince (*World Stories Retold*).

November

BAILEY, C. S., and LEWIS, C. M.: The Mince Pie (*For the Children's Hour*).
BALDWIN, JAMES: Grumbling Peter (*Second Fairy Reader*).
BRYCE, C. T.: The Travelers and the Bear (*Fables from Afar*).
LINDSAY, MAUD: The Visit, The Turkey's Nest (*More Mother Stories*).
O'GRADY, ALICE: A Good Thanksgiving (*The Story-Teller's Book*).
SCUDDER, H. E.: Diamonds and Toads (*Fables and Folk Stories*).
WIGGIN, K. D., and SMITH, N. A.: The First Thanksgiving (*The Story Hour*).
Grandmother's Thanksgiving, A Thanksgiving at Hollywood (*Half a Hundred Stories*).

December

Bryant, Sara Cone: Fulfilled, The Story of Jairus' Daughter (*How to Tell Stories to Children*).

Bryce, C. T.: The Old Woman and the Crowbar (*Fables from Afar*).

Cabot, Ella L.: St. Francis of Assisi and the Wolf (*Ethics for Children*).

Holbrook, Florence: Why the Fox Has a White Tip on His Tail (*Book of Nature Myths*).

O'Grady, Alice: Christmas Eve, Christmas Morning, The Christmas Story, The Christmas Tree (*The Story-Teller's Book*).

Olcott, F. J.: Little Wolf's Wooden Shoes (*Good Stories for Great Holidays*).

Wiggin, K. D., and Smith, N. A.: The First Christmas (*The Story Hour*).

January

Asbjørnsen, P. C.: Little Fred and His Fiddle (*Fairy Tales from the Far North*).

Bryant, Sara Cone: The Little Match Girl (*Best Stories to Tell to Children*).

Bryce, C. T.: Why the Cat Washes after Eating, Why Turtles Stay near Water (*That's Why Stories*).

Cabot, Ella L.: The Magic Mask (*Ethics for Children*).

Pierson, C. D.: The Lamb with the Longest Tail (*Among the Farmyard People*).

Scudder, H. E.: One Eye, Two Eyes, Three Eyes (*Fables and Folk Stories*).

Sly, W. R.: The Elephant and the Tailor, The Story without an End, The Flood and the Rainbow (*World Stories Retold*).

February

Baldwin, James: Saving the Birds (Lincoln), Going to Sea (Washington) (*Fifty Famous People*).

Kipling, Rudyard: How the Camel Got His Hump (*Just So Stories*).

Olcott, F. J.: The Cherry Tree, The Apple Orchard (*Good Stories for Great Holidays*).

Pierson, C. D.: The Story That Swallow Didn't Tell (*Among the Farmyard People*).

Stoddard, John L.: The Story of St. Valentine (*Lectures — South Tyrol*).

Wiggin, K. D., and Smith, N. A.: Little George Washington, Big George Washington (*The Story Hour*).

March

BRYANT, SARA CONE: Little Tavwots (*How to Tell Stories to Children*).

COOKE, FLORA J.: An Indian Story of the Mole (*Nature Myths*).

HOLBROOK, FLORENCE: Why the Evergreen Trees Never Lose Their Leaves (*A Book of Nature Myths*).

O'GRADY, ALICE: Titty Mouse and Tatty Mouse, The Sheep and the Pig That Built a House, The Straw Ox (*The Story-Teller's Book*).

OLCOTT, F. J.: The Little Tree That Longed for Leaves (*Good Stories for Great Holidays*).

SLY, W. R.: Why Boys Take off Their Hats in Church (*World Stories Retold*).

April

ÆSOP: The Fox and the Crow, The Jay and the Peacock (ADAMS: *Fables and Rhymes*).

BAILEY, C. S., and LEWIS, C. M.: The Red-Headed Woodpecker (*For the Children's Hour*).

COOKE, FLORA J.: How the Robin's Breast Became Red (*Nature Myths*).

LINDSAY, MAUD: Out of the Nest (*More Mother Stories*).

PIERSON, C. D.: The Wonderful, Shiny Egg (*Among the Farmyard People*).

SCUDDER, HORACE E.: The Jackdaw and the Doves (*Fables and Folk Stories*).

SLY, W. R.: The Woman Who Shared Her Last Loaf (*World Stories Retold*).

May

ANDERSEN, H. C.: The Snowdrop, The Little Butterfly Brothers, The Water Drop (OLCOTT: *Good Stories for Great Holidays*).

BRYANT, SARA CONE: How Brother Rabbit Fooled the Whale (*Best Stories to Tell to Children*).

COE, FANNY E.: The Story of the Anemone (*First Book of Stories for the Story-Teller*).

HART, A. S., and STEVENS, E.: A Boy Who Won the Cross (*Romance of the Civil War*).

HOLBROOK, FLORENCE: The Story of the First Butterflies (*Book of Nature Myths*).

SLY, W. R.: The Prince Who Hated Spiders and Flies (*World Stories Retold*).

June

Baldwin, James: The Boy and the Wolf, Another Bird Story, Speaking a Piece (*Fifty Famous People*).

Bryant, Sara Cone: Epaminondas and His Auntie (*How to Tell Stories to Children*).

Bryce, C. T.: The Four-Leaf Clover (*That's Why Stories*).

Grimm, Jacob: The Valiant Little Tailor, Snow White and the Seven Dwarfs (*German Household Tales*).

O'Grady, Alice: The Hop-About Man (*The Story-Teller's Book*).

Partridge, E. N. and G. E.: The Story of Harriet Ann, The Fox and the Crab, The Fairy Bird (*Story-Telling in the Home and School*).

Third Grade

September

Baldwin, James: Coco (*Second Fairy Reader*); Writing a Composition (Longfellow), The Whistle (Franklin), the Ettrick Shepherd (James Hogg) (*Fifty Famous People*).

Cabot, Ella L.: How Little Cedric Became a Knight, The Boy Who Wanted to Learn Climbing Alone, Hans, the Shepherd Boy (*Ethics for Children*).

Grimm, Jacob: The Little Flower Pot, Snow White and Rose Red (*German Household Tales*).

Holbrook, Florence: Why the Peacock's Tail Has a Thousand Eyes (*A Book of Nature Myths*).

Sly, W. R.: The Flood of Waters (*World Stories Retold*).

October

Baldwin, James: The Garden of Delight (*Old Stories of the East*); The Caliph and the Poet, Becos! Becos! Becos! (*Fifty Famous People*).

Bryant, Sara Cone: The Nightingale, The Burning of the Rice Fields (*How to Tell Stories to Children*).

Harrison, Elizabeth: Christopher Columbus (*In Story Land*).

Miller, Mrs. H.: How the Crow Baby Was Punished (*True Bird Stories*).

Nixon-Roulet, Mary F.: A Painter of Cats (*Japanese Folk Stories*).

Pumphrey, M. B.: The Jack o' Lantern (*Pilgrim Stories*).

SCUDDER, HORACE E.: The Wolves and the Sheep (*Fables and Folk Stories*).

The Story of Columbus (*Stepping Stones to Literature — Book 3*).

November

BAILEY, C. S., and LEWIS, C. M.: The Story of the First Corn, Little Cosette (*The Children's Hour*).

BALDWIN, JAMES: Sir Walter Raleigh (*Fifty Famous Stories Retold*); A Lesson in Humility (Haroun-al-Raschid), Another World Story (Israel Putnam), The Horseshoe Nails (*Fifty Famous People*).

HOLBROOK, FLORENCE: How Fire Was Brought to the Indians (*Book of Nature Myths*).

JORDAN, DAVID STARR: How the Flounder's Mouth Got Twisted (*The Book of Knight and Barbara*).

MACMANUS, SEUMAS: The Long Leather Bag (*Donegal Fairy Book*).

NIXON-ROULET, M. F.: The Goddess of Growing Things (*Japanese Folk Stories*).

PUMPHREY, M. B.: The First Thanksgiving (*Pilgrim Stories*).

SCHAUFFLER, R. H.: Grandma's Thanksgiving Story (*Book of Thanksgiving*).

WIGGIN, K. D., and SMITH, N. A.: The First Thanksgiving Day (*The Story Hour*).

December

ALDEN, R. M.: In the Great Walled Country (*Why the Chimes Rang*).

BALDWIN, JAMES: Bruce and the Spider (*Fifty Famous Stories Retold*); The Landlord's Mistake (*Fifty Famous People*).

DICKINSON, A. D., and SKINNER, A. M.: A Little Girl's Christmas (*Children's Book of Christmas Stories*).

HEBER, ELIZABETH: A Christmas Story, The First Christmas Tree (*A Child's Story Garden*).

JACOBS, JOSEPH: Cap o' Rushes (*English Fairy Tales*).

JORDAN, DAVID STARR: The Boy That Whacked the Witched Toad Stools (*The Book of Knight and Barbara*).

LINDSAY, MAUD: The Christmas Cake (*More Mother Stories*).

PARTRIDGE, E. N. and G. E.: Little Paulina's Christmas (*Story-Telling in the Home and School*).

Little Gretchen and the Wooden Shoe (*Storytellers' Magazine*, December, 1914).

The Christmas Visitor (*Storytellers' Magazine*, December, 1913).

January

BALDWIN, JAMES: The Shepherd Boy Painter, Two Great Painters, The King and the Bees, Our First Great Painter (*Fifty Famous People*); Peter Woodland (*American Book of Golden Deeds*); The Two Brothers (*Old Stories of the East*).

CABOT, ELLA L.: The Quails (*Ethics for Children*).

FARMER, J. F. V.: How Jean Found the Calf (*Boy and Girl Heroes*).

GRIMM, JACOB: Old Sultan (*German Household Tales*).

HOLBROOK, FLORENCE: The Story of the First Moles (*A Book of Nature Myths*).

PERRAULT, CHARLES: Beauty and the Beast (*Fairy Tales*).

SCUDDER, H. E.: The Stag at Stake (*Fables and Folk Stories*).

February

BALDWIN, JAMES: The Young Scout, The Lad Who Rode Sidesaddle (*Fifty Famous People*).

BRYANT, SARA CONE: The Jackal and the Camel (*How to Tell Stories to Children*).

CABOT, ELLA L.: Lincoln's Unvarying Kindness (*Ethics for Children*).

DAVIS, M. H., and CHOW-LEUNG: The Eagle and the Rice Birds (*Chinese Fables and Folk Stories*).

HARRIS, J. C.: How Brer Bear's Hair was Combed (*Little Mr. Thimble-finger*).

HOLBROOK, FLORENCE: The Lantern and the Fan (*A Book of Nature Myths*).

JACOBS, JOSEPH: Jack and the Golden Snuff Box (*English Fairy Tales*).

OLCOTT, F. J.: George Washington and the Colt (*Good Stories for Great Holidays*).

SCUDDER, HORACE E.: The Fair One with the Golden Locks (*The Children's Book*); The Four Bulls and the Lion (*Fables and Folk Stories*); An Old Man and His Sons (*Fables and Folk Stories*).

WILSON: The Virginia Boy (*Nature Study — Book 2*).

March

ANDERSEN, H. C.: The Loveliest Rose in the World (*Good Stories for Great Holidays*).

BALDWIN, JAMES: The Whisperers, How a Prince Learned to Read, Read and You Will Know, The Young Cupbearer (*Fifty Famous People*).

CABOT, ELLA L.: The Broken Flower Pot (*Ethics for Children*).

HARRIS, J. C.: The Grandmother of the Dolls (*Little Mr. Thimblefinger*).

HEBER, ELIZABETH: The Song of the Pine Tree (*A Child's Story Garden*).

JORDAN, DAVID STARR: Why the Parrot Was so Strong (*The Book of Knight and Barbara*).

MILLER, MRS. H.: My First Bird (*True Bird Stories*).

OLCOTT, F. J.: A Lesson of Faith (*Good Stories for Great Holidays*).

SLY, W. R.: The Generous Uncle and the Selfish Nephew (*World Stories Retold*).

STEVENSON, MRS. E. S.: The White Hare (*Days and Deeds*).

WIGGIN, K. D., and SMITH, N. A.: The Emperor's Bird's Nest (*The Fairy Ring*).

April

BALDWIN, JAMES: The Sons of the Caliph, The Boy and the Robbers (*Fifty Famous People*); The Bell of Atri (*Fifty Famous Stories Retold*).

BRYANT, SARA CONE: The Tailor and the Three Beasts (*Stories to Tell to Children*).

COWLES, J. D.: The Queen's Necklace (*The Art of Story-Telling*).

DAVIS, M. H., and CHOW-LEUNG: The Mule and the Lion, The Fish and the Flowers (*Chinese Fables and Folk Stories*).

FARMER, J. F. V.: A Brave Russian Girl (*Boy and Girl Heroes*).

LYMAN, EDNA: The Princess Moonbeam, The Boastful Bamboo, The Mirror of Matsuyama (*Story-Telling: What to Tell and How to Tell It*).

MILLER, MRS. H.: Doctor Dot, How the Dog Interfered (*True Bird Stories*).

May

BALDWIN, JAMES: A Clever Slave, The Story of a Great Story, The King and the Page, Why He Carried the Turkey, The Caliph and the Gardener, Saved by a Dolphin, The General and the Fox (*Fifty Famous People*).

DAVIS, M. H., and CHOW-LEUNG: The Wind, the Clouds, and the Snow (*Chinese Fables and Folk Stories*).

JUDD, M. C.: The Legend of the Arbutus (*Wigwam Stories*).

JUDSON, K. B.: The Miser of Takhoma (*Myths and Legends of the Pacific Northwest*).

LYMAN, EDNA: The White Hare and the Crocodiles, The Tongue-Cut Sparrow (*Story-Telling: What to Tell and How to Tell It*).

NIXON-ROULET, MARY F.: Princess Moonbeam (*Japanese Folk Stories*).
SCUDDER, HORACE E.: Clever Alice (*Fables and Folk Stories*).
SLY, W. R.: The Shepherd Boy Who Slew a Giant (*World Stories Retold*).

June

BALDWIN, JAMES: The Cowherd Who Became a Poet, The Lover of Men, The Charcoal Man and the King (*Fifty Famous People*).
BLUMENTHAL, VERRA X. K. DE: The Tsarevna Frog, Seven Simeons, The Language of Birds (*Folk Tales from the Russian*).
ENGLISH, THOMAS: The Ax of Ranier, The Black Cat (*Fairy Stories and Wonder Tales*).
GRIMM, JACOB: The Three Little Men in the Wood, The Three Languages, The Little Farmer (*German Household Tales*).
NIXON-ROULET, M. F.: The Boastful Bamboo (*Japanese Folk Stories*).
POULSSON, EMILIE: Knut Spelevink, The Princess Lindagull, Sikku and the Trolls, Sampo Lappelil (*Top of the World Series*).

FOURTH GRADE

September

BALDWIN, JAMES: The Great Chief (*Old Stories of the East*); The Charcoal Man and the King (*Fifty Famous People*).
BROWN, A. L., and BELL, J. M.: Why the White Bear Lives Alone (*Tales of the Red Children*).
BRYANT, SARA CONE: The Castle of Fortune (*Stories to Tell to Children*).
CABOT, ELLA L: The Two Travelers (*Ethics for Children*).
CATHER, KATHERINE DUNLAP: Pan and His Pipes (*Pan and His Pipes and Other Stories*).
GRIMM, JACOB: Six Soldiers of Fortune, The Little House in the Wood, The Three Trades (*German Household Tales*).
LANG, ANDREW: The Fisherman and His Wife (*Green Fairy Book*).
RAMASWAMI RAJU: The Hammer and the Anvil (*Indian Fables*).
DE LA RAMÉE, L.: The Nürnberg Stove (WIGGIN and SMITH: *The Story Hour*).

October

BALDWIN, JAMES: The Master of the Nile (*Old Stories of the East*); Partners (*American Book of Golden Deeds*); Which Was King? (*Fifty Famous People*).

BRYANT, SARA CONE: Why the Water in Rivers Is Never Still (*How to Tell Stories to Children*).

CABOT, ELLA L.: The Jack o' Lantern (*Ethics for Children*).

CATHER, KATHERINE DUNLAP: The Tortoise That Gave the World Music (*Pan and His Pipes and Other Stories*).

HARRIS, J. C.: The Witch of the Well (*Little Mr. Thimblefinger*).

JACOBS, JOSEPH: Mr. Fox (*English Fairy Tales*).

LANG, ANDREW: The Story of Caliph Stork (*Green Fairy Book*).

MABIE, H. W.: The Badger's Money (*Folk Tales Every Child Should Know*).

OLCOTT, F. J.: Shippeitaro, Burg's Hill's on Fire, The King of Cats (*Good Stories for Great Holidays*).

November

ALDEN, R. M.: The Knights of the Silver Shield (*Why the Chimes Rang*).

BALDWIN, JAMES: The Golden Tripod (*Fifty Famous People*).

CATHER, KATHERINE DUNLAP: The Holy Bird (*Story of Music in China — Pan and His Pipes and Other Stories*).

DAUDET, ALPHONSE: The Last Lesson (*How to Tell Stories to Children*).

HARRIS, J. C.: Brer Terrapin's Fiddle String (*Little Mr. Thimblefinger*).

HOWELLS, W. D.: Turkeys Turning the Tables (*Christmas Every Day*).

JUDD, M. C.: The Marriage of Mondahmin (*Wigwam Stories*).

LANG, ANDREW: Rosanella (*Green Fairy Book*).

MACMANUS, SEUMAS: Manis, the Miller (*Donegal Fairy Tales*).

SCHAUFFLER, R. H. (Ed.): The First Thanksgiving Day in New England, Jericho Bob, Ann Mary's Two Thanksgivings, Polly's Thanksgiving (*Thanksgiving*).

SLY, W. R.: The Little Lame Prince (*World Stories Retold*).

ZITKALA-SA: The Badger and the Bear (*Old Indian Legends*).

December

ANDERSEN, H. C.: The Little Match Girl (*Fairy Tales*).

BRYANT, SARA CONE: Fulfilled (*How to Tell Stories to Children*).

CATHER, KATHERINE DUNLAP: A Star and a Song, The Harp King Alfred Played (*Pan and His Pipes and Other Stories*).

COOLIDGE: Little Roger's Night in Church (SCHAUFFLER: *Christmas*).

DAVIS, M. H., and CHOW-LEUNG: The Proud Fox and the Crab, How the Moon Became Beautiful (*Chinese Fables and Folk Stories*).

DICKENS, CHARLES: The Christmas Goose at the Cratchits' (SCHAUFFLER: *Christmas*).

DODGE, M. M.: The Festival of St. Nicholas (SCHAUFFLER: *Christmas*).

MILLER, MRS. H.: Christmas in a Baggage Car, Lottie's Christmas Tree (*Kristy's Rainy Day Picnics*).

OLCOTT, F. J.: The Christmas Cuckoo (*Good Stories for Great Holidays*).

POULSSON, EMILIE: A Legend of Mercy (*Top of the World Series*).

STEIN, EVALEEN: Felix (*Troubadour Tales*).

January

CABOT, ELLA L., The Good Bishop, The Banyan Deer (*Ethics for Children*).

CATHER, KATHERINE DUNLAP: Stephen, the Child Crusader (*Pan and His Pipes and Other Stories*).

COWLES, J. D.: Robin Hood and Sir Richard at Lee, King Midas' Ears (*The Art of Story-Telling*).

DAVIS, M. H., and CHOW-LEUNG: The Melon and the Professor (*Chinese Fables and Folk Stories*).

FARMER, J. F. V.: Roland and the Jewel, David, the Brave Shepherd Boy (*Boy and Girl Heroes*).

JUDD, M. C.: The Face of Manitou on the Rock (*Wigwam Stories*).

MACMANUS, SEUMAS: Conal, Donal, and Taig (*Donegal Fairy Tales*).

PARTRIDGE, E. N. and G. E.: The Judgment Seat of Vikramaditya (*Story-Telling in the Home and School*).

POULSSON, EMILIE: The Testing of the Two Knights (*Top of the World Stories*).

February

BROWN, A. L., and BELL, J. M.,: The Cleft Mountain (*Tales of the Red Children*).

CABOT, ELLA L.: A Soldier's Pardon, The Sympathy of Abraham Lincoln (*Ethics for Children*).

CATHER, KATHERINE DUNLAP: When Knighthood Was in Flower (*Pan and His Pipes and Other Stories*).

DAVIS, M. H., and CHOW-LEUNG: The Children and the Dog (*Chinese Fables and Folk Stories*).

FARMER, J. F. V.: At the Ford of the Tribute (*Boy and Girl Heroes*).

GRIMM, JACOB: Jorinda and Joringel (*German Household Tales*).

LANG, ANDREW: The War Horse of Alexander (*The Animal Story Book*).

MOORE, CHARLES W.: A Backwoods Boyhood (*Abraham Lincoln*).
POULSSON, EMILIE: The Forest Witch (*Top of the World Stories*).
TAPPAN, EVA M.: Dolly Madison (*American Hero Stories*); How Cats Came to Purr (*Cat Stories Retold from St. Nicholas*).

March

BOYESEN, H. H.: Thorwald and the Star Children (*Modern Vikings*).
BRYANT, SARA CONE: The Dagada's Harp (*Stories to Tell to Children*).
CATHER, KATHERINE DUNLAP: The Violin Makers of Cremona (*Pan and His Pipes and Other Stories*).
FARMER, J. F. V.: Noel Duval, How a Boy Saved a Queen, The Sword of King Arthur (*Boy and Girl Heroes*).
KOROLENKO, Z.: Hot Cross Buns (*The Book of Easter*).
PARTRIDGE, E. N. and G. E.: Glooscap and the Great Wind Bird (*Story-Telling in the Home and School*).
RAMASWAMI RAJU: The Workman and the Trees (*Indian Fables*).
SLY, W. R.: Grace Darling, The Slave Girl Who Helped a Great Captain (*World Stories Retold*).

April

BLUMENTHAL, VERRA X. K. DE: Ivanoushka the Simpleton, Woe Bogotir, Baba Yaga, Dimian the Peasant, The Golden Mountain (*Folk Tales from the Russian*).
CATHER, KATHERINE DUNLAP: The Songs of Hiawatha (*Pan and His Pipes and Other Stories*).
FARMER, J. F. V.: The Young Hannibal (*Boy and Girl Heroes*).
LANG, ANDREW: Cowper's Hares (*The Animal Story Book*).
OLCOTT, F. J.: The Boy Who Became a Robin, The Quails, The Greedy Geese (*Good Stories for Great Holidays*).
PARTRIDGE, E. N. and G. E.: The Ride of Paul Revere (*Story-Telling in the Home and School*).

May

BALDWIN, JAMES: Androclus and the Lion (*Fifty Famous Stories Retold*).
CATHER, KATHERINE DUNLAP: The Holy Grail (*Pan and His Pipes and Other Stories*).
COWLES, J. D.: The Coming of Arthur (*The Art of Story-Telling*).
DAVIS, M. H., and CHOW-LEUNG: The Thief and the Elephant, The Hen and the Mountain Turtle (*Chinese Fables and Folk Stories*).

HARRISON, ELIZABETH: The Story of Decoration Day (*In Story Land*).
HOLBROOK, FLORENCE: The Story of the First Mocking Bird (*Book of Nature Myths*).
OLCOTT, F. J.: The Wonder Tree, The Blue Jay (*Good Stories for Great Holidays*).
STEVENSON, MRS. E. S.: The Origin of Memorial Day (*Days and Deeds*).
A Rat Tale (*Cat Stories Retold from St. Nicholas*).

June

BROWN, A. J., and BELL, J. M.: The Story of Ithenhiels (*Tales of the Red Children*).
FARMER, J. F. V.: Betty Lane (*Boy and Girl Heroes*).
PRICE, L. L.: The Legs of Duncan Ketcham (*Lads and Lassies of Other Days*).
SLY, W. R.: The Emperor and the Goose Boy, Betsy Ross and the Flag, How America was Named, The Fairy Godfather of the Orchards (*World Stories Retold*).
TAPPAN, E. M.: The Star-Spangled Banner, A Flag Incident, General Scott and the Stars and Stripes (*Good Stories for Great Holidays*).

FIFTH GRADE

September

BALDWIN, JAMES: Ezekiel and Daniel (*American Book of Golden Deeds*); The Forging of Balmung (*Hero Tales*).
BROWN, ABBIE F.: The Dwarf Giants (*In the Days of Giants*).
EASTMAN, C. A. and E.: The Buffalo and the Field Mouse (*Smoky Day's Wigwam Evenings*).
HARRIS, J. C.: Mr. Fox and Miss Goose (*Nights with Uncle Remus*).
JACOBS, JOSEPH: Master of All Masters (*English Fairy Tales*).
JUDD, M. C.: Wampum, or Indian Money (*Wigwam Stories*).
KINGSLEY, CHARLES: How They Built the Good Ship Argo in Icolos (*Greek Heroes*).
KIPLING, RUDYARD: Mowgli's Brothers (*Jungle Book*).
Bessie's Escape (*Panther Stories Retold from St. Nicholas*).

October

BALDWIN, JAMES: Columbus and the Egg (*Thirty More Famous Stories*); The Tombs Angel (*American Book of Golden Deeds*).

EASTMAN, C. A. and E.: The Frogs and the Crane (*Smoky Day's Wigwam Evenings*).

HIGGINSON, T. W.: How Diego Mendez Got Food for Columbus (*American Explorers*).

IRVING, WASHINGTON: Columbus at La Rabida (OLCOTT: *Good Stories for Great Holidays*).

JACOBS, JOSEPH: The Field Boliauns (*Celtic Fairy Tales*).

KIPLING, RUDYARD: Kaa's Hunting (*Jungle Book*).

LAMARTINE, DE: The Mutiny (OLCOTT: *Good Stories for Great Holidays*).

MILLER, JOAQUIN: A Bear on Fire (*True Bear Stories*).

MOORE, CHARLES W.: Guanahani (*Christopher Columbus*).

Bertholde (*Stories of the Middle Ages Retold from St. Nicholas*).

November

BALDWIN, JAMES: The Red Cross (*American Book of Golden Deeds*).

GRIMM, JACOB: The Robber Bridegroom, The Youth Who Could Not Shiver nor Shake (*German Household Tales*).

KIPLING, RUDYARD: How Fear Came (*First Jungle Book*).

PUMPHREY, M. B.: The Indians and the Jack o' Lantern, The Sword of Miles Standish, The Voyage of the Mayflower, Water Babies (*Pilgrim Stories*).

PYLE, HOWARD: How Robin Hood Became an Outlaw (*Some Merry Adventures of Robin Hood*).

WARNER, C. D.: The Coming of Thanksgiving (*Being a Boy*).

An Old-Time Thanksgiving (*Indian Stories Retold from St. Nicholas*).

The Story of the Sphinx (*Stories of the Ancient World Retold from St. Nicholas*).

December

BALDWIN, JAMES: Damon and Pythias (*Fifty Famous Stories Retold*).

KIPLING, RUDYARD: The Red Flower (*Jungle Book*).

OLCOTT, F. J.: The Thunder Oak (*Good Stories for Great Holidays*).

PYLE, HOWARD: Robin Hood's Adventure with the Tinker, The Sheriff's Shooting Match (*Some Merry Adventures of Robin Hood*).

STEIN, EVALEEN: Felix (*Troubadour Tales*).

STOCKTON, FRANK R.: Christmas before Last (*The Bee Man of Orn*).

WALSH, K.: St. Nicholas and the Robbers (*The Story of Santa Claus*).

WILDE, OSCAR: The Star-Child (*The Happy Prince*).

How Uncle Sam Observes Christmas (*Our Holidays Retold from St. Nicholas*).

The First Christmas Tree in New England (*Colonial Stories Retold from St. Nicholas*).

January

BALDWIN, JAMES: The Bootblack from Ann Street (*American Book of Golden Deeds*).

BRYANT, SARA CONE: The Red Thread of Courage (*How to Tell Stories*).

CABOT, ELLA LYMAN: The Persian and His Three Sons (*Ethics for Children*).

HARRIS, J. C.: Brer Fox Catches Brer Rabbit (*Nights with Uncle Remus*).

HOLLAND, R. S.: The Boys of Devon (*Historic Boyhoods*).

KIPLING, RUDYARD: Tiger! Tiger! (*The Jungle Book*).

MILLER, JOAQUIN: Music-Loving Bears (*True Bear Stories*).

PYLE, HOWARD: Robin Hood Saves Will Sutley's Life, The Sheriff's Visit to Robin Hood (*Some Merry Adventures of Robin Hood*).

The Boyhood of Michelangelo (*Stories of the Middle Ages Retold from St. Nicholas*).

February

BALDWIN, JAMES: Following the Surveyor's Chain (*Fifty Famous People*); The Great Law-Giver (*Old Stories of the East*).

BRYANT, SARA CONE: David and Goliath (*Stories to Tell to Children*).

KIPLING, RUDYARD: Letting in the Jungle (*Second Jungle Book*).

OLCOTT, F. J.: Young George Washington and the Colt (*Good Stories for Great Holidays*).

SCHAUFFLER, R. H.: Choosing Abe Lincoln Captain (*Lincoln's Birthday*).

TOMLINSON, EVERETT: How George Washington Was Made Commander in Chief (*The War for Independence*).

A New Leaf from Washington's Boy Life (*Colonial Stories Retold from St. Nicholas*).

How Moses Was Emancipated (*Civil War Stories Retold from St. Nicholas*).

March

BALDWIN, JAMES: The Story of Regulus (*Fifty Famous Stories Retold*).

BRYANT, SARA CONE: Tarpeia (*How to Tell Stories to Children*).

CATHER, KATHERINE DUNLAP: When Mozart Raced with Marie Antoinette (*Boyhood Stories*).

EASTMAN, C. A. and E.: The Falcon and the Duck (*Smoky Day's Wigwam Evenings*).

HARRIS, J. C.: How Brer Fox Was Too Smart (*Nights with Uncle Remus*).

KIPLING, RUDYARD: Red Dog (*Second Jungle Book*).

PYLE, HOWARD: Robin Hood and His Men before Queen Eleanor (*Some Merry Adventures of Robin Hood*).

SCHMIDT, CANON: The Easter Eggs.

The Fire Cat (*Panther Stories Retold from St. Nicholas*).

The General's Easter Box (*Our Holidays Retold from St. Nicholas*).

April

BALDWIN, JAMES: Ogier the Dane (*The Story of Roland*); Grace Darling, Alfred the Great (*Fifty Famous Stories Retold*).

BOLTON, S. K.: Garibaldi (*Lives of Poor Boys Who Became Famous*).

HARRIS, J. C.: Brer Rabbit's Astonishing Prank (*Nights with Uncle Remus*).

JACOBS, JOSEPH: Hudden and Dudden and Donald O'Neary (*Celtic Fairy Tales*).

KIPLING, RUDYARD: The Spring Running (*Second Jungle Book*).

PYLE, HOWARD: Robin Hood and Guy of Gisbourne (*Some Merry Adventures of Robin Hood*).

SETON, ERNEST THOMPSON: Monarch, the Big Bear of Tallac.

STOCKTON, FRANK R.: Old Pipes and the Dryad (LYMAN: *Story-Telling, What to Tell and How to Tell It*).

May

BALDWIN, JAMES: The Man Whose Eye Was Open (*Old Stories of the East*); La Salle (*The Discovery of the Old Northwest*); Ogier and Roland Knighted, How Ogier Won Sword and Horse, A Roland for an Oliver (*The Story of Roland*).

CATHER, KATHERINE DUNLAP: How a Boy Saved Lucerne, The Duty That Wasn't Paid.

OLCOTT, F. J.: The Legend of the Spring Beauty, The Fairy Tulips, Two Hero Stories of the Civil War (*Good Stories for Great Holidays*).

PYLE, HOWARD: The Death of Robin Hood (*Some Merry Adventures of Robin Hood*).

June

BALDWIN, JAMES: How Ogier Refused a Kingdom (*The Story of Roland*); William Tell (*Fifty Famous Stories Retold*); The Heroine of Fort Henry (*American Book of Golden Deeds*).

BROOKS, E. S.: William the Conqueror (*Historic Boys*).

CABOT, ELLA LYMAN: Margaret of New Orleans (*Ethics for Children*).
CATHER, KATHERINE DUNLAP: The Luck Boat of Lake Geneva.
OLCOTT, F. J.: General Scott and the Stars and Stripes (*Good Stories for Great Holidays*).
SLY, W. J.: Betsy Ross and the Flag (*World Stories Retold*).

SIXTH GRADE

September

BROWN, ABBIE F.: The Giant Builder (*In the Days of Giants*).
CABOT, ELLA LYMAN: David and Jonathan (*Ethics for Children*).
JUDD, M. C.: The Legend of Niagara Falls (*Wigwam Stories*).
KIPLING, RUDYARD: Weland's Sword (*Puck of Pook's Hill*).
LANG, JEANIE: The Story of General Gordon.
OLCOTT, F. J.: Bill Brown's Test, The Speaking Statue, The Champion Stone Cutter (*Good Stories for Great Holidays*).
RAGOZIN, Z. A.: Beowulf Comes to Daneland (*Siegfried and Beowulf*).
RHEAD, J. S.: The Story of the Fisherman (*Arabian Nights*).
TOLSTOÏ, LEO: Truth is Mighty and Will Prevail (CABOT: *Ethics for Children*).

October

GRIMM, JACOB: The Godfather (*German Household Tales*).
HARRIS, J. C.: Brer Rabbit Takes Exercise (*Nights with Uncle Remus*).
HAWTHORNE, NATHANIEL: Pandora (*Wonder-Book*).
IRVING, WASHINGTON: The Discovery of Land (*Life of Christopher Columbus*).
PERRY, E. L., and BEEBE, KATHERINE: George Rogers Clark (*Four American Pioneers*).
RAGOZIN, Z. A.: The Combat with Grendel (*Siegfried and Beowulf*).
RHEAD, J. S.: Abou Mohammed the Lazy (*Arabian Nights*).
TOLSTOÏ, LEO: Where Love Is, There God Is Also (CABOT: *Ethics for Children*).
All Hallow Eve Myths (*Our Holidays Retold from St. Nicholas*).
For additional Columbus Day material see "The Son of Columbus" by Mollie Elliot Seawell.

November

BRADLEY, WILL: Hans the Wise, Nip and Tuck (*The Wonder Box*).
BROWN, ABBIE F.: The Magic Apples (*In the Days of Giants*).
HARRIS, J. C.: Brer Wolf Says Grace (*Nights with Uncle Remus*).

OLCOTT, F. J.: The Ears of Wheat, How Indian Corn Came into the World (*Good Stories for Great Holidays*).

PUMPHREY, M. B.: Samoset, The Treaty of Peace, The Little Captives (*Pilgrim Stories*).

RAGOZIN, Z. A.: Grendel Avenged, Beowulf Returns to His Own Land (*Siegfried and Beowulf*).

RHEAD, J. S.: Abou Hassan the Wag (*Arabian Nights*).

December

DICKENS, CHARLES: Christmas at Fezziwig's Warehouse (SCHAUFFLER: *Christmas*).

DYER, WALTER: The Baby Camel That Walked to Jesus.

LAGERLÖF, SELMA: The Holy Night (*Christ Legends*).

PUMPHREY, M. B.: The Christmas Candle (*Pilgrim Stories*).

RAGOZIN, Z. A.: Beowulf's Victory and Death (*Siegfried and Beowulf*).

RICE, ALICE HEGAN: Betty's Best Christmas (*St. Nicholas*, December, 1916).

SKINNER, CHARLES M.: The Legend of the Mountain Ash (*Myths of Plants, Trees, and Flowers*).

TOLSTOÏ, LEO: Evil Allures but Good Endures (CABOT: *Ethics for Children*).

WALSH, K.: St. Nicholas and the Slave Boy (*The Story of Santa Claus*).

January

BRADLEY, WILL: Snip and Stitch (*The Wonder Box*).

CABOT, ELLA LYMAN: A Lesson for Kings (*Ethics for Children*).

EGGLESTON, EDWARD: The Troublesome Burglars (*Strange Stories from History*).

JUDD, M. C.: How Indians Came to Know Medicine Plants (*Wigwam Stories*).

MACLEOD, R.: A Great Feast and a Great Battle, The Marriage of Guinevere and Arthur and the Founding of the Round Table (*King Arthur and His Noble Knights*).

SLY, W. R.: The Golden Scepter in the Palace of the Lily (*World Stories Retold*).

STEVENSON, MRS. E. S.: A New Year's Talk (*Days and Deeds*).

STONE, G. L.: The Legend of the Oak (*Trees in Prose and Poetry*).

A Chinese New Year in California (*Our Holidays Retold from St. Nicholas*).

A Spanish Tale (*Fairy Stories Retold from St. Nicholas*).

February

BROOKS, E. S.: The Clary Grove Boys (*Abraham Lincoln*).

EGGLESTON, EDWARD: Young Washington in the Woods, How a Scullion Became a Sculptor (*Strange Stories from History*).

GALLAGHER, J. E.: Lincoln's Good Memory of Names (*Best Lincoln Stories*).

MACLEOD, R.: King Arthur and Sir Accalon, How King Arthur Fought with a Giant (*King Arthur and His Noble Knights*).

MOORE, CHARLES W.: Lincoln and the Unjust Client (*Abraham Lincoln*).

OLCOTT, F. J.: Washington at Yorktown (*Good Stories for Great Holidays*).

March

BALDWIN, JAMES: King Richard and Blondel (*Thirty More Famous Stories*).

BRADLEY, WILL: The Master Makes a Bargain (*The Wonder Box*).

EGGLESTON, EDWARD: The Prince Who Could Not Stay Dead (*Strange Stories from History*).

HAUFF, WILHELM: The Peddler and the Powder (*Caravan Tales*).

HOLLAND, R. S.: Daniel Boone (*Historic Boyhoods*).

MACLEOD, R.: Sir Brune, Sir Ivaine (*King Arthur and His Noble Knights*).

MARDEN, O. S.: How the Children Saved Hamburg (*Winning Out*).

PRICE, L. L.: Abraham and Isaac (*Wandering Heroes*).

April

BALDWIN, JAMES: As Rich as Crœsus (*Thirty More Famous Stories*).

BROWN, ABBIE F.: Saint Kentigern and the Robin (*Book of Saints and Friendly Beasts*).

DICKENS, CHARLES: A Child's Dream of a Star (OLCOTT: *Good Stories for Great Holidays*).

EGGLESTON, EDWARD: The Story of Catherine (*Strange Stories from History*).

HAUFF, WILHELM: The Mystic Word (*Caravan Tales*).

HOLLAND, R. S.: Lafayette, the Boy of Versailles (*Historic Boyhoods*).

MACLEOD, R.: Sir Balin, Sir Gareth the Kitchen Boy (*King Arthur and His Noble Knights*).

PRICE, L. L.: Joseph (*Wandering Heroes*).

May

ANDERSEN, H. C.: The Daisy (*Wonder Stories Told to Children*).

EGGLESTON, EDWARD: The Sad Story of a Boy King (*Strange Stories from History*).

GILBERT, ARIADNE: Beloved of Men and Dogs (*More than Conquerors*).

HAUFF, WILHELM: The Captive Owl (*Caravan Tales*).

HAWTHORNE, NATHANIEL: The Pomegranate Seeds (*Tanglewood Tales*).

MACLEOD, R.: Sir Launcelot and His Friends, Sir Tristram, How Sir Tristram Came to Camelot (*King Arthur and His Noble Knights*).

STEVENSON, MRS. E. S.: The Origin of Memorial Day (*Days and Deeds*).

June

BALDWIN, JAMES: Webster and the Woodchuck (*Thirty More Famous Stories*); Cornelia's Jewels (*Fifty Famous Stories*).

HAUFF, WILHELM: The Hall of Sorcerers (*Caravan Tales*).

JORDAN, DAVID STARR: The Story of a Salmon.

JUDSON, KATHARINE B.: Why the Sierra Nevada is Higher than the Coast Range (*Myths of California and the Old Southwest*).

MACLEOD, R.: The Quest of the Holy Grail, The Death of King Arthur (*King Arthur and His Noble Knights*).

PRICE, L. L.: Moses (*Wandering Heroes*).

SEVENTH GRADE

September

AUSTIN, MARY: The Basket Woman.

BRADISH, SARAH P.: Sigmund Wins the Sword (*Old Norse Stories*).

BROWN, ABBIE F.: St. Bridget and the King's Wolf (*Book of Saints and Friendly Beasts*).

CABOT, ELLA LYMAN: The Risks of a Fireman's Life (*Ethics for Children*).

MARDEN, O. S.: The Blacksmith's Boy (*Winning Out*).

PRICE, L. L.: Prince Siddârtha (*Wandering Heroes*).

RHEAD, J. S.: The Voyages of Sindbad the Sailor (*Arabian Nights*).

STEVENSON, MRS. E. S.: History of Labor Day (*Days and Deeds*).

WARMAN, CY: Jack Farley's Flying Switch (*Short Rails*).

October

BRADISH, SARAH P.: Sigmund and Sinfiotli, The Death of Sigmund (*Old Norse Heroes*).

HOLLAND, R. S.: Peter the Great, the Boy of the Kremlin (*Historic Boyhoods*).

MOORE, CHARLES W.: In Search of the Grand Khan, The Garden of Eden (*Christopher Columbus*).

PRICE, L. L.: The First Battle of Cyrus the Great (*Wandering Heroes*).

RHEAD, J. S.: Coga Hassan (*Arabian Nights*).

STEVENSON, R. L.: Black Andie's Tale of Tod Lapraik (*David Balfour*).

STEVENSON, MRS. E. S.: The History of Hallowe'en.

November

ABBOTT, J. S. C.: The Humanity and Self-Denial of Miles Standish. The Visit of Samoset (*Miles Standish*).

BALDWIN, JAMES: John Gutenberg and the Voices, The First Printer (*Thirty More Famous Stories*).

BRADISH, SARAH P.: Regin's Story, Forging the Sword (*Old Norse Heroes*).

CATHER, KATHERINE DUNLAP: Jacopo, the Little Dyer (*Boyhood Stories of Famous Men*).

HOLLAND, R. S.: Frederick the Great, the Boy of Potsdam (*Historic Boyhoods*).

PRICE, L. L.: The Khan of the Silver Crown (*Wandering Heroes*).

December

AUSTIN, MARY: The Christmas Tree (*The Basket Woman*).

BRADISH, SARAH P.: Brynhild (*Old Norse Heroes*).

LAGERLÖF, SELMA: The Wise Men's Well (*Christ Legends*).

OLCOTT, F. J.: The Three Kings of Cologne (*Good Stories for Great Holidays*).

RHEAD, J. S.: Aladdin and the Wonderful Lamp (*Arabian Nights*).

RICHARDS, LAURA E.: Tomorrow (*The Golden Windows*).

WALSH, K.: St. Nicholas and the Three Purses (*The Story of Santa Claus*).

WIGGIN, K. D.: The Ruggles' Christmas Dinner (*The Birds' Christmas Carol*).

January

BALDWIN, JAMES: King John and Prince Arthur (*Thirty More Famous Stories*).

BOUTET DE MONVEL, L. M.: The Story of Joan of Arc (*Joan of Arc*).
BRADISH, SARAH P.: Sigurd and the Niblungs, The Wooing of Brynhild, The Death of Sigurd (*Old Norse Stories*).
HOLLAND, R. S.: John Paul Jones, the Boy of the Atlantic (*Historic Boyhoods*).
LAGERLÖF, SELMA: The Animals' New Year's Eve (*The Further Adventures of Nils*).
OLCOTT, F. J.: The Twelve Months (*Good Stories for Great Holidays*).
PRICE, L. L.: Clovis the Frank (*Wandering Heroes*).
RHEAD, J. S.: Ali Baba and the Forty Thieves (*Arabian Nights*).

February

BALDWIN, JAMES: King John and the Magna Charta (*Thirty More Famous Stories*).
DRAKE, S. A.: The Washington Elm (*New England Legends*).
GILBERT, ARIADNE: The Matterhorn of Men (*More than Conquerors*).
HOLLAND, R. S.: Mozart the Boy of Salzburg, George Washington the Boy of the Old Dominion (*Historic Boyhoods*).
LODGE, HENRY CABOT: He Resigns His Commission (*George Washington*, Vol. I, page 338).
OLCOTT, F. J.: The Courage of His Convictions (*Good Stories for Great Holidays*).
PRICE, L. L.: The Dwarf of Attila the Hun (*Wandering Heroes*).
SCHAUFFLER, R. H.: Anecdotes and Stories (*Washington's Birthday*).
TAPPAN, EVA M.: A Winter at Valley Forge (*American Hero Stories*).
WHIPPLE, WAYNE: Lincoln's First Dollar, A Feat of Mercy and Strength (*The Story Life of Lincoln*).

March

BALDWIN, JAMES: Frederick Barbarossa (*Thirty More Famous Stories*).
BROWN, ABBIE F.: Saint Wartburg and Her Goose (*Book of Saints and Friendly Beasts*).
GILBERT, ARIADNE: Beethoven, the Blind Musician (*More than Conquerors*).
HAWTHORNE, NATHANIEL: The Liberty Tree (*Grandfather's Chair*).
JACOBS, JOSEPH: The Dream of Owen Mulready (*More Celtic Fairy Tales*).
PRICE, L. L.: The Saga of the Land of Grapes (*Wandering Heroes*).
STEVENSON, MRS. E. S.: What Easter Is (*Days and Deeds*).
WIGGIN, K. D., and SMITH, NORA A.: The Lion, the Fox, and the Story-Teller (*Talking Beast Fables from India*).

April

AUSTIN, MARY: The Merry-go-Round (*The Basket Woman*).
BALDWIN, JAMES: The Man in the Iron Mask (*Thirty More Famous Stories*).
BROWN, ABBIE F.: Gerasimus and the Lion (*Book of Saints and Friendly Beasts*).
BURROUGHS, JOHN: The Downy Woodpecker (*Bird Stories*).
HARRIS, J. C.: Why the Hawk Catches Chickens (*Uncle Remus and His Friends*).
HOLLAND, R. S.: Horatio Nelson, the Boy of the Channel Fleet (*Historic Boyhoods*).
JACOBS, JOSEPH: Jack, the Cunning Thief (*More Celtic Fairy Tales*).
KOROLENKO, Z.: The Procession of Passion Week in Seville (*The Book of Easter*).
PRICE, L. L.: Godwin and Knut (*Wandering Heroes*).
SETON, ERNEST THOMPSON: Arnaux, the Chronicle of a Homing Pigeon (*Animal Heroes*).

May

AUSTIN, MARY: The Coyote Spirit and the Weaving Woman (*The Basket Woman*).
BALDWIN, JAMES: Hannibal, the Boy of Carthage (*Thirty More Famous Stories*).
DYER, WALTER A.: The Opening of the Eyes of Jasper (*The Richer Life*).
HARRIS, J. C.: Brer Bear and the Honey (*Uncle Remus and His Friends*).
HAWTHORNE, NATHANIEL: The May Pole at Merry Mount (*Twice Told Tales*).
HOLLAND, R. S.: Robert Fulton, the Boy of Conestoga (*Historic Boyhoods*).
LANSING, M. F.: Godfrey, a Knight of the Crusades (*Page, Esquire, and Knight*).
PARTRIDGE, E. N. and G. E.: The Boy Abraham (*Story-Telling in the Home and School*).
SCUDDER, HORACE E.: The Monk and the Bird (LYMAN: *Story-Telling: What to Tell and How to Tell It*).

June

BALDWIN, JAMES: Friar Bacon and the Brazen Head (*Thirty More Famous Stories*).
GILBERT, ARIADNE: The Star Showers Baby (*More than Conquerors*).

HARRIS, J. C.: Why Brer Bull Growls and Grumbles (*Uncle Remus and His Friends*).

HOLLAND, R. S.: Andrew Jackson, the Boy of the Carolinas (*Historic Boyhoods*).

JORDAN, DAVID STARR: Agassiz at Penikese, A Cuban Fisherman, How the Trout Came to California, The Story of a Strange Land, The Fate of Icodorum (*Science Stories*).

LANSING, M. F.: St. George and the Dragon (*Page, Esquire, and Knight*).

PHELPS, E. S.: David and Jonathan (*David and Jonathan*).

SLY, W. R.: The Heroine of Gettysburg, The Man Who Wrote "America," Jenny Lind, Singer (*World Stories Retold*).

The Story of the Star-Spangled Banner (*St. Nicholas*, June, 1914).

EIGHTH GRADE

September

BROOKS, E. S.: Helena of Britain (*Historic Girls*).

CATHER, KATHERINE DUNLAP: The Boy of Cadore, The Joyous Vagabond (*Boyhood Stories of Famous Men*).

CHAPIN, ANNA ALICE: Parsifal, a Knight of the Grail (*The Story of Parsifal*).

DYER, WALTER A.: The Vision of Anton the Clockmaker (*The Richer Life*).

HOLLAND, R. S.: Napoleon Bonaparte (*Historic Boyhoods*).

MACMANUS, SEUMAS: Billy Beg and His Bull (*In Chimney Corners*).

RENNINGER, E. D.: Rustem, the Wonder Child, Rustem, the Young Warrior (*The Story of Rustem*).

October

DICKENS, CHARLES: The Speaking Rat (*The Uncommercial Traveller*).

IRVING, WASHINGTON: The First Landing of Columbus in the New World, The Building of the Fortress La Navidad, Reception of Columbus by the Spanish Court at Barcelona, Columbus and His Brothers Arrested and Sent to Spain, The Death of Columbus (*Life and Voyages of Christopher Columbus*); The Devil and Tom Walker (*Tales of a Traveller*).

RENNINGER, E. D.: The Seven Labors of Rustem, Rustem the Pehliva (*The Story of Rustem*). (Omit the romance in this last tale.)

STEVENSON, R. L.: The Bottle Imp (*Island Nights' Entertainments*).

November

ABBOTT, J. S. C.: The Mother of Kidnapped Indians, The Search for Corn, The Shipwrecked Frenchmen (*Miles Standish*).

CATHER, KATHERINE DUNLAP: When Mozart Raced with Marie Antoinette (*Boyhood Stories of Famous Men*).

RENNINGER, E. D.: Sohrab and the Youth (*The Story of Rustem*).

SCHAUFFLER, R. H.: The Thanksgiving Guest, Two Notable Thanksgivings (*Thanksgiving*).

SCUDDER, HORACE E.: The Flying Dutchman, King Cophetua and the Beggar, The Image and the Treasure (*Book of Legends*).

December

BOUTET DE MONVEL, L. M.: The Girlhood of Joan of Arc and the Call of the Voices, Attack and Delivery of Orleans (*The Story of Joan of Arc*).

BROOKS, E. S.: Edith of Scotland (*Historic Girls*).

HARTE, BRET: How Santa Claus Came to Simpson's Bar (*The Luck of Roaring Camp*).

HUGO, VICTOR: Cosette (*Les Misérables*).

MACMANUS, SEUMAS: Shan Beth and Ned Flyn (*In Chimney Corners*).

OLCOTT, F. J.: The Christmas Fairy of Strasburg (*Good Stories for Great Holidays*).

RENNINGER, E. D.: The Wrath of Rustem, Combat of Sohrab against Rustem (*The Story of Rustem*).

STOCKTON, FRANK R.: The Christmas Truants (*Fanciful Tales*).

VAN DYKE, HENRY: The Mansion (*The Mansion*); The First Christmas Tree (*The First Christmas Tree*); The Other Wise Man (*The Other Wise Man*).

WALLACE, LEW: The Journey of the Magi (*Ben Hur*).

January

CHURCH, ALFRED J.: The Adventure of Ulysses with the Cyclops, The Home of the Winds and the Palace of Circe, The Sirens, Scylla and Charybdis, What Happened in Ithaca, An Island Prison, A Princess Washing Clothes, Ulysses at Home (*Odyssey for Boys and Girls*).

GUERBER, H. A.: Charlemagne Blessing the Vineyards (*Legends of the Rhine*. Use also the poem, The Silver Bridge, in the same book).

SLY, W. R.: Horatius at the Bridge (*World Stories Retold*. Use also Macaulay's poem).

February

Cather, Katherine Dunlap: A Shepherd Lad of Tuscany, The Light of Guido's Lamp, A Bit o' Pink Verbena (*Boyhood Stories of Famous Men*).

Higginson, T. W.: The Story of Atlantis, Taliessin of the Radiant Bow (*Tales of the Enchanted Islands of the Atlantic*).

Holland, R. S.: James Fenimore Cooper (*Historic Boyhoods*).

Lodge, Henry Cabot: The British at Mount Vernon (*George Washington*, Vol. I, page 295); Washington Offered the Supreme Power (*George Washington*, Vol. I, page 328).

Olcott, F. J.: Training for the Presidency, George Picket's Friend (*Good Stories for Great Holidays*).

Rhead, J. S.: Adventures of Haroun al Raschid (*Arabian Nights*).

Stockton, Frank R.: The Clocks of Rondaine (*Fanciful Tales*).

March

Baldwin, James: Eureka (*Thirty More Famous Stories*).

Boutet de Monvel, L. M.: Joan's Trial and Death (*Joan of Arc*).

Brooks, E. S.: Woo of Hwang Ho (*Historic Girls*).

Cabot, Ella L.: Florence Nightingale (*Ethics for Children*).

Holland, R. S.: John Ericsson, the Boy of the Gotha Canal (*Historic Boyhoods*).

Korolenko, Z.: Easter Eve (*The Book of Easter*).

Renninger, E. D.: How Rustem Trained Saiwush and Avenged Him, The Later Feats of Rustem (*The Story of Rustem*).

Stevenson, Mrs. E. S.: What Easter Is (*Days and Deeds*).

April

Brooks, E. S.: Christina of Sweden (*Historic Girls*).

Burroughs, John: The House Wren, The Screech Owl, The Song Sparrow (*Bird Stories*).

Gould, F. J.: Why the Romans Bore Pain, The Second Founder of Rome (*The Children's Plutarch*).

Higginson, T. W.: The Swan Children of Lir, Usheen in the Island of Youth, Bran the Blessed (*Tales of the Enchanted Islands of the Atlantic*).

Holland, R. S.: Garibaldi, the Boy of the Mediterranean (*Historic Boyhoods*).

Lansing, M. F.: Chevalier Bayard (*Page, Esquire, and Knight*).

MacManus, Seumas: Rory the Robber (*In Chimney Corners*).
Renninger, E. D.: The Story of Isfendiyar, The Death of Rustem (*The Story of Rustem*).

May

Austin, Mary: The Stream That Ran Away (Olcott: *Good Stories for Great Holidays*).
Cabot, Ella L.: The Fight against Yellow Fever (*Ethics for Children*).
Cather, Katherine Dunlap: The Tomboy from Bordeaux (*Boyhood Stories of Famous Men*).
Gilbert, Ariadne: Through Failure to Success (*More than Conquerors*).
Gould, F. J.: The Man Who Waited (*The Children's Plutarch*).
Higginson, T. W.: The Castle of the Active Door, Maeldun's Voyage, The Voyage of St. Brandon, Harald the Viking (*Tales of the Enchanted Islands of the Atlantic*).
Holland, R. S.: Charles Dickens, the Boy of the London Streets (*Historic Boyhoods*).
Wilson, C. D.: How Rodrigo Was Knighted and Received the Name of Cid, The Banishment of the Cid (*The Story of the Cid*).

June

Brown, Abbie F.: Kenneth and the Gulls (*Book of Saints and Friendly Beasts*).
Cabot, Ella L.: Sister Dora (*Ethics for Children*).
Daudet, Alphonse: The Last Lesson (Bryant: *How to Tell Stories to Children*).
Gould, F. J.: How a Woman Saved Rome, A Roman Undismayed (*The Children's Plutarch*).
Higginson, T. W.: The Search for Norumbega, Bimini and the Fountain of Youth (*Tales of the Enchanted Islands of the Atlantic*).
Judson, K. B.: Why Grizzly Bear Goes on All Fours (*Myths of California and the Old Southwest*).
Lodge, H. C., and Roosevelt, T.: Remember the Alamo, The Flag Bearer (*Frontier Towns*).
MacManus, Seumas: Jack and the King Who Was a Gentleman (*In Chimney Corners*).
Tappan, Eva M.: Israel Putnam (*American Hero Stories*).
Wilson, C. D.: The Cid's Successors in the Land of the Moors, The Cid Returns Aid to the King (*The Story of the Cid*).

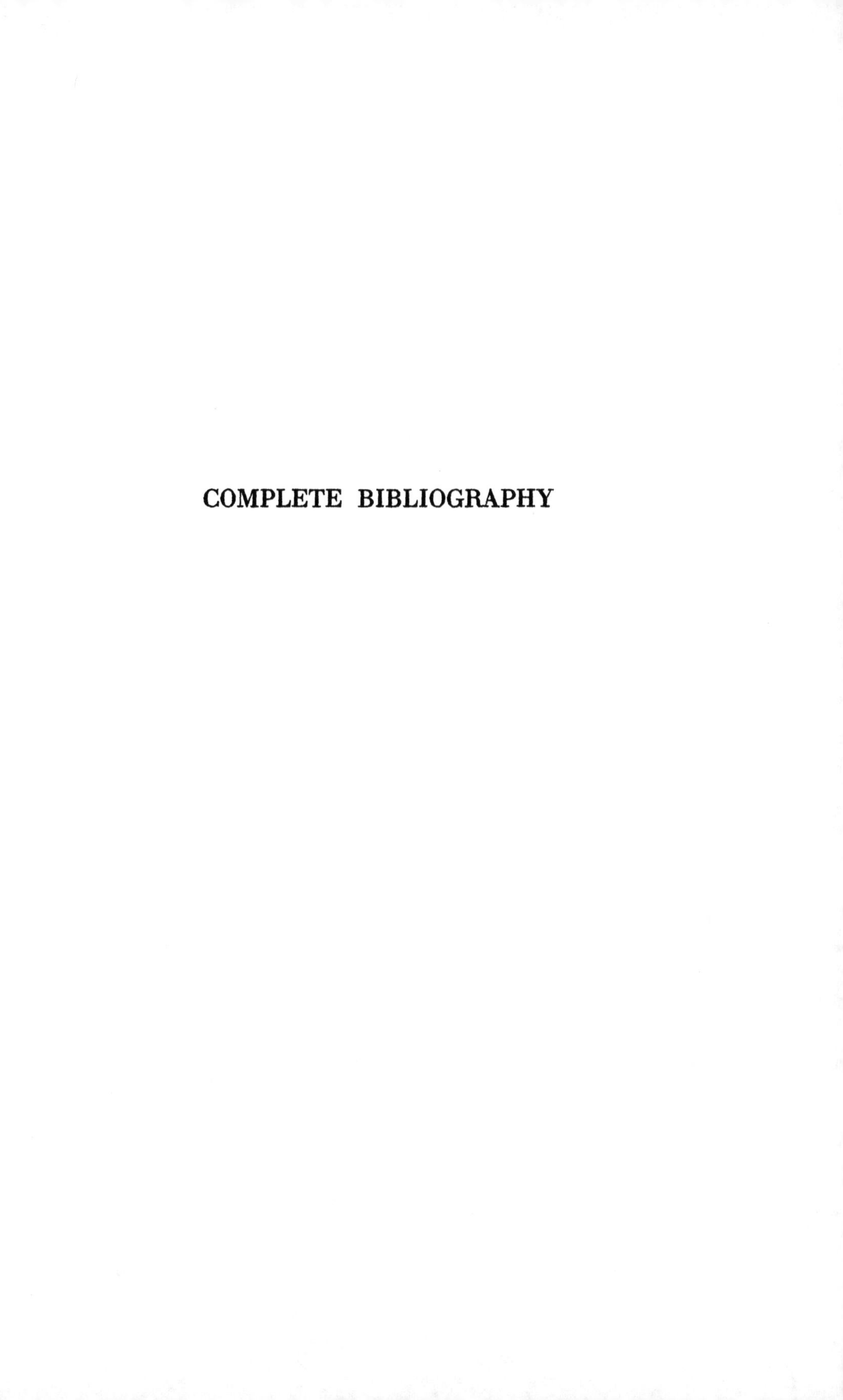

COMPLETE BIBLIOGRAPHY

COMPLETE BIBLIOGRAPHY

ABBOTT, JACOB: *Life of Genghis Khan.* Harper & Brothers.

ABBOTT, JOHN STEVENS CABOT: *Miles Standish.* Dodd, Mead & Co.

ABBOTT, LYMAN: *Life and Literature of the Ancient Hebrews.* Houghton Mifflin Co.

ADAMS, WILLIAM: *Fables and Rhymes — Æsop and Mother Goose.* American Book Co.

AGUILAR, GRACE: *The Women of Israel.* D. Appleton & Co.

ALDEN, RAYMOND MACDONALD: *Why the Chimes Rang.* Bobbs-Merrill Co.

ALLISON, S. B., and PERDUE, H. A.: *The Story in Primary Instruction.* A. Flanagan Co.

ANDERSEN, HANS CHRISTIAN: *Wonder Stories Told for Children.* Houghton Mifflin Co.

ANDERSON, RASMUS BJÖRN: *The Younger Edda.* Scott, Foresman & Co.

ANTIN, MARY: *The Promised Land.* Houghton Mifflin Co.

ARNOLD, SARA LOUISE, and GILBERT, CHARLES: *Stepping Stones to Literature — Book 3.* Silver, Burdett & Co.

ASBJØRNSEN, PETER CHRISTEN: *Fairy Tales from the Far North.* A. L. Burt Co.

The Fairy World. De Wolfe & Fiske Co.

AUSTIN, MARY: *The Basket Woman.* Houghton Mifflin Co.

BACON, MARY SCHELL HOKE: *Pictures That Every Child Should Know.* Doubleday, Page & Co.

BAILEY, CAROLYN SHERWIN: *Firelight Stories.* Milton Bradley Co.

For the Story-Teller. Milton Bradley Co.

Stories and Rhymes for the Child. Milton Bradley Co.

Story-Telling Time. Milton Bradley Co.

BAILEY, CAROLYN SHERWIN, and LEWIS, CLARA M.: *For the Children's Hour.* Milton Bradley Co.

BALDWIN, JAMES: *American Book of Golden Deeds.* American Book Co.

Discovery of the Old Northwest. American Book Co.

Fifty Famous People. American Book Co.

Fifty Famous Stories Retold. American Book Co.

Hero Tales Told in School. Charles Scribner's Sons.

Old Stories of the East. American Book Co.

Second Fairy Reader. American Book Co.

Story of Roland. Charles Scribner's Sons.

Thirty More Famous Stories. American Book Co.

BALLARD, SUSAN: *Fairy Tales from Old Japan.* Fleming H. Revell Co.

BARING-GOULD, SABINE: *Lives of the Saints.* 16 volumes. F. A. Stokes Co.

BARRIE, JAMES: *Peter Pan in Kensington Gardens.* Charles Scribner's Sons.

BEARD, JAMES CARTER: *Humor in Animals.* G. P. Putnam's Sons.

BECQUER, GUSTAVO ADOLFO: *Romantic Legends of Spain.* T. Y. Crowell Co.

BELL, FLORENCE EVELEEN: *Fairy Tale Plays.* Longmans, Green & Co.

BERGEN, FANNY DICKERSON: *Glimpses at the Plant World.* Ginn & Co.

BLAKEWELL, S. E.: *True Bird Stories.* Houghton Mifflin Co.

BLUMENTHAL, VERRA X. K. DE: *Folk Tales from the Russian.* Rand-McNally Co.

BOLTON, SARAH K.: *Famous Leaders among Men.* T. Y. Crowell Co.

Lives of Poor Boys Who Became Famous. T. Y. Crowell Co.

BOUTET DE MONVEL, L. M.: *The Story of Joan of Arc.* Century Co.

BOYESEN, HJALMAR HJORTH: *Modern Vikings.* Charles Scribner's Sons.

BRABOURNE, EDWARD KNATCHBULL-HUGESSEN, LORD: *River Legends.* E. P. Dutton & Co.

BRADISH, SARAH POWERS: *Old Norse Stories.* American Book Company.

BRADLEY, WILL: *The Wonder Box.* Century Co.

BROOKS, ELBRIDGE S.: *Abraham Lincoln.* De Wolfe & Fiske Co.

Historic Boys. G. P. Putnam's Sons.

Historic Girls. G. P. Putnam's Sons.

BROWN, ABBIE FARWELL: *Book of Saints and Friendly Beasts.* Houghton Mifflin Co.

In the Days of Giants. Houghton Mifflin Co.

BROWN, ABBIE FARWELL, and BELL, JAMES M.: *Tales of the Red Children.* D. Appleton & Co.

BROWNING, ROBERT: *Poems.* Houghton Mifflin Co.

BRYANT, SARA CONE: *How to Tell Stories to Children.* Houghton Mifflin Co.

Stories to Tell to Children. Houghton Mifflin Co.

BRYANT, WILLIAM CULLEN: *Poems.* D. Appleton & Co.

BRYCE, CATHERINE TURNER: *Fables from Afar.* Newson & Co.

That's Why Stories. Newson & Co.

BUELL, AUGUSTUS C.: *John Paul Jones, Founder of the American Navy.* 2 volumes. Charles Scribner's Sons.

BULFINCH, THOMAS: *The Age of Fable.* Lothrop, Lee & Shepard Co.
BUNCE, JOHN THACKRAY: *Fairy Tales: Their Origin and Meaning.* Macmillan Co.
BURGESS, THORNTON W.: *Bed-time Stories.* Little, Brown & Co.
BURNHAM, MAUD: *Descriptive Stories for All the Year.* Milton Bradley Co.
BURROUGHS, JOHN: *Bird Stories.* Houghton Mifflin Co.
Squirrels and Other Fur-bearers. Houghton Mifflin Co.
CABOT, ELLA LYMAN: *Ethics for Children.* Houghton Mifflin Co.
CANTON, WILLIAM: *A Child's Book of Saints.* E. P. Dutton & Co.
CARY, ALICE: *Poems.* Hurst & Co.
CATHER, KATHERINE DUNLAP: *Boyhood Stories of Famous Men.* Century Co.
Pan and His Pipes and Other Stories. Victor Talking Machine Co.
CHADWICK, MARA L. PRATT-, and FREEMAN, E. GRAY: *Chain Stories and Playlets.* World Book Co.
CHAPIN, ANNA ALICE: *Makers of Song.* Dodd, Mead & Co.
Masters of Music. Dodd, Mead & Co.
The Heart of Music. Dodd, Mead & Co.
The Story of Parsival. Harper & Brothers.
The Story of the Rhinegold. Harper & Brothers.
CHODZKO, ALEXANDER D. B.: *Slav Fairy Tales.* A. L. Burt & Co.
CHUBB, PERCIVAL: *Festivals and Plays.* Harper & Brothers.
CHURCH, ALFRED JOHN: *Odyssey for Boys and Girls.* Macmillan Co.
CLINCH, GEORGE: *Costume from Prehistoric Times to End of Eighteenth Century.* A. C. McClurg & Co.
COE, FANNY E.: *First Book of Stories for the Story-Teller.* Houghton Mifflin Co.
Heroes of Everyday Life. Ginn & Co.
COLLINS, ARCHIE F.: *The Book of Stars.* D. Appleton & Co.
COMSTOCK, JOHN HENRY: *Insect Life.* D. Appleton & Co.
CONVERSE, HARRIET CLARKE: *Myths and Legends of New York State.* N. Y. State Education Department, 1908.
COOKE, FLORA J.: *Nature Myths and Stories for Little Children.* A Flanagan Co.
COWLES, JULIA DARROW: *The Art of Story-Telling.* A. C. McClurg & Co.
CREIGHTON, LOUISE VON GLEHN: *Some Famous Women.* Longmans, Green & Co.
CROKER, THOMAS CROFTON: *Fairy Legends and Traditions of Ireland.* P. J. Kennedy & Sons.

CROWEST, FREDERICK JAMES: *Life of Verdi.* Charles Scribner's Sons.
CURTIN, JEREMIAH: *Myths and Folk Tales of the Russians, Western Slavs, and Magyars.* Little, Brown & Co.
CURTIS, ELNORA W.: *The Dramatic Instinct in Education.* Houghton Mifflin Co.
DANA, JAMES DWIGHT: *The Geological Story Briefly Told.* American Book Co.
DASENT, WALTER: *Popular Tales from the North.* G. P. Putnam's Sons.
DAVIS, MARY H., and CHOW-LEUNG: *Chinese Fables and Folk Stories.* American Book Co.
DEARMER, MABEL: *A Child's Life of Christ.* Dodd, Mead & Co.
DE LA RAMÉE, LOUISE: *Bimbi and Other Stories.* Ginn & Co.
DICKENS, CHARLES: *David Copperfield.*
Nicholas Nickleby.
Old Curiosity Shop.
The Christmas Carol.
The Uncommercial Traveller.
DICKINSON, ASA D., and SKINNER, ADA M.: *Children's Book of Christmas Stories.* Doubleday, Page & Co.
DILLINGHAM, ELIZABETH T., and EMERSON, ADELLE P.: *"Tell It Again" Stories.* Ginn & Co.
DOANE, T. W.: *Bible Myths.* Commonwealth Co.
DOLE, NATHAN HASKELL: *A Score of Famous Composers.* T. Y. Crowell Co.
DRAKE, SAMUEL ADAMS: *New England Legends.* Little, Brown & Co.
DU CHAILLU, PAUL B.: *The World of the Great Forest.* Charles Scribner's Sons.
DUMAS, ALEXANDRE, SAND, GEORGE, and Others: *Black Diamonds.* Harper & Brothers.
Golden Fairy Book. A. L. Burt Co.
DYE, CHARITY: *The Story-Teller's Art.* Ginn & Co.
DYER, WALTER A.: *The Richer Life.* Doubleday, Page & Co.
EASTMAN, CHARLES A.: *Indian Boyhood.* Doubleday, Page & Co.
Old Indian Days. Doubleday, Page & Co.
EASTMAN, CHARLES A. and ELAINE: *Smoky Day's Wigwam Evenings.* Little, Brown & Co.
Wigwam Evenings. Little, Brown & Co.
EDWARDS, CHARLES LINCOLN: *Bahama Songs and Stories.* Houghton Mifflin Co.

Eggleston, George Cary: *Strange Stories from History for Young People.* Harper & Brothers.

Eliot, George: *Silas Marner.*
The Mill on the Floss.

English, Thomas Dunn: *Fairy Stories and Wonder Tales.* Hurst & Co.

Ennis, Luna May: *Music in Art.* L. C. Page & Co.

Fabre, J. Henri: *Insect Adventures.* World Book Co.
The Hunting Wasps. Dodd, Mead & Co.
The Life of a Caterpillar. Dodd, Mead & Co.
The Life of a Fly. Dodd, Mead & Co.
The Mason Bees. Dodd, Mead & Co.

Farmer, Florence V.: *Boy and Girl Heroes.* Macmillan Co.

Fiske, John: *Myths and Myth Makers.* Houghton Mifflin Co.
The Great Epic of Israel. Houghton Mifflin Co.
The Myths of Israel. Houghton Mifflin Co.

Flagg, Wilson: *A Year with the Birds.* Educational Publishing Co.

Foa, Madame Eugénie: *Boy Life of Napoleon.* Lothrop, Lee & Shepard Co.

Forbush, William Byron: *Manual of Stories.* American Institute of Child Life.

Fortier, Alcée: *Louisiana Folk Tales.* Houghton Mifflin Co.

Foster, Mary H., and Cummings, Mabel H.: *Asgard Stories.* Silver, Burdett & Co.

Fryberger, Agnes: *Listening Lessons in Music.* Silver, Burdett & Co.

Frye, Alexis Everett: *Brooks and Brook Basins.* Ginn & Co.

Gallagher, James E.: *Best Lincoln Stories.* M. A. Donohue & Co.

Gatty, Margaret: *Parables from Nature.* E. P. Dutton & Co.

Gilbert, Ariadne: *More than Conquerors.* Century Co.

Gilchrist, Beth Bradford: *Life of Mary Lyon.* Houghton Mifflin Co.

Goldenberg, Samuel L.: *Lace, Its Origin and History.* Brentano's.

Gould, Frederick James: *The Children's Plutarch.* Harper & Brothers.

Graves, Alfred Perceval: *The Irish Fairy Book.* F. A. Stokes Co.

Grierson, E. W.: *Book of Celtic Stories.* Macmillan Co.
Tales from Scottish Ballads. Macmillan Co.

Griffis, William Elliot: *The Unmannerly Tiger and Other Korean Tales.* T. Y. Crowell Co.

Grimm, Jacob: *German Household Tales.* Houghton Mifflin Co.

GRINNELL, ELIZABETH and JOSEPH: *Birds of Song and Story.* A. W. Mumford.
Neighbors of Field, Wood, and Stream. F. A. Stokes Co.
GROOS, KARL: *The Play of Animals.* D. Appleton & Co.
GROSS, H.: *Lincoln's Own Stories.* Doubleday, Page & Co.
GUERBER, HELÈNE A.: *Legends of Switzerland.* Dodd, Mead & Co.
Legends of the Middle Ages. American Book Co.
Legends of the Rhine. A. S. Barnes Co.
Stories of the Wagner Operas. Dodd, Mead & Co.
Story of the English. American Book Co.
Story of Modern France. American Book Co.
Story of Old France. American Book Co.
HAIGHT, RACHEL WEBB: *Index of Fairy Tales.* Boston Book Co.
HALL, I. FREEMAN, and LENNOX, ELIZABETH D.: *Red Letter Days.* Silver, Burdett & Co.
HARDY, MARY H.: *Indian Legends from Geyser Land.* Rand-McNally & Co.
HARRIS, F. J.: *Plays for Young People.* Castle Co., London.
HARRIS, JOEL CHANDLER: *Little Mr. Thimblefinger.* Houghton Mifflin Co.
Nights with Uncle Remus. Houghton Mifflin Co.
Plantation Pageants. Houghton Mifflin Co.
Uncle Remus and His Friends. Houghton Mifflin Co.
HARRISON, ELIZABETH: *In Story-land.* Central Publishing Co.
HART, ALBERT B., and STEVENS, ELIZABETH: *Romance of the Civil War.* Macmillan Co.
HARTE, BRET: *The Luck of Roaring Camp.* Houghton Mifflin Co.
HARTLAND, E. SIDNEY: *The Science of Fairy Tales.* Charles Scribner's Sons.
HARTMANN, SADAKICHI: *Japanese Art.* L. C. Page & Co.
HASBROUCK, LOUISE S.: *Fabre's Insect Adventures.* World Book Co.
HAUFF, WILHELM: *Caravan Tales.* (Arabian Days' Entertainments). Houghton Mifflin Co.
HAWKES, CLARENCE: *Shovelhorns: the Biography of a Moose.* George W. Jacobs Co.
HAWTHORNE, NATHANIEL: *Grandfather's Chair.*
Tanglewood Tales.
Twice Told Tales.
HEARN, LAFCADIO: *Kwaidan.* Houghton Mifflin Co.
HEBER, ELIZABETH, and GARFIELD, GRACE: *A Child's Story Garden.* Scott-Miller Press, Indianapolis.

HENSEL, SEBASTIAN: *History of the Mendelssohn Family.* 2 volumes. Harper & Brothers.

HIGGINSON, THOMAS WENTWORTH: *American Explorers.* Longmans, Green & Co.

Tales of the Enchanted Islands of the Atlantic. Macmillan Co.

HODGES, GEORGE: *A Child's Guide to the Bible.* Baker & Taylor Co.

HOLBROOK, FLORENCE: *Book of Nature Myths.* Houghton Mifflin Co.

Round the Year in Myth and Song. American Book Co.

HOLDER, CHARLES F.: *Stories of Animal Life.* American Book Co.

HOLLAND, RUPERT SARGENT: *Historic Boyhoods.* George W. Jacobs Co.

HOUGHTON, LOUISE SEYMOUR: *Hebrew Life and Thought.* University of Chicago Press.

Telling Bible Stories. Charles Scribner's Sons.

The Bible in Picture and Story. American Tract Co.

HOURTICQ, LOUIS: *Art in France.* Charles Scribner's Sons.

HOWELLS, WILLIAM DEAN: *Christmas Every Day.* Harper & Brothers.

HOXIE, JANE: *A Kindergarten Story Book.* Milton Bradley Co.

HUGO, VICTOR: *Les Misérables.* 2 volumes. M. A. Donohue & Co.

HURLL, ESTELLE M.: *Child Life in Art.* L. C. Page & Co.

The Madonna in Art. L. C. Page & Co.

INGERSOLL, ERNEST: *Wild Life of Orchard and Field.* Harper & Brothers.

IRVING, WASHINGTON: *Tales from the Alhambra.* Ginn & Co.

The Life and Voyages of Christopher Columbus. A. L. Burt Co.

The Sketch Book. A. L. Burt Co.

JACKSON, E.: *History of Hand-Made Lace.* Charles Scribner's Sons.

JACOBS, JOSEPH: *Celtic Fairy Tales.* G. P. Putnam's Sons.

English Fairy Tales. G. P. Putnam's Sons.

Europa's Fairy Book. G. P. Putnam's Sons.

More Celtic Fairy Tales. G. P. Putnam's Sons.

JOHNSON, CLIFTON: *Oak Tree Stories.* Little, Brown & Co.

JOHONNOT, JAMES: *Ten Great Events in History.* American Book Co.

JORDAN, DAVID STARR: *Science Sketches.* A. C. McClurg & Co.

The Book of Knight and Barbara. D. Appleton & Co.

JUDD, MARY CATHERINE: *Wigwam Stories.* Ginn & Co.

JUDSON, KATHARINE B.: *Myths and Legends of the Great Plains.* A. C. McClurg & Co.

Myths and Legends of Alaska. A. C. McClurg & Co.

Myths and Legends of the Pacific Northwest. A. C. McClurg & Co.

Myths of California and the Old Southwest. A. C. McClurg & Co.

KEIGHTLEY, THOMAS: *Fairy Mythology.* Macmillan Co.

KENNEDY, HOWARD ANGUS: *The New World Fairy Book.* E. P. Dutton & Co.

KENT, CHARLES FOSTER: *Heroes and Crises of Early Hebrew History.* Charles Scribner's Sons.

KEYES, ANGELA M.: *Stories and Story-Telling.* D. Appleton & Co.

KINGSLEY, CHARLES: *Greek Heroes.* Henry Altemus.
Hypatia. Century Co.
Water Babies. Macmillan Co.
Westward Ho! A. L. Burt Co.

KIPLING, RUDYARD: *Jungle Book.* Century Co.
Just So Stories. Doubleday, Page & Co.
Puck of Pook's Hill. Doubleday, Page & Co.
Second Jungle Book. Century Co.

KNIGHT, JAMES: *Food and Its Function.* Charles Scribner's Sons.

KOROLENKO, Z.: *The Book of Easter.* Macmillan Co.

LABOULAYE, EDOUARD RENÉ: *Fairy Tales of All Nations.* E. P. Dutton & Co.
Last Fairy Tales. Harper & Brothers.

LAGERLÖF, SELMA: *Christ Legends.* Henry Holt & Co.
The Wonderful Adventures of Nils. Doubleday, Page & Co.
The Further Adventures of Nils. Doubleday, Page & Co.

LAMB, CHARLES and MARY: *Tales from Shakespeare.*

LANG, ANDREW: *Animal Story Book.* Longmans, Green & Co.
Blue Fairy Book. A. L. Burt Co.
Green Fairy Book. A. L. Burt Co.
Lilac Fairy Book. Longmans, Green & Co.
Orange Fairy Book. Longmans, Green & Co.
Red Fairy Book. A. L. Burt Co.
True Story Book. Longmans, Green & Co.
Yellow Fairy Book. Charles Scribner's Sons.

LANG, JEANIE: *Robert the Bruce.* E. P. Dutton & Co.
Stories from Shakespeare Told to Children. E. P. Dutton & Co.
The Story of General Gordon. E. P. Dutton & Co.

LANIER, SIDNEY: *The Boy's King Arthur.* Charles Scribner's Sons.
The Boy's Mabinogion. Charles Scribner's Sons.

LANSING, MARION FLORENCE: *Page, Esquire, and Knight.* Ginn & Co.
Quaint Old Stories to Read and Act. Macmillan Co.

LEA, JOHN: *Romance of Bird Life.* J. B. Lippincott Co.

LINDSAY, MAUD: *Mother Stories.* Milton Bradley Co.
More Mother Stories. Milton Bradley Co.
The Story-Teller for Little Children. Lothrop, Lee & Shepard Co.

LOCKHART, JOHN GIBSON: *Ancient Spanish Ballads*. E. P. Dutton & Co.

LODGE, HENRY CABOT: *George Washington*. 2 volumes. Houghton Mifflin Co.

LODGE, HENRY CABOT, and ROOSEVELT, THEODORE: *Frontier Towns, and Other Essays*. Charles Scribner's Sons.

LONGFELLOW, HENRY WADSWORTH: *Poems*. Houghton Mifflin Co.

LOWELL, FRANCIS CABOT: *Joan of Arc*. Houghton Mifflin Co.

LOWES, EMILY LEIGH: *Chats on Old Lace and Needlework*. F. A. Stokes Co.

LÜTKENHAUS, ANNA M., and KNOX, MARGARET: *Plays for School Children*. Century Co.

LYMAN, EDNA: *Story-Telling: What to Tell and How to Tell It*. A. C. McClurg & Co.

MABIE, HAMILTON W.: *Folk Tales Every Child Should Know*. Doubleday, Page & Co.

Norse Stories from the Eddas. Rand-McNally & Co.

MACDONNELL, ANNE: *Italian Fairy Book*. F. A. Stokes Co.

MACLEOD, R.: *King Arthur and His Noble Knights*. A. L. Burt Co.

MACMANUS, SEUMAS: *Donegal Fairy Tales*. Doubleday, Page & Co.

In Chimney Corners. Doubleday, Page & Co.

MCMURRY, CHARLES A.: *Pioneers of the Mississippi Valley*. Macmillan Co.

Special Method in Primary Reading. Macmillan Co.

MAETERLINCK, MADAME MAURICE: *The Children's Blue Bird*. Dodd, Mead & Co.

MAGRUDER, C. S.: *Tale of Ancient Persia*. Broadway Publishing Co.

MARCH, DANIEL: *Night Scenes in the Bible*. Seigler, McCurdy Co.

MARDEN, ORISON SWETT: *Winning Out*. Lothrop, Lee & Shepard Co.

MARSHALL, H. E.: *Stories of Roland*. E. P. Dutton & Co.

The Story of William Tell. E. P. Dutton & Co.

MATHESON, GEORGE: *Representative Men of the Bible*. 3 volumes. George H. Doran Co.

MATTHEWS, AGNES: *The Champions of Christendom*. Ginn & Co.

MENEFEE, MAUD: *Child Stories from the Masters*. Rand-McNally & Co.

MILES, ALFRED H.: *Animal Anecdotes*. F. A. Stokes Co.

MILLER, ELLEN R.: *Butterfly and Moth Book*. Charles Scribner's Sons.

MILLER, HARRIET: *Kristy's Rainy Day Picnics*.

True Bird Stories. Houghton Mifflin Co.

MILLER, JOAQUIN: *True Bear Stories.* Rand-McNally & Co.

MILLER, OLIVE THORNE: *The Second Book of Birds.* Houghton Mifflin Co.

MILLS, ENOS A.: *In the Beaver World.* Houghton Mifflin Co.

MITFORD, FREEMAN: *Tales of Old Japan.* Macmillan Co.

MOORE, CHARLES W.: *Abraham Lincoln.* Houghton Mifflin Co.
Christopher Columbus. Houghton Mifflin Co.

MORLEY, MARGARET W.: *Butterflies and Bees.* Ginn & Co.

MORRIS, WILLIAM: *Sigurd, the Volsung.* Longmans, Green & Co.

MORSE, FRANCES CLARY: *Furniture of the Olden Time.* Macmillan Co.

MOULTON, LOUISE CHANDLER: *Bed-time Stories.* Little, Brown & Co.

NEPOS, C.: *Tales of Great Generals.* Oxford Press.

NICHOLSON, J. S.: *Tales from Ariosto.* Macmillan Co.

NIEBUHR, BARTHOLD GEORG: *Greek Hero Stories.* Dodd, Mead & Co.

NIXON-ROULET, MARY F.: *Fairy Tales a Child Can Read and Act.* American Book Co.
Japanese Folk Stories. American Book Co.

NORTON, EDITH ELIZA: *Rugs in Their Native Land.* Dodd, Mead & Co.

NOYES, MARION I., and RAY, BLANCHE H.: *Little Plays for Little People.* Ginn & Co.

O'GRADY, ALICE: *The Story-Teller's Book.* Rand-McNally & Co.

OLCOTT, FRANCES J.: *Bible Stories to Read and Tell.* Houghton Mifflin Co.
Good Stories for Great Holidays. Houghton Mifflin Co.
The Arabian Nights. Henry Holt & Co.

OZAKI, YEI THEODORA: *Japanese Fairy Tales.* A. L. Burt & Co.

PARTRIDGE, EMELYN N. and GEORGE E.: *Story-Telling in the Home and School.* Sturgis & Walton.

PEABODY, JOSEPHINE PRESTON: *Old Greek Folk Stories.* Houghton Mifflin Co.

PERRAULT, CHARLES: *Tales for Children from Many Lands.*

PERRY, F. M., and BEEBE, KATHERINE: *Four American Pioneers.* American Book Co.

PERRY, STELLA GEORGE STERN: *When Mother Lets Us Act.* Moffat, Yard & Co.

PHELPS, ELIZABETH STUART: *David and Jonathan.* Harper & Brothers.

PIERSON, CLARA DILLINGHAM: *Among the Farmyard People.* E. P. Dutton & Co.

PITMAN, LEILA WEBSTER: *Stories of Old France.* American Book Co.

PLANCHÉ, JAMES ROBINSON: *History of British Costume.* Macmillan Co.
PORTER, GENE STRATTON: *Moths of the Limberlost.* Doubleday, Page & Co.
PORTER, JERMAIN G.: *Stars in Song and Legend.* Ginn & Co.
POTTER, BEATRIX: *Peter Rabbit.* Frederick Warne & Co.
Squirrel Nutkin. Frederick Warne & Co.
POULSSON, EMILIE: *Child Stories and Rhymes.* Milton Bradley Co.
In the Child World. Milton Bradley Co.
Top of the World Series. Lothrop, Lee & Shepard Co.
PRATT, M. L.: *Stories of Colonial Children.* Educational Publishing Co.
PRICE, LILLIAN LOUISE: *Lads and Lassies of Other Days.* Silver, Burdett & Co.
Wandering Heroes. Silver, Burdett & Co.
PRINGLE, MARY P., and URANN, CLARA A.: *Yule-Tide in Many Lands.* Lothrop, Lee & Shepard Co.
PUMPHREY, MARGARET B.: *Pilgrim Stories.* Rand-McNally Co.
PYLE, HOWARD: *Some Merry Adventures of Robin Hood.* Charles Scribner's Sons.
Stories of King Arthur and His Knights. Charles Scribner's Sons.
The Wonder Clock. Harper & Brothers.
QUILLER-COUCH, SIR ARTHUR THOMAS: *The Roll Call of Honor.* Sully & Kleinteich.
RAGOZIN, ZÉNAÏDE ALEXEÏEVNA: *Siegfried and Beowulf.* G. P. Putnam's Sons.
RAMASWAMI RAJU: *Indian Fables.* E. P. Dutton & Co.
RANSOM, CAROLINE LOUISE: *Studies in Ancient Furniture.* University of Chicago Press.
RENNINGER, ELIZABETH D.: *The Story of Rustem.* Charles Scribner's Sons.
RHEAD, J. S.: *Arabian Nights.* Harper & Brothers.
RHYS, ERNEST: *English Fairy Book* (Fairy Gold). E. P. Dutton & Co.
RICE, ALICE HEGAN: *Betty's Best Christmas.* Century Co.
RICHARDS, LAURA E.: *Five Minute Stories.* Dana Estes & Co.
Florence Nightingale, the Angel of the Crimea. D. Appleton & Co.
The Golden Windows. Little, Brown & Co.
The Pig Brother. Little, Brown & Co.
ROBERTS, CHARLES G. D.: *Kindred of the Wild.* L. C. Page & Co.
Kings in Exile. Macmillan Co.
Earth's Enigmas. L. C. Page & Co.
Haunters of the Silences. L. C. Page & Co.

St. John, Porter: *The Story in Moral and Religious Education.* Pilgrim Press.

Sangster, Margaret E., and Yonge, Charlotte M.: *Stories from the Best of Books.* Harper & Brothers.

Sawyer, Ruth: *This Way to Christmas.* Harper & Brothers.

Schauffler, Robert Haven: *Arbor Day.* Moffat, Yard & Co.

Book of Thanksgiving. Moffat, Yard & Co.

Christmas: Its Origin, Celebration, etc. Moffat, Yard & Co.

Lincoln's Birthday. Moffat, Yard & Co.

Memorial Day. Moffat, Yard & Co.

Washington's Birthday. Moffat, Yard & Co.

Scobey, Kathrine L., and Horne, Olive B.: *Stories of Great Musicians.* American Book Co.

Scott, Emma: *How the Flag Became Old Glory.* Macmillan Co.

Scudder, Horace E.: *Fables and Folk Stories.* Houghton Mifflin Co.

The Children's Book. Houghton Mifflin Co.

Seawell, Molly Elliot: *The Son of Columbus.* Harper & Brothers.

Seton, Ernest Thompson: *Animal Heroes.* Charles Scribner's Sons.

Sharman, Lyon: *Bamboo: Tales of the Orient Born.* Paul Elder & Co.

Shedlock, Marie L.: *The Art of the Story-Teller.* D. Appleton & Co.

Sidgwick, Ethel: *Four Plays for Children.* Small, Maynard & Co.

Singleton, Esther: *Furniture of Our Forefathers.* Doubleday, Page & Co.

Skeat, Walter W.: *Fables and Folk-Tales from an Eastern Forest.* G. P. Putnam's Sons.

Skinner, Ada M.: *Little Folks' Christmas Stories and Plays.* Rand-McNally & Co.

Stories of Wakeland and Dreamland. Rand-McNally & Co.

Skinner, Charles M.: *American Myths and Legends.* 2 volumes. J. B. Lippincott Co.

Myths and Legends beyond Our Borders. J. B. Lippincott Co.

Myths of Plants, Trees, and Flowers. J. B. Lippincott Co.

Slosson, Annie Trumbull: *Story-tell Lib.* Charles Scribner's Sons.

Sly, William J.: *World Stories Retold.* George W. Jacobs Co.

Smith, Bertha H.: *Yosemite Legends.* Paul Elder Co.

Smith, George Adam: *A Historic Geography of the Holy Land.* George H. Doran Co.

Smith, Nora A.: *Old, Old Tales from the Old, Old Book.* Doubleday, Page & Co.

Snedeker, Caroline D.: *The Coward of Thermopylæ.* Doubleday, Page & Co.

SOUTHEY, ROBERT: *Poems.* Oxford Press.
SPOFFORD, HARRIET E.: *Life of Nelson.* E. P. Dutton & Co.
The Fairy Changeling. Richard G. Badger.
STEEL, FLORA ANNIE: *Tales of the Punjab.* Macmillan Co.
STEIN, EVALEEN: *Troubadour Tales.* Bobbs-Merrill Co.
STERLING, MARY BLAKEWELL: *Story of Sir Galahad.* E. P. Dutton & Co.
STEVENSON, AUGUSTA: *Children's Classics in Dramatic Form.* Houghton Mifflin Co.
STEVENSON, ELIZABETH S.: *Days and Deeds.* Doubleday, Page & Co.
STEVENSON, R. L.: *David Balfour.* Charles Scribner's Sons.
Island Nights' Entertainments. Charles Scribner's Sons.
STOCKTON, FRANK R.: *Fanciful Tales.* Charles Scribner's Sons.
The Bee-Man of Orn. Charles Scribner's Sons.
STODDARD, JOHN L.: *South Tyrol.* Geo. L. Shuman & Co.
STONE, GERTRUDE LINCOLN: *Trees in Prose and Poetry.* Ginn & Co.
STRICKLAND, AGNES: *Queens of England.* American Book Co.
Queens of Scotland. 2 volumes. Macmillan Co.
SWEETSER, KATE D.: *Boys and Girls from Dickens.* Harper & Brothers.
Boys and Girls from George Eliot. Duffield & Co.
Boys and Girls from Thackeray. Duffield & Co.
SWEETSER, M. F.: *Artist Biographies.* 4 volumes. *Raphael and Leonardo, Angelo and Titian, Claude Lorrain and Reynolds, Turner and Landseer, Dürer and Rembrandt, Van Dyck and Angelico, Murillo and Allston.* Houghton Mifflin Co.
SWINTON, WILLIAM, and CATHCART, GEORGE R.: *Books of Tales.* American Book Company.
TAPPAN, EVA MARCH: *American Hero Stories.* Houghton Mifflin Co.
In the Days of Alfred the Great. Lothrop, Lee & Shepard Co.
In the Days of William the Conqueror. Lothrop, Lee & Shepard Co.
Robin Hood, His Book. Little, Brown & Co.
The Golden Goose. Houghton Mifflin Co.
TENNYSON, ALFRED: *Poems.* Houghton Mifflin Co.
THOMPSON, JEANETTE MAY: *Water Wonders Every Child Should Know.* Doubleday, Page & Co.
TOMLINSON, EVERETT: *Young Folks' History of the American Revolution.* Grosset & Dunlap.
TUCKER, LOUISE E., and RYAN, ESTELLE L.: *Historical Plays of Colonial Days.* Longmans, Green & Co.
UPTON, GEORGE P.: *William Tell* (*Life Stories for Young People*). G. P. Putnam's Sons.

VAN DYKE, HENRY: *The First Christmas Tree.* Grosset & Dunlap.
The Lost Boy. Harper & Brothers.
The Mansion. Harper & Brothers.
VAN DYKE, HENRY, and ABBOTT, LYMAN: *Women of the Bible.* Harper & Brothers.
VASARI, GEORGIO: *Lives of the Painters.* 4 volumes. Charles Scribner's Sons.
VERHOEFF, CAROLYN: *All about Johnny Jones.* Milton Bradley Co.
WALLACE, LEW: *Ben Hur.* Harper & Brothers.
WALSH, K.: *The Story of Santa Claus.* Moffat, Yard & Co.
WARMAN, CY: *Short Rails.* Charles Scribner's Sons.
WARNER, CHARLES DUDLEY: *Being a Boy.* Houghton Mifflin Co.
WARREN, HENRY PITT: *Stories from English History.* D. C. Heath & Co.
WARREN, MAUDE RADFORD: *Robin Hood and His Merry Men.* Rand-McNally & Co.
WATERS, CLARA ERSKINE CLEMENT: *Saints in Art.* L. C. Page & Co.
Stories of Art and Artists. Houghton Mifflin Co.
WEED, CLARENCE M.: *Bird Life Stories.* Rand-McNally & Co.
WELLS, CAROLYN: *Jolly Plays for Holidays.* Walter H. Baker.
WESTERVELT, W. D.: *Legends of Old Honolulu.* George H. Ellis & Co., Boston.
WHEELOCK, ELIZABETH M.: *Stories of the Wagner Operas.* Bobbs-Merrill Co.
WHIPPLE, WAYNE: *The Story Life of Lincoln.* John C. Winston Co.
WHITE, ELIZA ORNE: *When Molly Was Six.* Houghton Mifflin Co.
WIGGIN, KATE DOUGLAS: *The Birds' Christmas Carol.* Houghton Mifflin Co.
WIGGIN, KATE DOUGLAS, and SMITH, NORA E.: *Tales of Laughter.* Doubleday, Page & Co.
Talking Beast Fables from India. Doubleday, Page & Co.
The Children's Hour. Milton Bradley Co.
The Fairy Ring. Doubleday, Page Co.
The Story Hour. Houghton Mifflin Co.
WILDE, OSCAR: *The Happy Prince.* Frederick A. Stokes Co.
WILLISTON, TERESA P.: *Japanese Fairy Tales.* Rand-McNally & Co.
WILMOT-BUXTON, ETHEL M.: *A Book of Noble Women.* Small, Maynard & Co.
Stories from Old French Romance. F. A. Stokes Co.
Stories of Persian Heroes. T. Y. Crowell Co.

WILSON, CALVIN DILL: *The Story of the Cid.* Lothrop, Lee & Shepard Co.

WILTSE, SARA E.: *The Story in Early Education.* Ginn & Co.
Hero Folk of Ancient Britain. Ginn & Co.

WRADISLAW, A. H.: *Slavonian Fairy Tales.* Houghton Mifflin Co.

WRIGHT, MABEL OSGOOD: *Birdcraft.* Macmillan Co.
Gray Lady and the Birds. Macmillan Co.

WRIGHT, MABEL OSGOOD, and COUES, ELLIOTT: *Citizen Bird.* Macmillan Co.

WYCHE, RICHARD THOMAS: *Some Great Stories and How to Tell Them.* Newson & Co.

ZITKALA-SA: *Old Indian Legends.* Ginn & Co.

COLLECTIONS OF STORIES OF WHICH AUTHORS ARE NOT GIVEN

Cat Stories Retold from St. Nicholas. Century Co.
Civil War Stories Retold from St. Nicholas. Century Co.
Colonial Stories Retold from St. Nicholas. Century Co.
Dumpy Books for Children, The. Frederick A. Stokes Co.
Great Masters in Painting and Sculpture. George Bell & Sons.
Half a Hundred Stories. Milton Bradley Co.
Indian Stories Retold from St. Nicholas. Century Co.
Master Musician Series. E. P. Dutton & Co.
Our Holidays Retold from St. Nicholas. Century Co.
Panther Stories Retold from St. Nicholas. Century Co.
St. Nicholas Book of Plays and Operettas. Century Co.
Stories from the Classic Literature of Many Nations. Macmillan Co.
Stories of Chivalry Retold from St. Nicholas. Century Co.
Stories of the Ancient World Retold from St. Nicholas. Century Co.

INDEX

www.ingramcontent.com/pod-product-compliance
Lightning Source LLC
LaVergne TN
LVHW010531100826
845148LV00001B/158

* 9 7 8 1 4 2 5 5 7 3 3 9 3 *